Undocumented Politi

Undocumented Politics

PLACE, GENDER, AND THE
PATHWAYS OF MEXICAN MIGRANTS

Abigail Leslie Andrews

UNIVERSITY OF CALIFORNIA PRESS

University of California Press, one of the most distinguished university presses in the United States, enriches lives around the world by advancing scholarship in the humanities, social sciences, and natural sciences. Its activities are supported by the UC Press Foundation and by philanthropic contributions from individuals and institutions. For more information, visit www.ucpress.edu.

University of California Press
Oakland, California

Part of chapter 1 was originally published as Abigail L. Andrews, "Legacies of Inequity: How Hometown Political Participation and Land Distribution Shape Migrants' Paths into Wage Labor," *World Development* 87:318–32. Copyright © 2016 (Elsevier). Reprinted by permission of Elsevier. (https://doi.org/10.1016/j.worlddev.2016.07.003)

Parts of chapters 2 and 3 were originally published as Abigail L. Andrews, "Moralizing Regulation: The Political Effects of Policing 'Good' versus 'Bad' Immigrants," *Ethnic and Racial Studies.* Copyright © 2017 (Taylor and Francis). Reprinted by permission of Taylor and Francis. (https://doi.org/10.1016/j.worlddev.2016.07.003)

Part of chapter 5 was originally published as Abigail Andrews, "Women's Political Engagement in a Mexican Sending Community: Migration as Crisis and the Struggle to Sustain an Alternative," *Gender & Society* 28 (4): 583–608. Copyright © 2014 (Sage). Reprinted by permission of Sage Publications. (https://doi.org/10.1177/0891243214523124)

Library of Congress Cataloging-in-Publication Data

Names: Andrews, Abigail, author.
Title: Undocumented politics : place, gender, and the pathways of Mexican migrants / Abigail Leslie Andrews.
Description: Oakland, California : University of California Press, [2018] | Includes bibliographical references and index. |
Identifiers: LCCN 2018004217 (print) | LCCN 2018007346 (ebook) | ISBN 9780520971561 (ebook) | ISBN 9780520299962 (cloth : alk. paper) | ISBN 9780520299979 (pbk. : alk. paper)
Subjects: LCSH: Zapotec Indians—Mexico—Oaxaca (State)—Case studies. | Mixtec Indians—Mexico—Oaxaca (State)—Case studies. | Zapotec Indians—California—Los Angeles—Case studies. | Mixtec Indians—California—San Diego County—Case studies. | Emigration and immigration.
Classification: LCC F1221.Z3 (ebook) | LCC F1221.Z3 A53 2018 (print) | DDC 325/.27274097949--dc23
LC record available at https://lccn.loc.gov/2018004217

27 26 25 24 23 22 21 20 19 18
10 9 8 7 6 5 4 3 2 1

Dedicated to Rocío León (1975–2012) and the migrant families of Oaxaca, Mexico

Contents

Illustrations

Acknowledgments

Authors often say it takes a village to write a book. This book took two. I could not have done this work without the hundreds of migrant families who make up its pages or the slew of extraordinary mentors, supporters, and friends who saw it from start to end. First and foremost, I thank my mentors from UC-Berkeley, Raka Ray, Peter Evans, Michael Burawoy, Gillian Hart, and Irene Bloemraad. They taught me to be a scholar. Raka Ray brought sociology alive. She dared me to question my certainties. She also opened her heart, building a community of feminist scholars who kept one another going and deepened one another's work. Peter Evans steered me through graduate school with clarity, elegance, and unflagging enthusiasm. He waded through disarrayed notes for nuggets of insight. He never let go of agency—others' or my own—or the prospect of social change. Meanwhile, Michael Burawoy brilliantly connected my observations to theory and context. But I owe him more for his generosity and the gleam in his eye when he sees you might do something "subversive." Michael gave endlessly of himself: he was there at the final hour before job talks, funded me through intriguing international projects, and proffered twenty-five-year-old jugs of Russian liquor for graduate students, late into the night. By example, he showed us what it meant to teach. Gillian Hart was tough, and she never gave up on complexity, gender, process, space, or place. Through her commitment to communities in South Africa, she demonstrated the political stakes of how we interpret the world. Finally, Irene Bloemraad patiently guided me through the quagmire of academia, paying meticulous attention to my writing and helping to launch my career. Above all, they worked as a team. Thank you for believing in me. Thank you for insisting that I "think big" about power and possibilities. And thank you for showing me how brilliance is tied to heart.

I have also been blessed with inspiring, insightful, humane peers. In particular, my friendship with Fidan Elcioglu has been one of the decade's greatest gifts. Fidan brought brilliance, passion, and laughter into my life. Through ideas, uncertainties, and protests, she stood by my side. Jenny Carlson and Nazanin Shahrokni were also my sisters in feminist scholarship. Over wine we shared the thrill of discovery and the shock of disappointment. Ryan Calder, Graham Hill, Mike Levien, Marcel Paret, and Aaron Shaw made me cry laughing more times than I can count. They also pushed me to think, showing me by their actions what it meant to work for change. Lauren Duquette-Rury became a dear friend and ally as well, carrying me through as I finished this book. I am especially grateful to Lauren, Mike Levien, Marcel Paret, and Julia Chuang for their shrewd feedback on entire drafts of the manuscript. I also received important suggestions from Raka Ray's dissertation group: Kemi Balogun, Dawn Dow, Katie Hasson, Kimberly Hoang, Kate Maich, Kate Mason, Jordanna Matlon, Sarah Anne Minkin, and Gowri Vijaykumar, as well as Berkeleyites Dan Buch, Eli Friedman, Jacob Habinek, Juan Herrera, Gabriel Hetland, Simon Morfit, Tianna Paschel, and Heidi Sarabia. At UCSD I have been lucky to have the camaraderie of Kevin Lewis, Dan Navon, Juan Pablo Pardo Guerra, Danielle Raudenbush, Vanesa Ribas, and April Sutton. Finally, my group of academic mamas—Mary Doyno, Lauren Duquette-Rury, Rachel Haywood Ferreira, and Maria Alejandra Pérez—has helped me stay human along the way. It is a privilege to share this path with each of you.

Since I arrived at UCSD, my colleagues have gone out of their way to smooth the road, and several other sociologists have offered pivotal advice. In particular, David FitzGerald proved an ever-present mentor, reading drafts and connecting me to allies across the field. John Evans offered strategic consulting, while Amy Binder, Jeff Haydu, Isaac Martin, Nancy

Postero, Akos Rona-Tas, and others provided compassion and a focus on what mattered. At the University of California Press and Stanford University Press, I received excellent comments from Katrina Burgess, Pierrette Hondagneu-Sotelo, Leah Schmalzbauer, and three anonymous reviewers. Marie Berry, Laura Enríquez, Neil Fligstein, Nicholas de Genova, Tomás Jiménez, Cecilia Menjívar, Clarisa Pérez-Armendáriz, Michael Rodríguez Muñiz, Poulami Roychowdhury, Jeff Sallaz, Sandra Smith, and the participants of the Global Migration Workshop at UCSD also read chapter drafts, while Peggy Levitt, Isaac Martin, Tom Medvetz, and Roger Waldinger helped me hone the proposal for the book.

I also relied on other scholars to share their deep knowledge of Oaxaca and its migrants in the United States. In Mexico Ximena Avellaneda Díaz, Alejandra Aquino Moreschi, Salvador Aquino Centeno, Jack Corbett, Charlynne Curiel, Mike Danielson, Gudrun Dormann, Jorge Hernández-Díaz, Carlos Hernández Villalobos, Donato Ramos Pioquinto, Martha Rees, Laura Velasco Ortiz, and Holly Worthen taught me about the history and intricacies of indigenous life. In California Alegría de la Cruz, Jonathan Fox, Raul Hinojosa Ojeda, Irma Luna, Caitlin Patler, and Gaspar Rivera-Salgado helped introduce me to Southern California and the lives of Oaxacans there.

My ambition to understand four field sites would not have been possible without generous fellowships, including the National Science Foundation Graduate Research Fellowship, the Jacob K. Javits Graduate Fellowship, the Berkeley Fellowship for Graduate Study, the Phi Beta Kappa Dissertation Fellowship, the John Woodruff Simpson Graduate Fellowship, the Amherst College Graduate Fellowship, and the American Council of Learned Societies/Mellon Dissertation Completion Fellowship. I also received research grants from the University of California Institute for Mexico and the United States and, at UC-Berkeley, the Center for Latin American Studies, Center for Race and Gender, Sociology Department, and Andrew W. Mellon Foundation Program in Latin American Studies. At UCSD, funding from the Center for U.S.-Mexican Studies, Hellman Family Foundation, and Faculty Career Development Program gave me time and money to finish the book. Thank you to Carolyn Clark, Denise Gagnon, Solomon Lefler, Shanley Miller, Anne Meyers, Cindy Mueller, Martha Ponce, Michael Sacramento, Susan Taniguchi,

Kristen Walker, and Belinda Kuo White for their assistance with these grants.

I also had crucial institutional support. The Centro de Investigaciones y Estudios Superiores en Antropología Social in Oaxaca adopted me as a visiting scholar. The Mexican Migration Field Research Program at the University of California–San Diego's Center for Comparative Immigration Studies allowed me to join a survey team in Mexico, with particular help from Ana Minvieille. The Frente Indígena de Organizaciones Binacionales (formerly the Frente Indígena Oaxaqueño Binacional), California Rural Legal Assistance, the Coalition for Humane Immigrant Rights of Los Angeles, the Hub Oaxaca, the Casa de la Mujer Oaxaqueña, and the Welte Center for Oaxacan Studies also helped ease my entrée into Oaxacan communities. Finally, Adriana, Alan, Bernardo, Cat, Eric, Hilary, Itzel, Jen, Jimmy, Lionel, Nora, Ramona, Renato, Shorty, and Sonia took me into their homes.

Research assistants and editors also helped enormously with the work. In Oaxaca Alma, Antonio, Claudia, Edgardo, Erika, Hannah, Indira, Marco Antonio, Patricia, Ramses, Rebeca, Rosalia, Santiago, and Tania traveled to Partida with me, administered surveys, and transcribed hundreds of interviews. In the U.S. Johanna Torres cleaned data, Natalie Andrews and Karina Shklyan proofread the text and built the bibliography, and Rebecca Andrews designed a beautiful image for the front cover. Letta Page also did a bit of key editing, while Naomi Schneider, Benjy Malings, Susan Silver, and the team at UC Press helped bring the final product together.

Throughout the process my family and friends were my sanctuary. My parents, Jane and Hale, showed unwavering commitment and compassion, sharing the excitement and uncertainty that make up a scholar's world. Valerie, Emily, Dan, Rebecca, Natalie, and Bob also reminded me that I always had a home. In Mexico Aurelia, GNA, Holly, Josef, Lorena, Megan, Rebecca, Shane, and Whitney were companions in fieldwork, while Daniel provided moral support in uncertain moments and opened my eyes to the beauty and wonder of Oaxaca. In California Anna, Ashley, Ellen, Hilary, Jesse, Martina, Melanie, Naomi, and Sarah offered encouragement and support. Ben Sanoff saw me through the final six years with poise, sensitivity, and devotion. Loving Ben made me a softer person and brought levity and tenderness to the most toilsome days. Last but not least, Adrian Andrews-Sanoff lightened the stress of writing with his special, twinkling joy.

I owe the greatest debt of all to the communities of "Retorno" and "Partida." On both sides of the border, these *pueblos* adopted me as their own, nourished me with homemade tortillas, and offered a steady stream of potential suitors, should I take a mind to settling down. I especially want to thank (by pseudonym) Alejandro, Blanca, Benjamín, Bernardo, Carmen, Carolina, Celia, Consuelo, Eva, Juan, Leonel, Lourdes, Marcelo, María, Nadia, Nicolás, Pablo, Paula, Pilar, Ramiro, Ramona, Santiago, Sonia, Tamara, Teresa, Tomás, Violeta, Ximena, and all the others who went out of their way to reach out, taking me into their homes, hearts, and lives. Thank you for your friendship. Thank you for opening up. I will never forget your courage or wisdom, or the hope you gave me through dialogue.

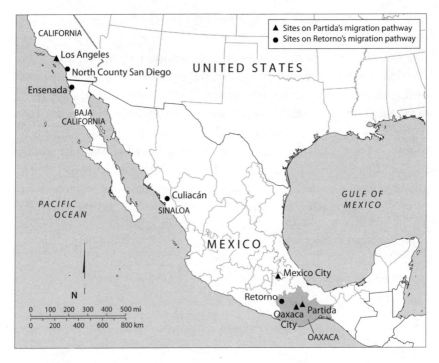

Map 1. Migration pathways of Partida to Los Angeles and Retorno to North County San Diego.

Figure 1. The village of Partida from above. Photo by the author.

Figure 2. The village of Retorno from above. Photo by the author.

Figure 3. Pacific Avenue, Huntington Park, California. Photo by the author.

Figure 4. North Santa Fe Avenue, Vista, California. Photo by the author.

Introduction

It would have been easy to think of Carmen Rojas as a victim of globalization.[1] By the time we met in Los Angeles in 2010, Carmen was thirty-four, and she had lived in the United States undocumented for almost twenty years. She subsisted by sewing pockets on jeans, seven cents apiece. In lean times she went without food, skipping dinner so her U.S.-born son would have enough to eat. Aside from that, Carmen kept her head down. She stopped at every crosswalk. She took pride that she had never asked for anything from the state.

Carmen was one of hundreds of undocumented immigrants who came to the United States in the 1990s from a village I call "Partida," deep in the mountains of Oaxaca, Mexico. Her parents were Zapotec farmers. For most of the twentieth century, her *pueblo* lived on the corn they grew, raising their children in one- or two-room adobe homes.[2] By the time Carmen was born, however, U.S.-backed policies of government privatization had pulled the bottom out from Mexico's subsistence farms. In the 1960s and 1970s people from Partida started to leave. First, they sought work in urban Mexico. Then, in the 1980s and 1990s, many went on to Southern California. Carmen hopped a bus to Mexico City in 1988, the year she turned twelve. Three years later she moved to Los Angeles. Carmen and her siblings, friends, and cousins crossed the border unauthorized. They had few other choices. By 2010 three-quarters of them still lacked legal papers.

Not since slavery had so many people lived in the United States with so few political rights. As of 2017 there were more than eleven million undocumented immigrants living in every state of the nation.[3] Two-thirds of them had been in the country for a decade or more.[4] Most, like Carmen, meticulously followed the law.[5] Nevertheless, very few had a way to "get in line" for legal authorization.[6] Their legal status kept them trapped in segregated neighborhoods and arduous, underpaid jobs. Federal laws barred them from most public services. Being undocumented also blocked them from traditional political advocacy. Without papers immigrants like Carmen could not vote or run for public office.

State violence reinforced their lack of political voice. Between 2009 and 2012, when I conducted this research, the United States deported nearly four hundred thousand people per year.[7] Most were Latinos, and less than half had ever been convicted of a crime.[8] Historically, immigration enforcement was considered federal jurisdiction and concentrated at the border. Starting in the late 1990s, however, federal programs began to define far more immigrants as "criminals."[9] The new laws also empowered police to seek out undocumented migrants and turn them over to Federal Immigration and Customs Enforcement (ICE) agents for removal. Local police played a key role in expanding deportation, helping extend immigration enforcement into the interior of the country. As police assumed greater roles in immigration control, they brought the threat of expulsion into migrants' everyday lives. In answer migrants like Carmen lived gingerly. Many hesitated to pick up groceries or take their children to school, let alone make claims on the state.

Nevertheless, Carmen did not play victim. Instead, she embraced what I call a *strategy of belonging*. From 2010 to 2011 I spent several days with Carmen as part of the field research for my doctoral dissertation. We talked, ran errands, and attended community events in Los Angeles and Huntington Park. The first time I visited Carmen's apartment, I had barely come in the door when she proclaimed, "I will never go back." For centuries Carmen's hometown of Partida had been governed communally under indigenous laws. These customs supported direct, participatory democracy, but they also barred women from political say. Like many of the women I came to know from Partida in my two years of fieldwork, Carmen now saw her hometown as too *machista* (patriarchal), too "stuck in the past." She questioned its exclusion of women, as well as its participatory traditions. She insisted that coming to California was a good thing, especially for women. She hoped that long-distance pressure might bring her village "into this century," even if it sparked backlash back home.

Carmen also fought for inclusion in the United States. She worked hard. She tried to learn English. She refused to depend on government services. And she participated in Los Angeles's giant marches for immigrants' rights. Yet when she did, she carried the U.S. flag. In the United States, she said, "I'm like a bird with wings. I spread my wings and I'm free."

. . . . .

Alma Sandoval disagreed. On paper Alma's story was much like Carmen's. Both grew up in indigenous pueblos in Oaxaca. Alma's hometown, a Mixtec village I refer to as "Retorno," lay less than a hundred miles from Partida. Alma also left Oaxaca by the time she was twelve. As in Partida, corn farming crumbled in Retorno starting in the 1970s, and people hemorrhaged out of the village. First they went to northern Mexico, then to Southern California. Alma also moved to the United States undocumented in the 1990s. She worked in the town of Vista, California, in a once-agricultural and now peri-urban region about thirty miles north of San Diego and ninety miles south of Los Angeles, known as North County San Diego. Holding factory jobs, she, too, kept out of the way of immigration control. Yet, unlike Carmen, Alma gave up on being undocumented in the United States.

Even though Alma spent nearly three decades working in northern Mexico and California, she never liked it. I met Alma in Retorno, on a dusty Sunday afternoon in 2010. I had just begun doing ethnographic fieldwork in the village, and I would wander its hills talking to people about their lives. Often women leaned out of their doorways to inform me, "Our people go to your country only to suffer, only to die." Alma concurred. While her husband and children still worked in Vista, Alma forsook the United States as hypocritical, racist, and unfair. She could not get used to the ways U.S. police and employers treated unauthorized immigrants:

"like slaves." Economic challenges aside, she felt it was better to go back to Mexico. So Alma adopted what I call a *strategy of withdrawal*.

Shortly after Alma returned to Mexico, she joined a road blockade for the first time in her life. One day a group of protestors aligned with Mexico's young opposition party, the Partido de la Revolución Democrática (PRD; Party of the Democratic Revolution), formed a barricade across the highway through Retorno. They cut off traffic and trade, demanding that Oaxaca's state government hand over resources it had promised indigenous villages but never delivered. The protestors refused to move until they received funds for irrigation, taxi licenses, and paved roads. Alma had never been in a protest before. But she was ready to do just about anything to avoid repeating the trauma she faced in the United States. The struggle was not just about resources; it was also about emigration. Debt had pushed Alma to leave. She hoped that state support might give her a means to stay. So Alma slung a *rebozo* (scarf) around her head and strode to the edge of the village, joining the fight for "the right not to migrate": *el derecho a no migrar*.

This fight was gendered in unexpected ways. Indigenous villages like Retorno and Partida had long blocked women from civic participation. This time, however, men asked for women's help. By the time the protests began, more than half the men born in Retorno worked in San Diego County. Like Alma, many of them were sick of U.S. policing. They hoped to return to Mexico. So they formed an organization in California that would pressure the Mexican state to give Retorno resources and help its people make a living at home. Yet because migrant men fought from afar, they needed boots on the ground. That was where people like Alma came in. Between the 1980s and 2010, many women had gone back to Retorno, whether from the agricultural fields of northern Mexico or from the United States. Migrants in the United States recruited these women to join their long-distance cause.

Alma was inspired after that first protest, and she eventually drew hundreds of other women into politics. Together with their migrant counterparts, these women won new rights to vote and hold public office in Retorno. Their movement propelled the first-ever indigenous representative into Oaxaca's state government. It also secured funding for indigenous hometowns. By rejecting U.S. repression and using their global ties to demand Mexican state support, the people of Retorno pursued what scholars call "alternative globalization."[10] Retorno, as Alma put it, was the place she could "be free."

.   .   .   .   .

From a bird's-eye view, the villages of Partida and Retorno were both isolated, indigenous, and patriarchal.[11] At the end of the twentieth century, economic restructuring in Mexico undermined their livelihoods, driving their people to migrate within Mexico and then to the United States. Upon arrival in California both sets of migrants confronted state violence and pounding political exclusion. Ultimately, both groups also wanted the same thing: inclusion in the process of globalization that was eroding their traditional lives. As they advocated for inclusion, both accomplished dramatic gender change.

Nevertheless, their political strategies diverged. Like Carmen, most immigrants from Partida pursued inclusion in the United States. Not only did they appreciate the U.S. government, but they also poured energy into demonstrating that they belonged. Many felt that moving to California offered a form of "progress," even for the undocumented. Women, in particular, associated gender empowerment with leaving their hometown "behind." In other words, most of these migrants accepted the dominant terms of globalization. They also grew polarized from their counterparts in Partida. In turn, emigrants' abandonment prompted people back in the village to reject the dominant version of globalization and defend their communal ways.

By contrast, migrants from Retorno withdrew politically from the United States. While most continued to live in California, they staked their hopes on returning home. Rejecting U.S. exclusion, they worked to build an alternative to undocumented migration. As they did, they forged a cross-border movement for inclusion on the Mexican side. Perhaps surprisingly, women like Alma led the way. In this case, both migrants and those in their hometown rejected the "American dream" and sought to create an alternative, more equitable form of globalization.

How did two excluded communities come to understand progress and "freedom" so differently? How did these perceptions translate into contrasting political strategies and modes of agency? And how did gender shape their attitudes and get reshaped by their actions? This book begins to answer such questions. For twenty-one months between October 2009 and July 2012, I lived among migrant families in Partida, Retorno, Los Angeles, and North County San Diego (their primary destinations). In Oaxaca I spent hours with families, hanging out in their houses, participating in political meetings, and talking about their relationships to migrants and emigration. In the United States I visited migrants' homes, drove them to work and errands, and attended their community meetings and festivals. Between the four places I also conducted more than a hundred life-history interviews, tracing how each group developed its own political strategies. I rotated between hometowns and destinations, often bringing videos of long-lost families who had not seen one another in years. In each village I also scoured archives and conducted surveys to map the history of migration. Though I focus on migrant communities, my main goal is not to explain the act of migration. Instead, I seek to better understand how excluded groups develop different approaches to politics. In the process, I rethink the interplay between gender, migration, and political voice.

THE PARADOX OF UNDOCUMENTED POLITICS

In many respects, undocumented people exemplify political exclusion. State laws and coercion deny them many of the rights that are fundamental to political action. Undocumented migrants cannot participate in elections, vote, or run for office. Like ex-felons, the colonized, and racial minorities, they have few channels through which to influence the governments where they live. Contemporary states also tend to treat such groups as objects of surveillance and control.[12] Not only do undocumented migrants lack rights; they also face the everyday violence of policing and the threat of deportation.

Pessimistic observers suggest that legal exclusion and state violence condemn the undocumented to silence. Often, studies of civic advocacy look at how protestors exercise their rights as citizens to make claims on the state.[13] Yet many migrants are too afraid of police to join the kind of emancipatory movements imagined in traditional social theory. Historically, foreign-born Latinos were among the least politically active residents in the United

States.[14] More recent research also shows that xenophobic laws can make undocumented people cynical about their host government and their prospects for legalization.[15] When migrants see U.S. laws as illegitimate and racially charged, some may give up on U.S.-oriented protests and focus their hopes on a future in Mexico.[16]

In social theory, political voicelessness is critical to migrants' social and economic marginality. Undocumented migrants are exploitable and socially excluded, most scholars argue, precisely because it is hard for them to speak out against the states and companies that oppress them.[17] The consequences can be especially bad for women. Not only are immigrant women subject to state violence; some also face "patriarchal backlash" (including domestic abuse) from immigrant men: the same people who ought—in theory—to be their allies.[18]

Recently, however, undocumented immigrants have shown surprising political agency. In the 1990s and the first decade of the 2000s, migrants' struggles brought them to the forefront of popular politics in both the United States and Mexico. By 2010 foreign-born Latinos in the United States reported *more* political advocacy than the native-born. In one survey 22 percent of Latino immigrants had participated in a protest in the past year, against just 6 percent of U.S. citizens.[19] Some research suggests that instead of producing cynicism and withdrawal, nativist legislation politicized Latino identity.[20] Of necessity, these politics went beyond the ballot box. Immigrants in the United States marched for rights, resources, and legal change. In 2006, led by organizations in Los Angeles, Chicago, and other major cities, 3.5 to 5 million immigrants and their allies went into the streets to demand legal inclusion in the United States.[21] Unauthorized migrants also innovated politically by coming out as "undocumented and unafraid" and declaring themselves American.[22] Others joined unions or canvased for congressional candidates.[23] Many of these activists showed an extraordinary commitment to working within mainstream U.S. policies and political practices. Like Carmen Rojas, they insisted that they were not criminals but deserving workers, families, and neighbors.[24] Two-thirds said they planned to stay in the United States.[25]

Migrants have also broken the bounds of traditional politics by acting transnationally. Many send money or ideas to their homelands, and some return themselves. Others create pressure groups to mobilize for homeland democratization.[26] One vehicle of such cross-border engagement is organizations called hometown associations. In these clubs migrants raise money to support local public works in their places of origin. Even though less than a third of migrants are active in transnational politics, their advocacy has had important impacts in migrant-sending countries like Mexico.[27] For most of the twentieth century, Mexico was ruled by a single political party, the Partido Revolucionario Institucional (PRI; Institutional Revolutionary Party). In the 1990s, however, other parties began to vie for political power. They reached out to emigrants in the United States for support, sparking new forms of long-distance citizenship.[28] Indigenous migrants like those from Retorno and Partida were especially active in transnational politics, drawing on their strong ethnic identities, traditions of communal self-governance, and histories of resistance within Mexico.[29] Many joined hometown associations and began to connect their own struggles to antiglobalization movements elsewhere in Mexico and Latin America, such as the Zapatistas.[30]

In this respect, migrants fit into a broader moment in which politics is being forged not just by rights-bearing citizens but also by the excluded and undocumented: those *outside* the formal political sphere.[31] Hopeful scholars suggest that migrants, in particular, are uniquely positioned to navigate between states, building the kinds of grassroots, transnational movements that some imagine as a counterweight to corporate globalization.[32] Like other marginalized groups, migrants exercise agency not only in visible acts of resistance or formal electoral politics but also in their day-to-day political identities, actions, and strategies. Such "everyday politics" are the focus of this book.

Finally, gender is critical to contemporary resistance. States often rely on ideas about gender to underwrite their strategies of control.[33] For instance, one might think of how U.S. government officials have invoked images of criminal, immigrant "bad *hombres* [men]" as it deports vast numbers of Latinos, most of them men.[34] Meanwhile, women often lead grassroots mobilization, even in historically patriarchal communities.[35] As Carmen's and Alma's stories suggest, migrants' activism can remake gender in dramatically different ways. To make sense of these distinct political strategies and their gendered effects, I compare and contrast the contexts in which they emerge.

UNDERSTANDING MIGRANTS' POLITICS THROUGH
RELATIONAL, CROSS-BORDER COMPARISON

This book traces the stories of Partida and Retorno from the mountains of Oaxaca, Mexico, to the barrios of Southern California and back. To understand how Carmen, Alma, and their communities built different strategies of activism, I set their recent histories side by side. Using what ethnographer Michael Burawoy (2009) calls the "extended case method," I pay special attention both to broader politics and to the local context. Studying four different field sites, past and present, posed significant practical challenges.[36] My answer was twofold: first, I concentrated on building close relationships with two relatively small communities (sets of people). Second, I triangulated observations with interviews, surveys, and others' accounts, which helped to extend my data beyond the reach of a single scholar. In this section I describe the cases of Partida–Los Angeles and Retorno–North County San Diego, as well as my approach to studying them. In the "Methodological Appendix," I go into more detail about how I got to know these communities and how my identity as a white, U.S.-born woman created dynamic tensions that helped to guide my analysis.

I focus on communities, meaning hometowns and their migrants, as key sites of political contention and collaboration.[37] The pueblo is the core of political and economic life in Oaxaca. Village networks also structure migration in Mexico and around the world, as migrants follow others from the same hometown and cluster together in the same destinations.[38] While not everyone in a migrant community shares the same political attitudes, individuals make sense of their experiences in relation to their families, friends, and enemies. Working through communities gave me access to migrants' backstage conversations about police, the state, work, and politics. It also enabled me to put multiple people's stories together, fleshing out how each group's strategies evolved over time.

I contrast *two* communities to illuminate the effects of different political contexts. Most ethnographers focus on a single case (sometimes transnational). Meanwhile, broader, statistical studies of immigration tend to use aggregate data to represent immigrants as a whole, homogenizing the undocumented experience. In contrast, I take variation as the point of departure. I use comparison to understand how conditions on the ground shaped internal community dynamics, leading two groups to interact differently with similar macrolevel dynamics.[39] Comparison also helps identify points where marginalized groups may gain leverage. Even in the context of neoliberal globalization and a xenophobic U.S. state, it shows, migrants are not inherently voiceless or condemned to exclusion.

I consider this book a *relational comparison*. I adopt this term from Gillian Hart (2002, 2016) and Fernando Coronil (1997), who emphasize that communities are not bounded units that can be divided and ranked as "better" or "worse" but interact with one another and evolve historically. Like many ethnographers, I find it almost impossible to control the complexities of the social world or hone in on a single cause for human action. Thus, my approach does not have the tight logic of some comparative studies of immigration, in which either the sending or receiving site is held constant.[40] Instead, I argue that hometowns and destinations are part of the same process: hometowns shape where migrants go, and destinations influence migrants' engagement with their natal homes. My goal in bringing two cases together is not to freeze one part of this process but to draw out communities' relationships to each other and to broader political and economic forces.[41] Thus, I compare their processes of migration as a whole.

The processual approach poses some limitations. For instance, I cannot conclusively weigh the impact of each individual place on migrants' journeys. Nor can I present a snapshot in time; migrants' histories are still in progress. Nevertheless, juxtaposing migrants' whole trajectories brings out critical turning points, in ways that an apparently controlled comparison would not. I use two key tools to identify the impacts of a given context: (1) I look at how the two migrant streams diverged as they encountered distinct destinations, and (2) I pay special attention to times when migrants adopted political strategies that would have been unexpected based on their prior histories. Thus, I show how inequalities do not just begin at the point of origin but also accumulate and shift over place and time.

Oaxaca and California as Iconic Sites of Migration

I focus on Oaxaca and California because they are iconic sites of undocumented migration, but they also have significant local-level contrasts that allow for comparative analysis.

Mexico is the key source of unauthorized U.S. migration: more than half of the undocumented migrants in the United States were born there. Within Mexico, Oaxaca is one of the largest sending states, as well as one of the poorest and most patriarchal.[42] Almost 60 percent of the state's population identifies as indigenous, and indigenous villages tend to be even poorer and more isolated than their mestizo (mixed-race) counterparts.[43] They are also notoriously patriarchal. As of 2004, 75 percent of indigenous villages in Oaxaca excluded women from voting, and only 9 percent had accepted a woman in public office.[44] Indigenous women faced Mexico's worst gender disparities in education and health, and roughly 75 percent had survived gendered violence.[45]

In the 1960s downward pressure on corn prices drove Oaxaca's rural population to begin emigrating within Mexico and to the United States. Due to their poverty and lack of networks, most Oaxacans moved within Mexico first, then to California, in what scholars refer to as a "stepwise" pattern.[46] By the 1990s Oaxaca was one of the top migrant-sending states in Mexico. By 2004 its primary sources of income were no longer corn farms but (1) remittances, (2) tourism, and (3) Mexico's national welfare program, Oportunidades, in that order.[47] As of 2010, roughly a million indigenous Mexican migrants lived in the United States.[48] Almost all of them crossed the border undocumented, and almost all worked in manual jobs.

Within Oaxaca, however, local political dynamics and migration patterns varied dramatically. Oaxaca lies at the gnarled convergence of Mexico's two massive mountain ranges. For centuries Spanish colonists and the Mexican government used divide-and-conquer strategies to control its indigenous people. This combination kept villages so isolated that some neighboring communities could not understand one another's spoken dialects. Long-term state neglect also left indigenous people to run their own affairs under a system known as Usos y Costumbres (Ways and Customs). In 1995 Oaxaca formalized this system, giving roughly three-quarters of its municipalities the right to run their own elections and staff their own governments. Usos y Costumbres is often associated with communal governance, in which members make decisions by democratic assembly and rotate into local civil service posts. However, self-government also left room for dramatic variation. In some places, village elites co-opted Usos y Costumbres, so their pueblos came to look more like the despotic haciendas that predominated elsewhere in Mexico.[49] Thus, even though indigenous villages were subject to the same state and federal laws, local practices ranged from collective governance and landholding to elite control and dispossession. Because Oaxacan villages were isolated, each community also followed a relatively independent pattern of migration.

Southern California is also an emblematic site of undocumented Mexican migration. The region is an immigrant gateway: until the 1990s, 85 percent of Mexican migrants went to California, Texas, or Illinois.[50] In 2010 almost 40 percent of California's population was Latino. That same year Los Angeles and San Diego were among the top ten counties in the nation by total number of immigrants. Roughly one in ten working adults in the area was unauthorized, the largest concentration of undocumented immigrants in the United States.[51] This early experience with undocumented immigrants put cities in California at the vanguard of local immigration policy and enforcement.

As in Oaxaca, California's practices diverged at the city level.[52] When this book went to press in 2018, California was arguably the most immigrant-friendly state in the country, offering undocumented immigrants benefits like drivers' licenses and student financial aid. Yet it was not always so welcoming. In fact, in the 1990s California passed some of the nation's most restrictive policies. When I conducted this research in 2009–12, California had a Republican governor and little statewide legislation around immigration, leaving room for local variation. Cities like Los Angeles, Escondido, and Vista had created their own local immigration policies starting in the 1980s and 1990s. Other cities and states later followed suit, passing thousands of local immigration laws in the first decade of the 2000s.[53] On one end of the spectrum, places like Maricopa County, Arizona expanded policing and passed laws to target immigrants. On the other end, Los Angeles was among the first of what are now more than five hundred "sanctuary cities" in the United States, including New York, Chicago, San Francisco, and most other major metropolitan areas. While "sanctuary" is not a legal designation, most such cities promised not to share information about people's legal status with federal immigration agents. Many also extended services to immigrants.[54]

On the ground, police, service providers, and other state agents also exercised significant discretion toward immigrants. During the period of this study, ICE had only about six thousand agents dedicated to deportation, so it relied on local police to identify migrants for removal.[55] Formally, programs such as 287(g) and Secure Communities charged police with reporting undocumented immigrants to ICE.[56] In practice, however, some city police used these programs to pursue immigrants, while others refused to participate altogether.[57] Though Los Angeles and North County San Diego both adopted 287(g) and Secure Communities, Los Angeles police refused to check detainees' legal status until after criminal conviction. In contrast, North County police frequently checked people's papers right at their stops in the field. Likewise, even though federal laws blocked undocumented immigrants from most public services, providers in some areas extended education, health care, and welfare to the unauthorized.[58] To do so, they framed immigrants as hardworking and law abiding. In such areas migrants were significantly better protected from crime, labor violations, and domestic violence.[59] By contrast, as scholars such as Seth Holmes (2013) and Leah Schmalzbauer (2014) demonstrate, migrants in rural, agricultural, and anti-immigrant communities faced far harsher exclusion. Because cities in California created local immigration policies before most other parts of the United States, they may hint at dynamics in the pipeline in newer destinations.

The Cases of Partida–Los Angeles and Retorno–North County San Diego

I selected Partida–Los Angeles and Retorno–North County as case studies because they exemplified the variations in Oaxaca-California migration. Using Mexican census data, I created a list of migrant-sending communities to use as possible cases.[60] After visiting roughly a dozen pueblos, I chose Retorno and Partida because the hometowns were similar in size and status, but their experiences of migration diverged.

From the economic and demographic perspectives often used in migration research, Partida and Retorno resembled each other and other rural pueblos in Oaxaca. Both villages had roughly 1,500 inhabitants in 2010, and both were located just over fifty miles from the nearest city. Both were also municipal seats, held communal titles to their land, and self-governed under Usos y Costumbres. When I began researching this book, more than

60 percent of people in Retorno and Partida still lived in homes with dirt floors.[61] For most of the twentieth century, women in both hometowns had been blocked from attending political meetings, beaten at home, and required to ask their husband's and father's permission to work or leave the house.

The people of Partida and Retorno also migrated at similar times and volumes. While almost all Oaxacan villages now send migrants to the United States, these communities were among its earliest "high-expulsion" pueblos (as defined by the Mexican census), enabling me to study their dynamics over time. Like most indigenous migrants, their members lacked the money or social networks to go directly to the United States.[62] Instead, they migrated within Mexico in the 1960s and 1970s. Both began coming to the United States in the 1980s, with U.S. migration peaking in the early 1990s and declining in the first decade of the 2000s as border control intensified. By 2011 roughly two-thirds of respondents surveyed in each hometown had an immediate family member living in California.

In the United States, migrants from Partida and Retorno concentrated in nearby cities, with 99 percent of those from Partida settling in Los Angeles and 65 percent of those from Retorno moving to North County San Diego.[63] As was typical among Oaxacans, more than 95 percent of both groups crossed the border undocumented. By 2010 just over 70 percent remained unauthorized. The other 25–30 percent had become lawful permanent residents, almost all of them in mixed-status families. Both sets of migrants settled in cities where the population was roughly 50 percent Latino as of 2010 (50 percent in Los Angeles and 48 percent in Vista and Escondido).[64] They also lived in segregated neighborhoods where almost everyone spoke Spanish. In turn both encountered relatively similar cultural influences, including Spanish-language radio, television, and social-media sites.[65]

But Partida and Retorno also exemplified two contrasting streams of unauthorized migration from Oaxaca to the United States: one of permanent migration to Los Angeles, largely of Zapotecs, and the other of circular movement to rural California, mostly of Mixtecs.[66] While other scholars have puzzled over these differences, this book traces the contrasts to hometown power dynamics. I note that while these patterns tended to break down along ethnic lines, there were exceptions as well. Some Mixtec communities flouted the trend by moving to Los Angeles, while some Zapotec groups migrated to rural California.[67] Ethnicity alone could not explain their divergence.

As destinations, Los Angeles and North County San Diego also stood at opposite (if not extreme) ends of a continuum of U.S. cities, from pro- to anti-immigrant. Los Angeles had a long history of Chicano and Mexican immigrant organizing. It was the original and most vibrant site of the contemporary immigrants' rights movement, which is now represented in every major city in the United States. In the 1990s in particular, pro-immigrant organizations in Los Angeles, including the Coalition for Humane Immigrant Rights of Los Angeles, the Central American Resource Center, the Instituto de Educación Popular del Sur de California, and the Movimiento Estudiantil Chicano de Aztlán, among others, began collaborating with unions, faith organizations, and left-wing academics to expand local support for immigrants, including labor protections and access to state services.[68] In 2006 LA-based advocates built on these long-standing ties to lead the national immigrants' rights movement, mobilizing more than a million local residents to march in the span of two months. Starting in the 1990s Los Angeles also extended significant labor protections to undocumented workers.[69] Finally, migrants to Los Angeles tended to live in heavily Mexican neighborhoods like Koreatown, Echo Park, South and East Los Angeles, and Huntington Park, which was 94 percent Latino as of 2009. Although these cities did police, exploit, and deport large numbers of migrants, the local social context mitigated federal-level exclusion.

In contrast, Escondido, Vista, and other towns in North County San Diego were at the vanguard of restrictionism. Unlike Los Angeles, San Diego County lies within a hundred miles of the Mexican border. In this "zone of exemption," Border Patrol officers have license to search for undocumented immigrants without warrants or probable cause. In the 1980s and 1990s, while most of the United States turned a blind eye to undocumented migration, San Diego County's Border Crime Prevention Unit became notorious for murdering migrants. During the 1990s thousands of unauthorized immigrants in San Diego County lived beside the fields where they worked and were persecuted by immigration control.[70] North County San Diego also had far fewer pro-immigrant organizations than Los Angeles. Instead, Republicans and vocal anti-immigrant activists dominated local politics. Driven by these militants, cities in North County became some of the first in the nation to pass exclusionary local immigration measures, such as requiring that employers electronically verify workers' identities, criminalizing day labor, and prohibiting parking in Latino neighborhoods. Escondido also integrated ICE agents directly into its police department, and area police often used regular traffic stops to detain the undocumented.[71]

A study of two communities cannot represent the experiences of all Oaxacans or of Mexican migrants to Los Angeles, North County San Diego, or the United States as a whole. Partida and Retorno do not stand in for all communal or exclusionary villages, nor Los Angeles and San Diego County for all tolerant or restrictive sites. There may be hybrids between them as well as more extreme cases, particularly as the United States has grown more openly polarized. Nevertheless, their contrasts offer a starting point to understand how local state practices affect migrants' cross-border politics.

Methods and Data

To tell this story, I draw on almost two years of ethnographic fieldwork, 104 oral histories, original hometown surveys, archival research, and background from historical and ethnographic studies. I began my fieldwork in the hometowns of Partida and Retorno. In the fall of 2009 I took collective taxis to each village, asked town leaders for permission to do research, and began wandering around introducing myself.[72] After I had spent several months in each hometown, villagers put me in contact with their friends and relatives in Los Angeles and North County San Diego. Many U.S.-based respondents opened up when they learned I knew their families back home. Working through close-knit communities also made it possible for members to "check up on" me with one another, reinforcing their trust. Finally, going through migrants' hometowns enabled me to study their political attitudes independently of their participation in schools, service providers, NGOs, activist organizations, or labor unions.[73]

I lived in each field site for a total of about five months. In the villages I stayed with families. In California I rented apartments in Vista and Echo Park, Los Angeles.[74] In each place I joined community festivals and political meetings; visited members' homes; tagged along on errands, hospital visits, and school pickups; and had hundreds of conversations about people's experiences of migration, politics, gender, and work. Because most unauthorized migrants avoid U.S. government officials, I rarely observed direct interactions with state agents. Instead, I analyzed migrants' relationships to the state through hearsay and perceptions, paying special attention to (1) migrants' discussions about the police and bureaucrats, (2) their "backstage" reactions to officials, and (3) their "legal consciousness," or expressed, commonsense understandings of the law.[75]

Interviews brought my observations into dialogue with migrants' own voices. I conducted twenty-eight in-depth interviews in Partida, twenty-eight in Retorno, twenty-five in Los Angeles, and twenty-three in San Diego County. I focused on interviewing key players in each community who could remember its biggest accomplishments as well as its biggest fights. I then used surveys to check that I had interviewed people who reflected the distribution of age, legal status, and migration experiences in each community. Interviewees ranged from age twenty to seventy, 57 percent were women, 62 percent were married, and 68 percent lived in or had previously migrated to the United States. Over 70 percent of the migrants were undocumented as of 2011. They averaged six years of schooling, and less than half had completed primary school. Because I was concerned with unauthorized adults, I focused on people who arrived in the United States as teenagers or older.[76] Throughout, I treated respondents as participants in a common process rather than individual units that could be aggregated.[77] For instance, I often included several members of the same family, comparing their stories. By playing accounts against one another, I helped counter the bias of memory and reconstruct each community's history as a whole.

I conducted interviews in Spanish at a time and place of migrants' choosing, usually their homes.[78] Before each interview I visited respondents several times, getting to know them and their families. During the interviews I asked about their decisions to migrate or not, perceptions of policing and social services, feelings of belonging, ideas about gender, and political actions. While respondents may have been inclined to present rosier views of the United States to me than to their peers, comparison served as a resource. Even if both groups tempered what they said to me, I could gain insights from the differences between them.

I used systematic surveys or censuses in each hometown and snowball surveys in each destination to map their migration paths. In January 2011 I joined about forty faculty members and students from University of California, San Diego (UCSD), and the Universidad Autónoma de Benito Juárez de Oaxaca to conduct a census of adults age fifteen to sixty-five in Retorno (N = 717) and snowball surveys of Retorno's migrants in North County San Diego (N = 121).[79] The survey lasted about an hour and asked about migrants' histories, occupations, family relations, experiences in the United States, and political participation. It also gathered migration histories of respondents' family members (N = 1924). The team also conducted more than fifty in-depth interviews in Retorno and North County, augmenting my own qualitative research. The following month I hired six undergraduates from the Universidad Autónoma de Benito Juárez de Oaxaca and replicated UCSD's survey in Partida. We selected every third household and randomly identified a member age fifteen to sixty-five to participate (N = 121). I then did a snowball survey of Partida's migrants in Los Angeles (N = 51), gathering family members' migration histories on both sides of the border (N = 686).[80]

Finally, I drew on archives and secondary sources to understand how Partida and Retorno fit into the landscape of Oaxaca and U.S. migration. A vast body of ethnographic research about Oaxaca and its migrants in the United States provided context, enabling me to start fieldwork from what other scholars already knew.[81] I also checked respondents' recollections against records at Oaxaca's National Agrarian Registry, its National Institute for Statistics and Geography, and Partida and Retorno's municipal archives. This mix of sources extended my reach beyond a single field site, making it possible to trace communities' pathways as a whole.

PATHWAYS TO POLITICS

Based on these data, I make three key arguments about migrant communities' politics. First, local-level practices of power mediate migrants' decisions to move, as well as their attitudes about U.S. exclusion. Second, political agency is processual, evolving as migrants navigate their local histories and their particular destinations. Third, gender informs both state control and migrants' fights for inclusion.

I refer to these gendered processes as *pathways to politics*. Like a path through the woods, migrants' pathways are shaped by "landmarks," which mold their twists and turns. Political scientists refer to such landmarks as "critical junctures," points where two similar groups diverge. For indigenous Mexican migrants, key landmarks include local power dynamics in their hometowns as well as in their destinations in the United States. A political pathway is similar to other scholars' idea of "path dependence" in that it uses historical trajectories to help explain present actions.[82] But in a pathway migrant communities are not just driven by historical legacies. Rather, their politics reflect a *series* of local conditions.

A "pathway" is also a sequence or course of action. On one hand, people from Partida lived in places that set them on a path of relative inclusion— from a communal starting point to a comparatively tolerant destination. Those from Retorno, on the other hand, faced one exclusion after another, from a hierarchical hometown to a hostile U.S. extreme. Yet migrants not only face different interplays between sending and receiving sites; they also engage with and react to those conditions. Their actions shift the trajectories one might have expected at the outset. For instance, given Retorno's exclusion of indigenous villagers and its abuse of women, outsiders might assume that migrants like Alma would never return. Instead, they came back to remake the village. Understanding such shifts requires examining how migrants respond to both the places they go and the places they leave behind.

Modes of State Control

As Carmen's and Alma's stories suggest, unauthorized migrants confront distinct practices of power, both in their hometowns and in the United States. State policies also intertwine with the local economy, shaping people's experiences at work. I call these local contexts *modes of control*. Different modes of control, I argue, inspire distinct attitudes about the homeland and the United States. Partida and Retorno demonstrate how.

Before people migrate abroad, local power dynamics in Mexico influence who leaves and why. For instance, Partida's redistribution of land and political power enabled villagers to avoid agricultural labor and hold out for urban jobs. Young people—especially women—were able to leave to seek opportunity. In urban areas, in turn, women built the social ties to connect their community to Los Angeles. By contrast, Retorno's local inequality forced its residents into the hands of farm recruiters. There, local political bosses appropriated power and land for themselves, driving poorer villagers into debt. Whole families often left to work on Mexico's industrial farms. While there, women suffered so much that many returned to the village, leaving only men to move on to California. Farm recruiters brought these men from Mexican ranches to the then-agricultural area of North County San Diego.

Once migrants arrive in the United States, contrasting local modes of control mold their political identities. Los Angeles represents one extreme, in which migrants perceive state treatment as *conditional* on their behavior. Observing a combination of deportation and state support, migrants think of the policing as punishment for "bad" behavior, while associating services with "being good." For those from Partida, such good/bad contrasts offered a sense of control, diminishing fear and promoting belonging, particularly among women. Yet the binary also encouraged them to act according to state norms of hard work and self-sufficiency. Many, like Carmen, strove to distance themselves from their "bad" counterparts and Mexican roots. North County San Diego, meanwhile, exemplifies a different, more *arbitrary* mode of control. There, migrants from Retorno believed that police and bureaucrats targeted migrants by race, regardless of their behavior. Most felt terrified and powerless. Many resigned themselves to perpetual exclusion, even as they continued to live in the United States.

Local modes of control also shape migrants' experiences at work. Migrants from Partida entered Los Angeles through the service sector, while those from Retorno came to North County through farmwork. By the time of my research, however, most people in both sites worked in factories or domestic service. Still, each city's political environment conditioned the bosses' treatment. In Los Angeles employers were regulated by local labor controls, so they often used rewards or competition to motivate workers. At work as in public, migrants tended to believe hard work would earn them rewards. By contrast, foremen in North County San Diego relied on fear, threatening to call immigration control if migrants did not do as they bid. As a result, people from Retorno tended to feel like "slaves."

Migrants' Political Strategies

As migrant communities like Partida and Retorno confront contrasting modes of control, they adopt distinct *political strategies*. Depending on the terms of local state power and the resources available to them, members take different approaches to seeking inclusion in the process of globalization. Thus, their politics vary in the United States, across borders, and in their hometowns.

For one, migrants have different ways of dealing with "illegality" in the United States. Under conditional control in Los Angeles, most immigrants from Partida embraced a *strategy of belonging*. They trusted that if they acted "good" they could earn economic and political inclusion. Perhaps counterintuitively, this faith in the U.S. government encouraged some of them to join marches for immigrants' rights. At the same time, many also sought to earn recognition, rights, and resources by performing "good" behavior and hard work. Good/bad distinctions also pitted migrants against their peers, marking those deported as "bad" and even legitimating ongoing exclusion. By contrast, North County's arbitrary control made immigrants from Retorno feel alienated. Most were cynical about their prospects for inclusion in the United States, so they reverted to a *strategy of withdrawal*. Giving up on changing California, they looked to Mexico for hope. Though few of them actually returned, they stoically awaited the promise of "home."

Different pathways also encourage distinct transnational practices. For instance, as migrants from Partida struggled to prove they belonged in Los Angeles, they distanced themselves from their hometown and Mexican politics, sparking cross-border *polarization*. By contrast, Retorno's migrants looked for escape from North County San Diego, building *solidarity* with their hometown and opposition parties in Mexico. It seems surprising that migrants like Alma would want to return to the debt, inequality, and violence from which they fled (even in the face of U.S. exclusion). But Mexico had also changed, reaching out to include migrants in homeland politics. For those from Retorno, therefore, Mexico came to seem more dynamic and open to their influence than the United States.

Finally, people in migrants' hometowns react to migration, redefining their relationships with the Mexican state. Hometowns are not simply objects of migrants' long-distance actions. They, too, respond to migrants' pathways. In some places, like Partida, those remaining see emigration as a threat to local traditions and adopt an *antiglobalization* stance. Indeed, as migrants distanced themselves from Partida, villagers rejected outside efforts to change their communal history, led by both migrants and the Mexican state. By contrast, pueblos like Retorno may see migration itself as "suffering." There, returnees like Alma joined long-distance migrants to wage a movement for *alternative globalization*, demanding resources and representation from Mexico. In neither case did ideas simply flow from North to South, United States to hometown. Instead, homeland politics reflect the dynamic contentions between hometowns, migrants, and the Mexican and U.S. states.

Gendering Fights for Inclusion

Gender is critical to migrants' pathways, in both the modes of control they face and the strategies they adopt for change. For one, local power dynamics affect women and men differently. On the hometown side both Partida and Retorno were deeply patriarchal. Nevertheless, Partida's urban migration pattern helped women escape abuse. By contrast, Retorno's inequity forced whole families to leave together, offering no such relief. In Los Angeles, in turn, women from Partida often had more access to public services and police protection than men. They were preferred in local, feminized service and garment jobs. In light of these advantages, women like Carmen tended to feel "empowered" in the United States and grateful to their adopted home. Meanwhile, men in Los Angeles often felt more ambivalent about their prospects for U.S. inclusion. These differences sometimes pitted women against men. In North County, by contrast, arbitrary enforcement made women afraid to leave home, reinforcing their isolation. Though women from Retorno also worked in service and factory jobs, many arrived later than their male counterparts, leaving them more dependent on men. With little access to state protection, women like Alma remained vulnerable to male abuse. Thus, like men, they rejected the United States and hoped to return. Understanding how modes of control are gendered helps explain variations in men's and women's perceptions of the United States.

As women and men struggle for inclusion, they also transform gendered power dynamics. Yet they do so in different places and ways. Like Carmen, women from Partida became politically active in the United States, embracing the support it offered them. As they struggled for rights as immigrants, they also demanded influence as women. They used relations with their hometown to display this empowerment, such as by pushing for gender equity in the village. But many men in Partida rejected women's newfound independence, further dividing the hometown and its migrants. By contrast, women from Retorno often looked to their hometown for reprieve from North County's isolation and abuse. Yet men in North County *also* wanted to return to Mexico. As a result, men from Retorno helped mobilize women in the village to advocate on their collective behalf. In both cases women gained political voice in and through their efforts to navigate state control. But the character of their political strategies shaped whether women felt "free" in the United States, like Carmen, or in Mexico, like Alma.

RETHINKING THEORIES OF MIGRATION, GENDER, AND GLOBAL ADVOCACY

The political-pathways framework—and the concept of modes of control— help shed new light on migrant legal status, globalization, gender, and grassroots advocacy. For students of immigrant "illegality," I highlight the importance of local state practice. A wealth of recent research exposes how undocumented status, policing, and deportation keep migrants marginal in the United States. Scholars demonstrate that U.S. immigration policies mark undocumented people as criminals, justifying the use of force against them and their exclusion from rights.[83] In what sociologists Cecilia Menjívar and Leisy Abrego (2012) call "legal violence," state laws normalize the physical abuse and symbolic dehumanization of immigrants.[84] I show how local policing and bureaucratic practices mediate such legal violence. Building on the concept of *contexts of reception,* which refers to a receiving community's openness or hostility to immigrants, I emphasize the importance of the local *state.*[85] In particular, I demonstrate how local protection can give migrants hope. Yet when combined with force, such support can push migrants to act "good" or even accept the subordination of other "bad" immigrants as fair. I also underscore how arbitrary enforcement can reinforce the violence of deportation, making migrants feel they are suffering. These subjective understandings of the state are central to immigrants' politics: undocumented people are likely to seek inclusion in the United States when they see its government as reasonable, as did those from Partida, and look elsewhere when they reject U.S. state laws as illegitimate, as did those from Retorno. In turn, people's attitudes toward the United States inform their feelings about their homelands.

For global, transnational, and development sociologists, I draw attention to the relationship between U.S. exclusion and sending-country politics. Scholars of development have long debated the impacts of migration. Some argue that migration creates a political "safety valve," allowing people to "vote with their feet" instead of protesting unfair policies in their homelands.[86] Others hail the promise of migrants' remittances, suggesting that emigrants can help the sending country by sharing both money and new ways of thinking, such as about civic participation or gender.[87] Albeit unintentionally, such analyses often tie sending communities' prospects for economic development, democracy, and gender equity to money and ideas from the United States. I show that transnational and homeland advocacy are more complex. In some cases, such as Partida, the westernization of migrants may spark hometown defiance rather than emulation. In other cases, migrants may use transnational advocacy to build alternatives to the United States, "remitting resistance," as did those from Retorno. Transnational advocacy must be therefore be contextualized in terms of communities' pathways, particularly the modes of control they face in the United States. At the same time, transnational engagement (or disengagement) is processual, building not only on the U.S. context but also on ever-evolving hometown dynamics. People who remain in the homeland are also agents of change in their own right. They may reject their emigrants' abandonment, as in Partida. Or, as in Retorno, they may sympathize with their migrant counterparts and seek to insulate themselves from similar suffering. Sending communities' engagement in home-country politics is also shaped by this complex interplay between particular sending and receiving sites.

My focus on place and process also helps advance theories about gender and migration. Early scholars in this area argued that women gained standing when they migrated, thanks to the wages and egalitarian norms they encountered in the United States. Some could also "remit" (U.S.) gender equity back to their hometowns.[88] More recently, intersectional theorists have highlighted how gender overlaps with legal status, race, and class. Instead of focusing on women's empowerment, they highlight how fear, isolation, and family separation can create new burdens for migrant women and even *worsen* domestic patriarchy.[89] I extend this line of inquiry by examining how women's and men's understandings of gender—and their feelings of "empowerment"—vary with local structures of power. I show that tolerant and equitable state treatment can support women's mobility and help them feel "free." By contrast, arbitrary, unequal, and anti-immigrant practices make women more vulnerable, whether or not enforcement is specifically directed at them. These varying gendered experiences shape how and whether migrants participate in activities associated with immigration, including hometown associations and cultural incorporation.

At the same time, I underscore how the cross-border dynamics of gender intertwine with migrants' politics. Traditionally, scholars evaluated gender and migration by comparing people's gendered practices in the sending country (which often appeared as backward) with their practices in the receiving country (which emerged as "enlightened"). While gender *is* transnational, I demonstrate, it is also malleable, in *both* the homeland and the United States. As men and women work to challenge exclusion, both of them transform old patterns of patriarchy. In particular, women gain political voice in and through their efforts to navigate dislocation.

Finally, this work offers a novel perspective on the collective identities and political strategies of excluded groups. In recent years political theorists have celebrated the agency of the disenfranchised and the struggles they wage outside the formal political sphere. In the context of global migration in particular, people fight for membership within and beyond their original nation-states. Migrants have thus become famous for their transnational advocacy.[90] As a result, the *politics of belonging* have grown increasingly important.[91] I bring such theories into conversation with studies about how place and local organizing shape people's political identities.[92] In particular, I illustrate how local power dynamics weigh on excluded populations' desires and abilities to pressure a given state for rights and resources. In both receiving sites and places of origin, I show, local state practices lay the foundation for different aspirations, movements, and kinds of social change. In turn, migrants' battles hinge on their hopes for inclusion.

MAP OF THE BOOK

The following chapters set Carmen, Alma, and their counterparts from Partida and Retorno side by side at five key landmarks. The first two chapters analyze local practices of power in each of the four field sites. Chapter 1 traces how hometown dynamics set the stage for migrants' entry into the United States. In Partida, I show, communal governance helped migrants enter urban Los Angeles. By contrast, Retorno's elites appropriated land and political power, driving poorer villagers into the hands of farm-labor recruiters in rural California. Chapter 2 then compares the modes of control in Los Angeles and North County San Diego. In Los Angeles, I argue, migrants from Partida saw state and labor treatment as conditional on their behavior, giving them a sense of hope. By contrast, North County's arbitrary policing left those from Retorno feeling alienated, cynical, and afraid.

The last three chapters turn to migrants' own struggles. In Chapter 3 I look at each community's approach to political integration in the United States. I show that in Los Angeles, migrants like Carmen adopted a strategy of belonging, working to prove they deserved inclusion. In North County San Diego, by contrast, migrants like Alma reverted to a strategy of withdrawal. Though few people from Retorno left the United States, they grew stoic and looked to their hometown for hope. Chapter 4 considers how the two groups of migrants approached cross-border ties. While those in Los Angeles grew polarized from Partida, I show, those from Retorno built solidarity with their counterparts on the Mexican side. Finally, Chapter 5 looks at each hometown's response. I explore how migrants' Americanization in Los Angeles sparked antiglobalization back-lash in Partida and how Retorno joined its migrants to fight for alternative globalization. Thus, I illustrate how migration remade the villages where it began. In the conclusion I explore how a focus on political pathways and local modes of control can illuminate spaces for agency. I highlight how— even in the face of exclusion—U.S. cities, Mexican hometowns, and undocumented men and women can carve out political voice.

1 Legacies of (In)Equity

For most of the twentieth century, villagers in Partida and Retorno lived by growing corn. Neither hometown had roads, let alone electricity or running water. Only one in four people owned shoes, and less than 20 percent could read.[1] To access urban markets or schools, Carmen's and Alma's parents had to walk for two or three days through the mountains. The Oaxacan government neglected such villages almost entirely. As long as the pueblos delivered votes to the ruling Partido Revolucionario Institucional (PRI; Institutional Revolutionary Party), they were free to run their own affairs. In principle, indigenous people followed the customary system of communal governance known as Usos y Costumbres. In practice, men ruled, blocking women from voting or holding property and demanding that they ask their husbands' permission to leave the house. In some villages, including Retorno, a few men took over the local government, using their power for personal gain.

Then, in the 1950s and 1960s, labor recruiters came to Oaxaca.[2] In the state of Sinaloa, 1,300 miles to the north, Mexico had begun building a vast, new agroindustry, whose growers needed cheap labor (see map at front). Recruiters trekked into Oaxaca to tap its isolated, indigenous population. They promised the peasants cash advances and double or triple the wages earned at home. As Mexico urbanized, demand for urban service workers soared as well. Oaxacans began to leave for such paid work. By the 1980s pioneer migrants from both Partida and Retorno had gone on to California, almost universally crossing the border without legal authorization. By the 1990s almost 90 percent of the villages' migrants were headed, undocumented, for the United States.[3]

Though farm recruiters came to both villages, they got little traction in Partida. Instead, people from Partida held out for urban jobs.[4] They became servants in middle-class homes in Oaxaca. They cleaned houses in Mexico City. Eventually, they found themselves in Los Angeles.[5] Instead of traveling as families, most left as young people, alone, in search of opportunities before they settled down. More than half were women.

In contrast, Mixtec families poured into farmwork. By the 1970s Alma, her parents, and three-quarters of Retorno were making a yearly trek to the tomato fields in Sinaloa. Winters they worked; summers they came back to the village. From Sinaloa, labor contractors drew them farther north, funneling them into the hostile, rural area of North County San Diego. In Mexico, women and children had worked alongside the men. Yet when men from Retorno went on to the United States, women sought reprieve from the trials of industrial farms. Many returned to Oaxaca, refusing to go on.

HOW HOMETOWN POWER DYNAMICS SHAPE EMIGRATION

These histories stand in for a broader trend, in which Zapotec migrants tended to move to Los Angeles, while Mixtecs went to farmwork. Though other scholars have traced these differences, few offer a clear explanation. If both groups were poor and isolated, and both left at the same times and volumes, how did they come to take such different paths? In general, researchers know that industrialization pushes emigrants out of rural towns.[6] Typically, those with more money, skills, education, and networks have the best prospects as migrants. By contrast, the poor often have to move within their home countries to build cash and contacts before they can continue abroad.[7] Theorists of social networks also show that family and hometown ties play critical roles in defining where individuals end up—and in which jobs. Migrants from rural areas, in particular, follow others from their hometowns.[8] Indeed, it is common to find an entire restaurant or ranch in Southern California staffed entirely by migrants from a single Mexican village.

Many scholars also assume that Mexico-U.S. labor migration follows a relatively standardized process. First, men move into U.S. farmwork, then they bring their families, and eventually migrants branch into different places and jobs.[9] Some researchers contend that even when two communities appear to have different migration patterns, they may just be at different stages of this process.[10] Those with migrants living in cities may simply have had more time to branch out. As for different starting points, this model implies that variations are due to chance. For instance, some scholars argue that an early migrant "in the right place at the right time" might help his whole village find contacts in New York City, while those of a neighboring pueblo remained consigned to farmwork.[11] In this rendering, landing in Los Angeles or North County San Diego appears almost accidental.

This chapter shows that, in fact, hometown power dynamics shape the choices available to a village's early migrants—and thus to its networks as a whole. In the twentieth century, Partida and Retorno faced similar poverty and isolation. Technically, both villages governed themselves under Usos y Costumbres and held communal titles to their land. Yet they practiced autonomous governance in starkly different ways. Partida followed a traditional model of indigenous participation, running itself as a commune (albeit a patriarchal one).[12] It redistributed land, insulating families from debt. As a result, when farm recruiters came to the village, its residents had just enough resources to refuse their overtures. Men in Partida also rotated into local leadership posts like village president or secretary. While serving in such positions, they gained access to Oaxaca City and learned of urban opportunities. Soon they began sending their children to the city for education and jobs. Thus, men in Partida were able to reject farm labor and build a pattern of independent, urban migration. Later these urban ties also helped women from Partida flee male control.

In contrast, Retorno was unequal, pressing whole families into farmwork. Even though Retorno technically followed Usos y Costumbres, in practice, it was ruled by caciques, or local political bosses. These caciques used their positions to strip other villagers of land, converting the poor into sharecroppers. By the time farm recruiters arrived in Retorno, most of its residents were destitute, landless, and in debt. Elites also monopolized access to cities. As a result, poorer families had little choice but to accept farm jobs. Driven by debt, men, women, and children cycled back and forth to northern Mexico for seasonal agricultural work.

Each community's internal migration patterns then channeled it into a different destination in the United States.[13] Like many Sierra Zapotecs, young men and women from Partida began to work as housekeepers in Mexico City. While there, women met wealthy U.S. families who offered them work in Los Angeles.[14] Even though men from Partida were recruited into farmwork in the United States, just like those from Retorno, women's housekeeping ties gave them both an alternative. By contrast, as migrants circled between Retorno and northern Mexico, they met few contacts except for farm recruiters. Even when they went on to the United States, they stayed trapped in agroindustry. Still, these patterns were not inevitable once they began. Rather, migrants reacted to their internal migration experiences, reinforcing or altering their paths. Partida's and Retorno's shifting gender dynamics illustrate this dynamism.

Scholars have generally argued that men dominate Mexico-U.S. migration thanks to (1) Mexico's "patriarchal culture" and (2) the U.S. government's recruitment of men as temporary farmworkers after World War II, in what is known as the Bracero Program.[15] Indeed, most migrants from rural Mexico to the United States in the second half of the twentieth century were men. Women tended to either stay in Mexico or come to the United States after their male counterparts.[16] But Partida and Retorno reveal that this trend was not universal. Whether or not women migrated was not just a reflection of patriarchal culture but also of whether village-wide migration paths enabled the women to escape. In particular, urban opportunities attracted women migrants, while farmwork deterred them from further migration.

Women's experiences in housekeeping (from Partida) and farmwork (from Retorno) sparked very different responses. Those from Partida could use hometown networks in Oaxaca City and Mexico City to leave independently, escaping the violence of their families of birth. As women from Partida found urban jobs, more of them chose to leave, tipping the balance among migrants toward women.[17] In turn, women's access to feminized housekeeping and garment work helped the whole community set roots in Los Angeles. At first, in the 1960s and 1970s, women from Retorno also migrated in almost equal numbers to men. Yet patriarchy traveled with them. In farmwork, they shouldered labor violations alongside sexual abuse and household beatings. They also had to raise families in squalid labor camps. Migration was no escape. Instead, women from Retorno found relief by separating from their husbands and returning to their village of origin. Ironically, their decisions to opt out of U.S. migration left the people of Retorno as a whole with little access to feminized service work in the United States. Still, the women of Retorno were not "left behind," as accounts of Mexican migration sometimes imply. In the face of family farm labor, they *chose* to go home for relief.

EMIGRATION IN THE CONTEXT OF MEXICO'S AGRARIAN TRANSFORMATION

Migrants left Oaxaca as part of Mexico's agrarian transformation. From 1929 until 2000 a single party—the Partido Revolucionario Institucional—held power in Mexico, ruling through a centralized state and corrupt elections without real competition.[18] In the 1950s and 1960s this party began seeking to "modernize" the nation. It invested in industry, agricultural technologies, energy, and transportation, driving a three-decade period of 3–4 percent economic growth known as the "Mexican miracle." In 1941, with support from the Rockefeller Foundation, Mexico began the Green Revolution: a project to revolutionize agriculture through environmental restructuring, fertilizers, chemical pesticides, irrigation, and railroads to the United States.[19] The Valley of Culiacán, Sinaloa, a sparsely populated area in the middle of Mexico's western coast, became a lynchpin of this growth. To fuel the agroindustrial machine, growers in Sinaloa began importing labor, mostly from Oaxaca. Over time Oaxacan workers also moved on to nascent agroindustries in the states of Baja California and Sonora, just south of the U.S. border.[20] By 1980 more than five hundred thousand Oaxacans were serving as seasonal farmworkers in Sinaloa, Sonora, and Baja California, the three most concentrated sites of Mexican agroindustry.[21] They worked fourteen-hour days, up to their knees in mud, growing more than half the winter vegetables sold in North America.[22]

The Mexican miracle also fueled rapid urbanization. In the 1940s more than 80 percent of Mexicans lived in rural pueblos without running water or electricity. By 1970 the country was almost half urban. In particular, Mexico City's population grew from 1.4 million in 1900 to more than 22 million in 1970, making it one of the largest cities in the world.[23] As the urban upper classes expanded, they began wanting household help. To fill this demand, peasant boys and girls came to cities as housekeepers, starting work as early as age eight or ten. Though household workers in Mexico had typically been young boys, in the 1960s employers began demanding single women. Migrant women found they could establish themselves as servants, even as their male counterparts struggled to find stable urban jobs.[24]

Mexico's policies also drove peasants *out* of subsistence farming. In the 1940s and 1950s the government introduced primary schools, piped water, and dirt roads in rural Oaxaca. It also began to require fiscal accounting from indigenous villages.[25] Then, in the 1960s, Mexico imposed price controls on corn, decreasing its value by a third.[26] In the 1970s the large-scale borrowing that had fueled Mexico's "miracle" drove the country into debt and runaway inflation. Prices for seeds and farm equipment increased dramatically. In the late 1970s world oil prices plummeted, sending Mexico into crisis. The government responded by reducing farm subsidies and opening local markets to mass-produced U.S. food.[27] By 1981 Mexico was importing more corn than it exported, even as production reached record highs. In August 1982 Mexico defaulted on its debt. In exchange for a bailout by the International Monetary Fund (IMF) and World Bank, the government devalued the peso by 100 percent.[28] In the coming decade, in a series of reforms demanded by the World Bank and IMF, and referred to as "structural adjustment," Mexico privatized government firms, deregulated markets, reduced public-sector spending, eliminated price supports for basic crops, and pushed peasants to sell communal land.[29] The passage of the North American Free Trade Agreement in 1994 put the final nail in the coffin of the nation's small-scale corn farms, removing remaining subsidies and trade barriers.[30]

By the mid-1990s it was cheaper for farmers in rural Oaxaca—the birthplace of maize—to buy corn from the United States than to grow it themselves.[31] By 2003 peasants in pueblos like Retorno and Partida earned a mere 11 percent of what they had just a decade before. Meanwhile, the indigenous population boomed, fueling land shortages.[32] Thus, Oaxaca became a prime target for labor recruitment. In the 1980s and 1990s indigenous peasants flooded out of the state.[33]

At the same time, employers in the United States also began seeking new low-wage workers. In the 1970s the U.S. market for fresh produce started to boom. Women also entered the U.S. workforce in unprecedented numbers. The effect was to radically increase U.S. demands for farm and household labor, doubling the number of gardeners and housekeepers in Los Angeles, for instance, between 1980 and 1990.[34] Then, in 1986, the U.S. Immigration Reform and Control Act legalized many of the unauthorized immigrants who were already in the United States, enabling earlier waves of migrants to obtain higher-paying jobs. Thus, there opened up a new market for undocumented migrants with little choice but to do low-wage work.[35]

THE ROLE OF LOCAL GOVERNMENT

Local power dynamics mediated rural villages' experiences of economic transformation. While the PRI was highly centralized, with no formal local government in Mexico until the 1990s, in practice it ruled through various regional arrangements, combining bargaining, coercion, and alliances in different sites.[36] State power was especially variegated in Oaxaca, where the PRI relied on indirect rule to manage remote, indigenous villages. To keep the indigenous from organizing, the state often pitted nearby communities against one another. At the same time, it gave each village autonomy to run its own affairs.[37] As a result, local governance practices diverged.

Formally, Partida, Retorno, and most indigenous pueblos used (and still use) the system of Usos y Costumbres, or "Ways and Customs." Practiced since the colonial era, Usos y Costumbres allows indigenous villages to run their own elections and staff their governments in the way they see fit. In theory Usos y Costumbres is associated with collective governance. Whereas Western governments define citizenship in terms of individual rights, members of Usos y Costumbres communities earn rights through public service to the pueblo.[38] In an ideal-type village, adult men serve in unpaid civic posts (known as *cargos*), do collective labor on public-works projects *(tequio)*, and make decisions in community assemblies.[39] A male villager might rotate into a new cargo once every few years, starting at the lowest rank, such as night watchman, and moving up to town president. While these posts confer traditional status, they are also onerous. Thus, the name *cargos,* meaning "burdens." Historically, Usos y Costumbres has also been entwined with collective landholding.[40] As of 2007, 72 percent of Oaxacan land was technically communal, 61 percent held under communal titles granted in the colonial era (including Partida and Retorno), and the rest as *ejidos,* collective holdings granted during Mexican land reform in the 1930s.[41] Villagers typically had usufruct rights to parcels of communal land. If they reneged on their political duties, the pueblo could expel them or reclaim the plots they tilled.

Despite this "standard," the combination of local autonomy and state neglect meant that nearby pueblos could be run in starkly different ways.[42] On one extreme, communities like Partida redistributed land and rotated political posts. In such villages, the cargo system mediated class hierarchies by assigning burdensome positions to those who were best off.[43] Collective practices also helped these villages resist co-optation by the state, landlords, corporations, and even NGOs.[44] On the other extreme, pueblos like Retorno converted ostensible participation into exploitation, clientelism, and elite control. As mentioned, the Mexican state tolerated Usos y Costumbres as part of a clientelist bargain, in which peasant communities delivered votes to the PRI in exchange for autonomy.[45] In the process it converted some indigenous leaders into PRI clients and political bosses, who managed their pueblos arbitrarily and with little accountability.

INDEPENDENT URBAN MIGRATION FROM PARTIDA

In Partida, as in much of the Sierra Norte region, villagers clung fiercely to collective control, resisting the land grabs and evangelization that occurred elsewhere in Oaxaca.[46] Their obstinacy dates to the colonial era. Zapotecs in the region fought Spanish colonists for more than thirty-five years, murdering invaders and Catholic evangelists.[47] By Mexican Independence in 1821, Partida remained 99.5 percent indigenous, with just a "tiny, impoverished group of Spanish colonists," as historian John Chance puts it (1989, 13).

In the nineteenth and early twentieth centuries, Partida's leaders had little influence, living like commoners and using their positions to promote populist projects such as infrastructure. When members attempted to monopolize influential positions in the pueblo, villagers rioted. The would-be caciques had demanded that civic posts be made hereditary, so that fathers could pass their status to sons, rather than letting them work their own way up the cargo hierarchy. Other villagers refused. Likewise, the community assembly insisted on holding leaders accountable for funds, and it expelled those who accepted patronage or defied community decisions.[48] In the late 1800s and early 1900s, the new Mexican state began to seek rural intermediaries. Again the people of Partida dismissed would-be go-betweens as "pimping" and drove them out of the village. Later, when the government of Porfirio Díaz began to push land privatization, Partida invoked the 1589 colonial title that had granted its communal land.[49] In the 1930s, Sierra Norte villages also led an anticlerical movement in Oaxaca, pushing to delink local politics from the demands of the Catholic Church.[50] Thus, Partida sustained collective governance and rebuffed outside incursion.

The Collective Foundation for Urban Ties

Samuel Luna—a jocular, silver-haired man in his seventies—remembered what it was like to grow up in this environment. When Samuel was born in Partida in 1942, the village was built entirely of adobe. Aside from attending school in Oaxaca City in the 1950s, Samuel had lived in Partida his entire life. Today he ran one of the pueblo's two public phone stands. On the side, he also sold Cheetos and chili-flavored lollipops, which he would gift me if I stayed long enough and business was slow. We talked often during my fieldwork. Samuel's parents had been illiterate farmers. When I asked him what life was like in Partida when he was a child, he recounted,

> There were one or two people who didn't have any land, but, yes, the majority had land—if even just a few parcels, but they had it.[51] Yes, my father had

land, but the way he planted—well, here, in those days, there was what they call *gozona,* a kind of work that you do with several people. So, you come help plant my land, and in ten or twenty days they would plant the land, and after that they would go plant someone else's. . . . So my father would go to help other people in order to bring his own work along. . . . We worked through reciprocal labor; that's how we all got corn.

As Samuel came of age in the 1950s, each family in Partida had use of about nine acres of farmland.[52] By combining communal land with shared labor, villagers produced just enough to support a family of nine or ten (typical for the time).[53] As a result, almost no one in Partida had to work for wages.[54]

Though Samuel's parents had never gone to school, they sent him to Oaxaca City to learn Spanish when he turned ten years old. Like most villagers at the time, his parents spoke almost exclusively Zapotec, making it hard for them to communicate with urban Mexicans. Samuel explained,

It was precisely because sometimes it's our turn to carry out cargos in the town government. My father was a town councilman, policeman, and so on. He had to be on the education committee, to sponsor the village festival, to be the judge. He's a farmer, but he never even went to school. . . . And because we spoke Zapotec here, we felt stunted in our language capacities. The teaching in the village school was really bad, so our parents felt an obligation to send us to Oaxaca City. With the goal of us learning Spanish, they sent us to work as servants. . . . The families used to go to Oaxaca City, and there would be ads up saying "servant boy wanted," so parents would just go there and say, "We have a boy that can work for you."

In the 1950s and 1960s the state of Oaxaca began demanding that rural villages report on their affairs. Several times a year village representatives had to read government documents, travel to Oaxaca City, and interact with urban bureaucrats. Since people in Partida rotated through leadership posts, a different person reported to city officials each year. As Samuel's father faced these demands, he began to feel an urgent need for literacy and Spanish language. During one trip to the city, he saw an ad for servant boys, offering work in exchange for room and board, so he sent his son.

Samuel's story highlights two effects of Partida's communal structure. First, because farmland was distributed, most people had enough to subsist. Rotating political control also helped reduce economic inequality. Partida's cargos were so burdensome—and its collective oversight of leaders so stringent—that nominating someone to a leadership post could curb his accumulation. Juan Pablo Menéndez, a former village president explained that if someone began to amass wealth the village assembly would nominate him to a demanding cargo, which would take up his time, prevent him from working, and thus even out wealth disparities.[55] Even though migrants often came from large, poor, corn-farming families, most had food on the table. As one longtime migrant put it, as a child in Partida, she "never wanted for anything."

Second, rotating political posts gave villagers access to urban ties. Each year Partida's leadership shifted hands, so almost every household head in the village eventually became town secretary or treasurer. When they did, the pueblo paid for them to go to the city on public business. Even though few were literate, these visits exposed them to ads and hearsay about urban jobs.

Migrating for Opportunities in the City

The combination of basic subsistence and urban access enabled men like Samuel Luna and his father to reject farm labor and seek urban alternatives. In hundreds of conversations and two years of fieldwork, I did not hear one interviewee from Partida attribute his or her departure to debt. While migrants from Partida admitted that they were better off in the city, hometown poverty did not *force* them to leave. Lane Hirabayashi, an anthropologist who studied the Sierra Norte in the 1970s, reported a similar pattern: "By general agreement of both early and later migrants, [villagers] were not starving and did not flee the village out of dire necessity" (1993, 64).

When farm recruiters came to Partida, therefore, villagers refused.[56] Though a few tried farmwork, they gave up fast. Alfonso Salas, for instance, was one of the few to try agricultural labor in the 1950s. After two months he returned to Partida. He could not stand the work. Although the foreman cajoled Alfonso to stay, he recalled, "I said, 'basta (enough).' I didn't like that work, so I came back. The work was really hard." Alfonso remembered the experience as a turning point, convincing him that his children had to study before having children of their own. In the coming years Alfonso ordered his children like a broken record: "Study, study, so you don't have to migrate [as farmworkers]. . . . You get up at 5:00 A.M., and they don't treat you well." He added to me, "I always told [my daughters], 'You're going to study; you're going to have a career. Marriage will be later.' And yes, they obeyed." Meanwhile, Alfonso himself used his urban ties to start a clothing store on the main street of town, earning money that would help send his children to school. Other villagers told similar stories, saying that though they briefly tried farmwork, they never got used to it. The work was "really hard, really backbreaking," as one put it. Those who had gone did not go back, and they did not let their families do similar work.[57]

Instead, migrants from Partida sought to "improve themselves," as they put it, through urban schooling and jobs. At first, fathers like Samuel's sought training for their adolescent sons, so the boys could do cargos and trade more effectively. For instance, fifty-five-year-old Otilio Santos recalled that his parents began trying to trade cattle but were swindled along the way, due to their lack of Spanish. Then Otilio's father sent him to Oaxaca City, explaining, "Son, you're not going to end up like me, ignorant, without knowing how to write. You have to study." "So," Otilio continued, "they put my clothing in a little bag, and *vámonos* [let's go]." Thus boys of eight or ten were sent off to Oaxaca alone to acquire the skills they needed to govern and trade.[58]

While Samuel, Otilio, and other men of their generation eventually returned to Partida, they created a pipeline for information and an appetite for urban life. As children in the village came of age, boys *and girls* began to notice that those who went to the city not only learned Spanish but also enjoyed material commodities. Children of eight, ten, or twelve began to covet this urban "fun." At the age of eleven, Cora Romero left for Oaxaca City, eventually going on to Mexico City and then Los Angeles. By the time of my fieldwork, she had returned to Partida to care for her aging mother. She often puttered among the chickens in her front yard, plunking down a stool among them as we talked. As a girl, Cora remembered, the city dazzled her. She began working in Oaxaca as a maid. Though Cora worked hard, her *señora* (woman, in this case employer) gave her all manner of things unknown in the village: Jell-O, papayas, pastries, and chocolate. The woman also taught Cora Spanish, insisting that she repeat words like *ajo* (garlic) over and over to herself as she shopped in the market. Though Cora's jobs were hardly a walk in the park, they gave her Spanish skills and access to commodities that children in Partida had never enjoyed. As other young people heard of such perks, they left for cities as well.

Blanca Martínez told a similar story. In 1968 Blanca left Partida on the back of a pickup truck, as it rolled down the newly cut road to Oaxaca. The eldest daughter of a family of eight, Blanca was twelve years old. Later she would be one of the first migrants from Partida to set roots in Los Angeles. Sitting at Blanca's glistening dining-room table in South Los Angeles, I asked how she got the courage to leave. She recalled, "I had seen my cousin come back with pretty clothes and shoes and a purse, and I wanted to experience that too, because I had always been poor, and I had no changes of clothes, no shoes. . . . For me all of that was like a shop window, filled with things I longed for."

Imelda Hidalgo's eyes twinkled as well. Before going to Oaxaca City as a housekeeper in 1957, Imelda explained, "I had never had underwear! Just imagine—and suddenly I could have underwear, shoes, dresses." Juan Serrano, a later migrant, added that he left Partida *despite* his family's economic stability: "Economically, we were fine; I can't say I needed a job . . . but I wanted to see things, to experience things. . . . My seventeen-year-old friends would come back here [to Partida] well dressed, with their sneakers, and they talked differently. So all of that dazzled me. . . . I said, I don't think this is my future, just to be trapped here in these mountains."

Partida's urban networks enabled young people to leave alone, first for Oaxaca City and then for Mexico City. In the 1950s, 80 percent of young urban migrants were boys, leaving on behalf of the family, just like Samuel Luna. Sometimes, parents also sent girls, finding the children jobs at places like food stalls in the market in Oaxaca City. There they would clean, bring out food, and study Spanish at night. Young girls quickly realized that they too could go to the city to get away from their father's abuse. By the 1960s, 50–60 percent of Partida's urban migrants were women. Both boys and girls then used the village's urban networks to run away, seeking opportunities apart from their families. Once Partida got roads in the 1960s, so many villagers were transiting back and forth to Oaxaca City that kids as young as ten could get to town by jumping on the back of a passing truck.

There, migrants like Cora Romero and Blanca Martínez met other women or female cousins, who helped them find higher-paying housekeeping jobs in Mexico City. By the 1970s most of Partida's migrants moved on to Mexico City, where they earned higher wages for similar work.[59]

Women's Escape

Nearly half of interviewees from Partida—including almost all of the women and some of the men—left to escape its gendered abuse. When Cora Romero was almost fourteen, she returned to Partida from Oaxaca City, and her parents arranged a marriage. The relationship quickly degenerated. Cora remembered how it drove her to leave:

> [My husband] went to bring the belt, and he said, "Who gave you permission to step outside?" Because I had taken the onions and the chilies outside to wash them in the sun. . . . He just wanted me behind the door, in the corner, as if I were a crook, shut in. . . . I didn't want to be in the pueblo; I wanted to get ahead. My mother had so many children, and I spent all my time working with them, taking care of the kids. And, my mom—if one of her boys fell, well, she came to hit *me*. So I said, "I have to be different."

Strapping her newborn son to her back, Cora ran away with her female cousins to Mexico City and found work as a live-in maid. Often, she worked from five in the morning to two at night, ironing, washing, cleaning, cooking, and taking care of the family. Nevertheless, she said, "I liked it. The lady liked how I worked; she said I cleaned well and all. Of course she really cared for me. She would even take my son in her bed and buy him Clavel [store-brand] milk—pure Clavel milk." Compared to Cora's husband and parents, her employer was relatively caring. *And* she had store-brand milk. Even working twenty-one hours a day, Cora was far happier in Mexico City than in Partida.

Older women—deprived of such chances—also helped push their daughters out. Claudia Vega, a tiny dynamo in her midseventies, lived near the house where I stayed in Partida, and I often stopped by her place on my way in and out. She would whiz around her patio as she talked, cutting up raw chicken to sell to the neighbors, her white braids swinging almost as fast as the flies that buzzed around her. Claudia was smart as a whip, and as a girl, she had wanted to be a teacher. Yet her father prevented her from studying. "Get rid of that idea!" he told her, "That's a stupid idea you have. Women were made *para el metate* [to grind corn]. Your husband will go out to work in the fields, and you will follow behind. Your brother, since he's a man, will go to study in Oaxaca City." Claudia cursed her father, vowing, "When I have daughters, female children, they will be teachers."

As fate would have it, Claudia bore seven daughters. Just after the second girl was born, her first husband died, and she demanded to keep their house. Then, insisting that women did not have the right to property, Partida's town government locked Claudia and her two young children in jail. Claudia was undeterred. When her eldest turned five, though Claudia had never left the village before, she escorted the girl to a school in Mexico City. In the coming decades she would push dozens of other girls to leave Partida as well. "You have to study," she would tell them. "You will go to a boarding school so that you don't suffer, because here in the village you suffer too much. . . . Go study, all of you. Go study, girls; don't stay here."[60]

Elvia Aguilar was one of these girls, fleeing in 1964, the year she turned twelve. With smile lines stretching behind her small, round glasses, Elvia described, "I wanted to get out of [Partida]—to have a better life than my mother had, because she had so many children. I thought, I'm not going to have so many kids, like my mom . . . because my mother suffered a lot of abuse from my father. He would drink. When he was home he went out drinking, and he would come back and beat my mother. So I decided I didn't want that kind of life." Instead, Elvia hopped a truck. She went back to Partida only once, to pull her sister Inés from the village. Though Inés was nervous, Elvia urged, "Don't be afraid. You're going to go with me. You have to find another life, not the life you have here." Thus, women created a chain, pushing one another to leave.[61] By the 1970s more than half of Partida's migrants were women, and 86 percent left before they were married.[62] Their access to urban areas allowed them to flee patriarchy, breaking the usual pattern of Mexican male migration.

Women also helped link the community of Partida to Los Angeles. Rosa Reyes was one of the first. As a housekeeper in Mexico City, Rosa slowly got to know other domestic workers. In one household her friends met a couple from Los Angeles, who were looking for Mexican maids.[63] By the late 1960s the women had used these contacts to go on to California. In 1971 Rosa followed their lead. She was one of the first three people from Partida to go to Los Angeles, all of them women. She explained,

> [In Los Angeles] there was work for women, to work cleaning houses ... jobs where we could earn good money compared with what we earned there [in Mexico City]—to come here [to Los Angeles] and earn two or three times that.... There wasn't much for men and that's how we decided I would go with my female cousin to the United States, and my husband would work in Mexico City.... [My housekeeper friends] gave me the opportunity to find work quickly [in Los Angeles], because they already knew the person that helped women find work.

Families like Rosa's strategized for women to take advantage of feminized, urban U.S. jobs. In later years women also found garment work, following signs on the factories with phrases like *se busca muchachas* (hiring young women). The opportunities for women quickly became well known. Even during my fieldwork, villagers reiterated, "There are a lot of opportunities for women in LA" or "In Los Angeles women make more money than men." As Raquel Moreno, who moved to Los Angeles in the 1980s, recalled, "My mother suffered a lot of domestic violence, so she didn't want that for me.... So she said, 'You know what? If these girls went to the United States, and they're telling you they work sewing jeans.... Sewing buttons is nothing you can't do.'"

These women created channels for both themselves and their male counterparts to get out of farmwork. They did not follow male counterparts, as studies of Mexican migration often assume. Instead, as migrants arrived in Los Angeles, pioneer women migrants like Rosa Reyes gave them lodging, job contacts, and even money. For instance, Elvia Aguilar's brother Vicente moved to Los Angeles a few years after she did, and she helped him and his wife find jobs at the garment factory where she worked. Likewise, by the time Epifanio Cruz arrived in Los Angeles in the mid-1980s, two of his sisters had been working in California for almost a decade, one in housekeeping and another in garment factories, where she got him a job. Bruno Torres also came through female relatives, who found him work washing dishes. Though men sometimes spurned these feminized jobs, the work was far more stable than farm labor and had the added benefit of being in urban Los Angeles. Even though a few Sierra Zapotecs had worked on farms at first, by the early 1980s all of them shifted into LA service and industry.[64] Partida's co-ed networks—and the cross-class that cities they allowed—helped the pueblo as a whole opt into this more desirable destination.

FAMILY FARM MIGRATION FROM RETORNO

In Retorno, meanwhile, local elites excluded most villagers from land and politics, driving them into farmwork.[65] In the early 1900s, even though Retorno legally held land in common and governed itself collectively, mestizo (mixed-race) outsiders moved into the village to buy up communal land.[66] The newcomers crushed rebellions by the Mixtec majority and positioned themselves as political bosses (caciques) and privileged liaisons to the ruling PRI.[67] Local priests then buttressed the caciques' control. Retorno had operated as a regional center for Catholic evangelization since the 1600s.[68] Its powerful church leaders affirmed the mestizos' control by insisting that indigenous people address them in the same terms one would speak to God. The village came to refer to the mestizos as "people of reason" *(gente de razón)* and to everyone else as *naturales*, or native, simple, indigenous people.[69] Elites reciprocated church support by demanding that villagers give money and labor to more than twelve Catholic festivals a year.[70] When anticlerical uprisings swept Oaxaca in the 1930s, mestizos in Retorno and nearby pueblos crushed the rebellions. By the middle of the twentieth century, caciques in the Mixteca region were stronger than local leaders anywhere else in Oaxaca.[71]

The Yoke of Local Exclusion

Today Rogelio Méndez lives in a ranch house in San Diego County and stocks produce at a grocery chain. For most of his life, though, Rogelio was a farmworker. When Rogelio was born in Retorno in 1956, his parents had already lost their land. As he described in a bitter, wistful interview with sociologist Laura Velasco Ortiz,

What made us migrate was that my mother did not have any piece of land. All of my uncles were poor, because the owners of the lands were the *caciques*, the "people of reason," the *mestizos*, including the direct descendants of the Spanish. No one—no indigenous person—had a piece of land in the center of the *pueblo*. The indigenous were where it's communally held land on the steep slopes or where there are rocks. . . . The indigenous people had to abandon their *pueblo* for not paying tributes, ever since those times when [mestizos] used to demand so much from them—and because they were humiliated, mistreated, and their families raped. . . . So then they abandoned their lands, their wealth, and they [mestizos] kept it all. . . . When a family member got sick, when someone had an emergency, [the poor] would say: "Lend me money, and I'll give you the papers for my land." . . . For example, if someone had a very sick little girl, he would have to take her to the *cha za'a*, that is, to the [mestizo] healer, so that he would cure the girl. They would have to treat them with luxury, sometimes even give them land. That's how people slowly lost their lands. When the epidemics and sicknesses came, they [mestizos] hunted, surrounded [the people], and they took their land from them. By every means, they took possession of the land (2005a, 61–62).

As Rogelio emphasized, Retorno's caciques used sickness, emergency, and debt to force indigenous villagers to hand over land. As a result, Rogelio and his brothers had barely enough to eat. They worked for the rich men of the village, planting, weeding, and harvesting maize from May through December. For this, their salary was a single sack of corn.

Not only did mestizos appropriate land, Rogelio added; they also twisted Usos y Costumbres to their own benefit. Instead of rotating political posts, as villagers did in Partida, Retorno's elites monopolized the local positions of influence, leaving only undesirable cargos for the others. Rogelio continued, "The *mestizos* always held the posts of judge, president, secretary, and they used everyone else to be assistants and such. . . . The *cargos* were mandatory, obligatory only for those [lower] positions. That was the evil, that they used the customs for their own benefit and *Usos y Costumbres* only helped the *gente de razón*" (Velasco Ortiz 2005a, 61). Elites also distorted the custom of communal labor to their own benefit. When the state government brought running water to Retorno, for instance, wealthy families demanded that indigenous people dig the ditches. People like Rogelio's father spent months working to lay pipes for the water. Yet in the end the pipes reached only the center of the village and the homes of elites.

Rogelio's story reveals how, in Retorno, landlords' control of lending, religious tributes, and political posts fueled land dispossession. In the early 1900s, in Retorno and across the Mixteca, mestizos appropriated thousands of hectares of indigenous land, far more than in other parts of Oaxaca.[72] Weaving palm mats in his courtyard in Retorno, eighty-year-old Heladio Contreras echoed Rogelio's story. In the 1940s, he croaked, "My father held communal land up on the mountains. But he had to sell it when I got sick. All his money disappeared, so I don't have land, just a little plot for my house." Not only did the caciques appropriate land, but they also used their control over the village government to delegitimize common holdings. In a 1960 report to Mexico's National Agrarian Registry, for instance, Retorno's mestizo municipal secretary Juan Coronado stated that despite the pueblo's communal land title, "In this village, all of the lands that belong to the population have been used for many years as if they were private property, to make money for the owners, and there is very little remaining communal land."[73] By the time of my fieldwork, respondents in Retorno reported that even though land was communal, it had "always" been treated as private property. Only the rocky, arid terrain on the hillsides was left for common use.

By the 1950s the median landholding in Retorno was around six-tenths of a hectare (less than 1.5 acres) and almost no one owned more than one hectare.[74] In other words, most families had less than one fifth of the four or five hectares they would need to get by. Though 92 percent of Retorno made a living by farming, a typical family could grow only 20 percent of the corn they needed to live.[75] As the population expanded, the land crisis grew even worse. To make ends meet, villagers became sharecroppers or *jornaleros* (hired day labor). Families borrowed to buy food.[76] They also borrowed to buy medicine, cover slow seasons, and contribute (as required) to the village government and the Catholic Church. By the 1960s, without enough jobs to go around, three-quarters of Retorno was in debt.

At the same time, mestizos kept a lock on political power. Throughout much of the twentieth century, the Coronado family dominated key village offices, especially that of municipal secretary. This position allowed them to control information and money from the state and the ruling party, the

PRI. Basilio Ramos, a longtime U.S. migrant who returned to the village from Vista, California, in 2009, leaned back on a plastic chair in his cement patio. He reflected that when he was young, "They [mestizos] were the teachers, the priests, and the landlords. The judges. The mayors. They were the owners of the town." Even as late as the 1980s, the village leaders "were the descendants of those families that had been in power the whole time. . . . Juan Coronado had been municipal secretary for about twenty or thirty years, so he knew all the ins and outs of the municipality. . . . He *was* the town government." In a conversation described by anthropologist Charlynne Curiel, another villager added, "Juan Coronado . . . had a lot of power because he was the one who knew how to write, do paperwork, get funding, and talk with the PRIistas in the capital (Oaxaca City). It was a *cacicazgo* of 20 years" (2011, 75). Mestizos' literacy enabled them to keep a stranglehold on leadership posts, and with them on access to cities. Only civil leaders could travel on the municipality's dime, meaning only elites built urban ties. Even if poorer villagers *wanted* to go to the city, they had very few contacts or money to pay for rides.

Economic Refugees into Farmwork

Retorno's stratification echoed in its patterns of emigration. In the 1960s, just as indigenous people left the village for farmwork, mestizos began moving to Mexico City. Basilio Ramos explained,

> There were some mestizo people from here in the village who were really influential, people who arrived after the [Mexican] Revolution, according to what people here in the pueblo say—the Peñas, the owners of those old houses that are just above the town hall. Those are some palaces! These people with a lot of money. . . . They were used to being businessmen, to being rich, so the place seemed small to them, and they left for other places, too. . . . The mestizos went to Mexico City, as an ethnic group, and the "natural" people—the ones they called "Indians"—to the farms.

These elites—who made up about 25 percent of Retorno's migrants—used their urban ties to move to either Mexico City or the nearby town of Huajuapan de León. As in Partida, they left as independent young people, seeking education or to "better themselves." Yet unlike those from Partida, almost none of these urban migrants went on to the United States. Instead, they used family resources to attend high school and even college and to become accountants, nurses, or operatives for the ruling PRI. For instance, Sonia Márquez, the self-proclaimed daughter of a cacique, studied nursing in Mexico City before returning to the village to care for her aging parents. Sonia and I took several long walks together, to the cross on the hillside above Retorno. When I asked why she never considered going to the United States, Sonia replied, "Why would you go to have them exploit you, when here you can be the boss? At least here you're the lion's head; there you'd end up being a rat's tail." Other elites added that "sweeping dollars" was too degrading.

Meanwhile, Retorno's indigenous, poor majority moved to farmwork, primarily in the Valley of Culiacán, Sinaloa. Landless, barred from urban ties, and barely able to eat, these villagers became what James Stuart and Michael Kearney call "economic refugees" (1981, 7). More than half attributed their departure to debt. Then, the meager wages in Mexican agroindustry trapped them in a circuit between farmwork and the village. Desperate for money, almost all of Retorno's indigenous migrant families took women and children along.

When Alma Sandoval was a girl in the 1960s, for instance, her parents scraped by as sharecroppers, planting and weeding corn for other families in Retorno. Alma tried to go to school one year, but the local teachers wouldn't let her in without shoes. So she joined her parents at work. One hot afternoon, as I lazed around Alma's taco shop, she described how the family landed in farmwork, "Here [in Retorno] we went around working day to day. Pulling weeds, growing corn. Except it was half the salary [as in Culiacán, Sinaloa]. We didn't have land. We wanted to work, but it was always sharecropping, other people's land. That was what you did. . . . And here it was not every day, just the days we found work. And the days we didn't, well, that was the problem. That's why we had to leave." In 1968, when Alma turned twelve, she and her parents left for Sinaloa. When labor recruiters came to the village, Alma's parents felt they had no choice but to go along.

In Sinaloa the migrants worked like dogs. Every day, at three in the morning, Alma and her mother got up and made tortillas, before leaving at dawn to pick tomatoes. After sunset they made their way back to the corrugated chicken sheds where they slept and drew water from irrigation runoff to drink and wash. Alma continued,

> We used to go to Sinaloa seasonally [to pick tomatoes]. We'd leave in November or December and come back in May or June. It became a custom: we came home from the north, my father paid his debts, and then he took out more loans; so by November or December we had to go again in order to pay them back. We were always coming and going; we never went to [Sinaloa] to stay. Just to stay a few months, even though we spent every winter there for years.

Marcelo Sánchez also started working in Sinaloa when he was ten years old. Lingering over a tepid coffee in Vista, California, in 2010 Marcelo sighed, "On that steep slope allotted to us we got to keep maybe 25 percent, and 75 percent would go to them [the landlords]. . . . My parents went into debt a lot. Among the people in the town, the ones that had money at that time made great profit off this, because they would charge high interest. We wouldn't make enough [in Sinaloa] to pay off what my father owed, so again we had to go." Marcelo begged his parents to send him to school. But his father refused. He needed Marcelo to work. So Marcelo went to school for two months, and then he moved to Sinaloa. By the time Marcelo was fifteen, he was picked up by tomato recruiters, first from Baja California and then from San Diego County.

Like Alma and Marcelo, most poorer migrants left Retorno together as families. Women worked beside men, and infants and toddlers were too young to be left behind. By the time children were eight or ten, they could earn wages as well. Even when parents sought alternatives, their children pleaded not to be left at home. Dante León, who became a farmworker at eleven, remembered that though his parents wanted him to study, "I left school after third grade. I didn't want to stay [in Retorno] anymore. My parents told me to stay, but I felt really lonely there. . . . So I worked, and the water [around the tomato plants] came up to my knees. My shoes would fall apart—just to earn some money to help my parents." Paloma Pacheco added, "My parents didn't want to bring me to Culiacán, because I was in school and they said, 'You can't go. You're studying and we'd prefer that you stay.' But I said, 'No, I want to go wherever you go, because with you I'll be okay. It doesn't matter if I have to work or whatever I have to do." Such children longed to be with their mothers and fathers. Yet circular movements cut short their schooling, leaving them few future choices outside the farms.

When migrants got to Sinaloa, they faced notoriously squalid conditions and labor abuse. To pick tomatoes, the primary crop, workers had to stand up to their knees in water or mud and bend over all day long. Many suffered head, neck, and back pain. If migrants stepped on the dry tomato beds, foremen beat them. Every migrant I interviewed remembered such mistreatment. At the time pesticides banned in the United States were routinely sprayed on tomatoes in Mexico, fueling rashes, headaches, and respiratory and mental problems. At night up to seven thousand workers would cram into cardboard huts or long poultry sheds made of corrugated tin, in camps with no electricity or running water. Toxic runoff from the fields and latrines emptied directly into the irrigation ditches that served as migrants' source of water, leading to diarrhea, vomiting, and fevers.[77] When workers attempted to strike, growers hired mercenaries to crush the revolts.[78]

Therefore, migrants retreated to Retorno for relief. For instance, Ximena Ortíz cycled back and forth from Sinaloa for thirteen years, with her husband and all eight children. Ximena had been so poor in Retorno that when she fought with her mother-in-law (whose house she shared), she had to sleep outdoors. Culiacán pushed her back. Tears streamed down Ximena's cheeks when she described her life in Culiacán:

> The water was so dirty! There were these canals [flowing by the sheds], and we used to go do our washing in that water. We would be washing, and the ' people that were nursing were washing baby diapers. The poop was just floating right there, and we drank that water. It wasn't filtered, nothing. We drank it like that. We would just grab a piece of cloth like this so it didn't catch any shit, and we drank it. Ay, no! [Abigail: You didn't get sick?] Of course we got sick! Really sick, because that was toxic. That water was filled with filth, with infection, and that was the water we drank. So we suffered so much, until we saved our selves—until, well, I don't know, we paid our debts and came back.

One year there were rebellions in the fields, and Ximena watched an activist get killed. That's when she lost heart. Going back to the village, she explained, was a way to "save herself" from Culiacán. Others did the same.

Whatever money they earned poured into doctors' bills—and to the extortionate vendors who sold food to farmworkers. Teenage mothers lost babies to diarrhea in the fields. So they never stayed long, or even a year. From December to May they worked in Sinaloa and from June to November they returned.

Ironically, circulation kept migrants trapped in the 1,300-mile circuit between Sinaloa and Retorno, tomatoes and debt. Whereas migrants from Partida built their *own* networks to Mexico City and Los Angeles, those from Retorno followed labor contractors from the village to Sinaloa, Baja California, and ultimately San Diego County.[79] In the 1970s many moved to Baja California, just south of the U.S. border. Irrigation technology had fueled agricultural growth in the area, and recruiters began sending buses to Sinaloa to poach workers directly from the fields. David Molina, who was born in Retorno and then worked in each of these areas in turn, recalled,

> First we went to Sinaloa, and then from Sinaloa we would come to San Quintín [Baja California]. The bosses themselves transported people in pickup trucks with walls or in carts. They would bring people in for the harvest, and from there they would take them to Vizcaíno in Baja California and then cross them back again in a boat to Culiacán. That's how people started working in the San Quintín Valley, and then crossing over to the United States—the youngest ones. That was the circuit.

San Diego was the crossing point from Mexico, its farms integrated into the same corporate networks. Yet on U.S. ranches men could earn up to three times the wages offered in Sinaloa or Baja California.

Migrants had few alternatives. Because farmworkers were home only six months a year—and Sinaloa's labor camps had no schools—not one of those surveyed finished primary school. With elites monopolizing ties to the city, almost none were familiar with urban areas. Instead, the only recruiters they met were farm-labor contractors, first from Baja California and then from the United States.[80] Many Mexican farms were owned by U.S. corporations. As a result, both used the same techniques and materials, down to the packing boxes.[81] In Sinaloa and Baja California, migrants got trained in U.S. farming procedures. So when tomato growers in San Diego County ran out of cheap labor in the mid-1980s, they turned to

Mexico. When migrants arrived, many were too poor to pay smugglers the extra $200 to cross the checkpoint separating San Diego from Los Angeles.[82] So they stayed in San Diego County. Then, in the 1990s and the first decade of the 2000s, following the common pattern among Mexican migrants, many branched out of agriculture and into factories and domestic work. By the time of my fieldwork, less than 20 percent still worked on farms. Nevertheless, their roots in North County San Diego tied them to a hostile receiving site.

Patriarchy Traveled with Them

Retorno's history illustrates the complexity of the relationship between gender and migration. Like Partida, Retorno was profoundly male dominated throughout the twentieth century, barring women from even leaving the house. As in Partida, this history did not stop women from leaving: fully half of Retorno's internal migrants were women. Yet their mobility was limited because patriarchy traveled with them, even intensifying in Culiacán. Farmwork gave women like Alma Sandoval anything but relief. Not only did they pick tomatoes for fourteen-hour days in the fields; they also cooked, cared for children, and tended to the ubiquitous sick. They usually did so in the wee hours of the morning, always under sordid conditions. Both on the fields and off, they were often abused.

Sexual violence was rampant in Sinaloa. Alma, for instance, got married at age seventeen. Days later she went back to Sinaloa to work with her husband in the fields. There, she recalled, "The men abused the women a lot. For example, there were many who raped the women or touched them. They harassed them like that. And they would say things to them—who knows what. Our husbands were really jealous too, because men and women worked together there. So when the women arrived home, they would hit us. They would accuse their wives of seeing other men." So, when Alma's husband emigrated to California in the late 1980s, she opted out.

After Sinaloa many women returned home. Angela Cantú, a heavyset mother of five, worked as a tomato picker in Culiacán throughout the 1970s and into the 1980s, alongside her husband and children. When her husband moved to California in 1988, however, Angela stayed in Retorno.

Though her husband circulated for decades, Angela never crossed the border. One day I sat in Angela's cool, cement kitchen as she slapped together homemade tortillas. She reflected,

> I went to Culiacán and that killed my desire [to go to the United States]. Because of that, I imagine what it might be like. . . . So I said to my husband, "Oh, no, I will not go around like that with my children. It's so sad. If you go to the United States, so be it. But, I do not want to migrate anymore." So, that's how our separation began; he started living in the United States and me here. . . . My husband would say that he used to live with lots of men—all in one room, many of them together. He said, "Where else could we live?" Because he didn't have papers, my husband never went to the city. He always stayed in the country. They used to make little caves in the hills. . . . He says they dug caves, then they crawled inside, and that's where they slept. Ah!

Life was not easy. Though Angela's husband made double the wages in the United States, she continued to struggle. She went on, "Oh, how much debt we were in sometimes, so the work [in California] would pay off what we owed. And when he had paid it off he came back [to Retorno], and then he would go into debt, and once again he would leave for the United States. So it was really hard for us, because as soon as you pay things off, here comes something else." Nevertheless, Angela refused to repeat the suffering she had faced or enter the all-male, homeless encampments promised in North County San Diego.

Dolores Muñoz went back to Retorno as well. Dolores had started working in farm labor when she married in the late 1970s. In northern Mexico, she explained, "My husband started to drink a ton. He would beat me, he would verbally assault me, and the only thing I wanted was to come home to my parents." When her husband went to California, Dolores returned to the village with her three sons. "I no longer loved him," she added. "I hated him, and there things fell apart." By returning alone, Angela, Dolores, and others hoped to escape the miseries of both farmwork and household abuse.

As women opted out, they transformed family migration into family separation (even though most remained married). Once men from Retorno started moving to the United States, most women and children went back to the village. Of respondents who worked in Culiacán, 60 percent of men eventually went to California, while 80 percent of women stayed in Mexico. As a result, though migration to Culiacán had been roughly fifty-fifty, more than 90 percent of Retorno's pioneer migrants to the United States were men. This pattern reflected not just a history of patriarchy but also the conditions and constraints women from Retorno faced on the ground.

Eventually, however, some women from Retorno went to the United States as well. More than 90 percent were associational migrants, meaning they came with their husbands or fathers, with 71 percent arriving married and 90 percent living with their spouses.[83] They moved not for opportunity, like those from Partida, but to pay family debts or accede to their husbands' demands. In 1986 some of the earliest male migrants from Retorno obtained lawful permanent-resident status through the agricultural-worker provision of the Immigration Reform and Control Act. Several encouraged their wives or children to join them in the United States. For instance, Marcelo Sánchez insisted that his wife, Teresa, move to California in 1988. Teresa resisted. She recalled, "I felt ill! I didn't want to join him, because it was never my plan to come here [to the United States]. . . . I felt really horrible leaving my pueblo." Marcelo threatened that if she refused, he would find another wife. Male migrants from Retorno were notorious for taking mistresses while living far from their wives. So Teresa conceded. Though Camila Mejía had lived in California more than a decade, she echoed these sentiments, telling me, "I never imagined I would come here [to the United States]—I never had that desire to get to know it . . . but when I got married to my husband, he said, 'You're coming,' so I didn't have any other choice, and I came." Should women refuse, they risked losing their husbands and their sources of economic support.

Other women came to the United States because their husbands did not send adequate funds to pay off the family debt. Dora López, for instance, who now sells weight-loss products in Vista, California, lived as a de facto single mom in Retorno in the 1990s while her husband was gone. Eventually, she came to California join him. She explained,

[My husband] would get drunk and take out money—take out loans [in the village] . . . at a rate of 10 percent interest, so, of course, his debts grew and grew. Then he came here [to the United States]. At times he had a little money, so he sent it, but what he sent was to pay debts and more debts. So then I would end up with nothing again. I cried and cried. It filled me with rage—I couldn't figure out what to do. I was so ashamed when people would come to charge me—I don't like owing. . . . So finally it made me so angry that eventually I picked up and came to the United States to help him pay off those debts.

Coming against their will, through networks controlled by men, such women had little access to the feminized garment and service jobs held by women from Partida. Without such alternatives Retorno's first migrants—both men and women—were consigned to working on farms.

THE POWER DYNAMICS BEHIND MIGRANTS' PATHS

This chapter shows how in migrant communities, hometown power dynamics shape who migrates and where they go. Even before migration begins, local political and economic arrangements affect people's desperation to leave. Hometown practices also influence members' access to urban jobs. Land distribution—like that in Partida—can give prospective migrants an economic base to be choosy about where they go. Collective governance also helps rural villagers build networks into cities. Therefore, communal social protection is not just a hindrance to an inevitable process of proletarianization, as scholars once thought.[84] Rather, collective control offers migrants advantages as they enter the industrial economy. By contrast, inequity may force migrants into farmwork or other unwanted jobs. Agricultural labor likely became the "standard" pattern of migration from rural Mexico due to the widespread hacienda system, in which landlords monopolized productive farmland and excluded peasants from political power.[85] Even though Retorno was indigenous, it operated similarly to these haciendas, with oligarchy and land dispossession fueling debt and restricting urban networks to the elite. Research by other scholars suggests that similar patterns held in other villages, regardless of ethnicity.[86]

Hometown (in)equity also has critical implications for the gender and family dynamics of migration. Women's migration is not simply a reflection of different levels of hometown patriarchy. Partida was just as patriarchal as Retorno. Yet over time women came to predominate among migrants from Partida because their hometown supported independent, urban migration. This pattern offered young women an outlet for escape, especially since they had feminized, service-sector jobs. In turn, women gave their whole community access to urban work in the United States. In Retorno, by contrast, debt forced men, women, and children to leave together. When people migrated as families, patriarchy traveled with them, even getting worse in farm-labor camps. For women from Retorno, the only means of escape was to leave the fields, separate from their husbands, and return to their village of origin. As they did, they transformed coed internal migration into almost all-male movement to the United States. These different dynamics of female "escape" reflected the two communities' power structures and their contrasting patterns of family migration.

For both, hometown histories shaped who moved to the United States, where they went, and which attitudes and capabilities they brought in. As other scholars have shown, the skills and experiences migrants bring with them weigh on their prospects in the United States.[87] In the early years of Partida's U.S. migration, more than half of its migrants were women. Almost universally, they went to Los Angeles. While they were undocumented and hardly prosperous, they had more stable jobs, faced less harassment, and built deeper civic ties to the United States than their counterparts from Retorno. Couples rarely divided across borders. Migrants from Partida also brought a sense of opportunity. Women, in particular, arrived in Los Angeles predisposed to feel "free."

By contrast, more than 70 percent of Retorno's U.S. migrants were men. Roughly 65 percent of them settled in North County San Diego and another 30 percent in other rural areas of California. Prior to 1986, 78 percent of these migrants worked on farms and almost all of them returned to Mexico at least once, many circulating ten times or more. They grew strawberries and tomatoes for brands like Kirk, Sunshine, Sunrise, and Sundance, which processed berries to Kraft, Heinz, and Knott's Berry Farm.[88] Advocates argued that farm-labor conditions in San Diego were even worse than in other parts of the state, with growers often failing to pay minimum wage or overtime or refusing to pay workers at all.[89] Thus, Retorno's pioneer migrants faced lower wages, less consistent employment, and more labor abuse than their counterparts in urban jobs.[90] Over time they diversified into other sectors, and circulation diminished. Nevertheless, in North County San Diego they suffered greater anti-immigrant hostility and remained more isolated than their urban peers.[91] Driven by debt, many entered California already feeling under attack.

The chapter also reveals how oppressive U.S. industries like agriculture rely on sending-side exclusion to make people desperate enough to accept grueling work.[92] By contrast, hometown redistribution and shared urban ties offer low-wage migrants a degree of choice. To the extent that sending nations or villages can promote such local equity, they may be able to mitigate migrants' entry into the global economy.

Yet legacies alone do not predict migrants' paths. Migrants also react to conditions in their destinations, and their reactions change their trajectories over time. During stepwise migration women from Partida and Retorno responded to opportunities or distress by choosing to stay, move on, or return home. So doing, they altered the gendered character of migration as well as the choices available to their communities in the United States. The following chapters show how political and economic contexts on the receiving end transformed each group's attitudes and goals, both reinforcing and shifting the pathways that began on the Mexican side.

2 "Illegality" under Two Local Modes of Control

Carmen Rojas left Partida in the early 1990s, in search of opportunities in Los Angeles. Like 99 percent of her *paisanos* (fellow migrants), she crossed without papers. She was fifteen. For most of the next twenty years, she sewed jeans in the garment plants that lined Alameda Street, just south of downtown Los Angeles. In her off hours, she shared a cramped two-bedroom apartment with her uncle, two sisters, nephew, and five-year-old son, on a treeless street near the railroad tracks. About a third of the migrants from Partida lived within a ten-block radius of Carmen, in the town of Huntington Park. Once a white, working-class suburb, Huntington Park was now more than 90 percent Latino. Roughly a third of its residents were undocumented, and a full 30 percent worked in factories nearby.[1] Earlier arrivals from Partida, meanwhile, had settled in Koreatown and Echo Park, while later ones landed in the rougher sections of South Los Angeles. With their poor, immigrant populations, all of these areas attracted steady police attention.

Nevertheless, "illegality" seemed to recede into the background for Carmen. When I visited her house one afternoon in 2011, the street chattered with life. Women were out watering their gardens, and young boys swerved by on bikes. Though I was the only white person in the area, several people called out *buenas tardes* (good afternoon) as I stepped out of my Toyota Camry. Carmen was waiting by her screen door. "How did she feel about not having papers?" I wondered, as she swept laundry aside to clear me a place on the sofas that doubled as beds. "Well," she replied,

> I think it is fine as long as we do what the law asks, follow the speed limits, the steps they ask for, not go faster or slower, not drink, not do drugs. I say that as long as one is following the law, everything is fine. But if you go around messing here, messing there, not paying tickets . . . If [police] see someone is going to work, [they say], "How good, go ahead"—maybe a ticket and that's it. But if they see people drunk, or drugged, if they see them making a mess and a half *[haciendo barbaridad y media]*, then let them take them [out of the United States] as they should. That doesn't bother me. . . . I'm not afraid of the police, because they're doing their jobs. No, I'm not uncomfortable. On the contrary, we know we're protected by someone when we need it. I don't avoid them either. No, I feel free; I feel calm.

I was surprised. Most reports suggested that since September 11, 2001, intensified immigration policing had terrorized the undocumented. For Carmen, however, there were two different camps. "Bad immigrants" who behaved like "barbarians" would be deported, and rightfully so. Yet Carmen trusted police to take a different approach with "good immigrants" who worked hard, didn't drink, and followed the law. "This country of America is really nice," she added. "It gives us everything we need." As long as Carmen acted "good," she felt "free."

Living in North County San Diego, thirty-year-old Lupita Suárez saw things differently. Lupita was born in Retorno, and, like many of those from her village, she spent her childhood circling between Retorno and Sinaloa. Loath to suffer any more, Lupita's mother, Angela Cantú, eventually returned to the village, while her father continued on, undocumented, to the United States. When Lupita got married in 1998, she crossed the border to Vista, California, as well. Her husband had already been working in the area for seven years, picking strawberries, before he switched to construction. Though Vista was once primarily agricultural, by 2010 it had a population of almost a hundred thousand, half of them Latino. During my fieldwork, the area was dotted with Starbucks, El Pollo Loco, and Southern California strip malls. Lupita, her husband, and their two children shared a one-bedroom apartment near several of the migrants from Retorno. Others had trailers or ramshackle houses on the outskirts of town or in nearby Escondido or Oceanside. As with those from Partida, only about a quarter had legal authorization.

Though I called Lupita twice before visiting, it took her five long minutes to come to the door. Earlier in the year I had spent several languid days talking, sewing, and making tortillas with Lupita's mother, Angela. I had also met Lupita at a community festival before visiting her house. Still, she peeked hesitantly through her peephole. We sat at the kitchen table, waiting until it was time to get her U.S.-born son and daughter from school. Toying with a string on her tea bag, Lupita reflected,

> When I arrived [in the United States] I felt despair sometimes, and I would sit in the house and cry. I wasn't familiar with anything, and I was afraid to go out. Then he [my husband] would tell me, "Don't go out much, because *la migra* [immigration control] hangs out down there at the corner." . . . I was afraid to walk outside alone. It was very hard. Except when I went to work, I just stayed locked in my room. . . . I'm not really informed about where [it's safe] to go, so I waited for the weekends to go out with [my husband].

Lupita had worked in a range of jobs, from babysitting to the kitchen of a pie shop. She had also grown bolder over the years. When the time came to pick up her kids, however, Lupita handed me her keys. Lupita owned a small sedan. Nevertheless, whenever I visited, she prevailed on me to chauffeur her to grocery runs, school pickups, and village festivals. A few years back a police officer had stopped Lupita as she pulled out of her driveway to take her five-year-old daughter to school: the girl was not wearing a seatbelt. He impounded Lupita's car for a month, leaving her no way to get around. She didn't dare risk it again. She went on, "When someone sends you a text message to say, 'Don't go out; la migra is in such and such a place,' why are you going to go looking for it, right? So, you try not to go out and to stay in the house." Though Lupita had lived her whole adult life in the United States, she said, "I want to return to Mexico. I like my village; I like it a lot. There, you don't have this fear of going out like here. There, no, because you're free."

LOCAL STATE POWER AND THE SEARCH FOR BELONGING

In the United States Carmen, Lupita, and their fellow migrants were treated as "illegal." Beginning in the 1990s federal programs such as 287(g) and Secure Communities empowered local police to identify immigrants and turn them over to Immigration and Customs Enforcement (ICE). Both Los Angeles and San Diego Counties implemented these programs, deporting some of the highest numbers of immigrants in the country. Nevertheless, like Carmen, most of those from Partida to Los Angeles felt free. By contrast, those from Retorno to North County often went so far as to describe themselves as "slaves."

One might assume that these attitudes reflected different cultural or economic contexts: the media migrants consumed, for instance, or the scope of Latino social networks in their destinations. Indeed, San Diego County was more spread out and isolated. Nevertheless, both Los Angeles and North County San Diego were roughly 50 percent Latino during the time of my fieldwork. In both areas migrants lived in segregated, Latino neighborhoods. Both also saw similar Latino TV and radio programs, social media, and Internet feeds.[2] One might also ask about the impacts of different labor sectors. Migrants often spend up to fifteen hours a day at work, five or six days a week, so work experiences weigh heavily on their senses of self. As described in chapter 1, migrants from Partida entered the United States via housekeeping and garment factories, while those from Retorno came through farmwork. Yet by the time Carmen and Lupita arrived in the early 1990s, more than 60 percent of migrants from Retorno *also* worked in housekeeping or factory jobs, with another 24 percent in construction and less than 15 percent still on farms. In this chapter I argue that migrants' experiences in the social landscape and at work were deeply intertwined with their perceptions of the state.

Focusing on the state may also seem counterintuitive because most undocumented people avoid interacting directly with ICE, police, or public-service providers. Nevertheless, they remain on constant alert, using piecemeal interactions and hearsay to get a sense of their risks of deportation, as well as their social and economic prospects. Local laws and practices also shape employers' impunity to violate labor laws or use threats for labor control.[3] Thus, understanding local policies helps explain why migrants in similar sectors had such different experiences at work.

I refer to local state and labor practices as *modes of control*. Across the United States police, service providers, and city lawmakers have used personal discretion and local ordinances to reshape federal immigration control. For instance, even though Los Angeles deports large numbers of immigrants, its pro-immigrant advocates have defended "good immigrants" and offered support to subsets of the unauthorized. In particular, they have pushed for limits on police involvement with ICE and for greater labor protections for undocumented workers.[4] In this context, respondents perceived state treatment as *conditional*. Based on hearsay, interactions with police, and observations of other migrants, they suggested that bad behavior provoked deportation while good behavior earned services, steady employment, or police protection. The meaning of *good* was not always clear. To make sense of this category, immigrants drew on their own beliefs, valuing working hard, deferring to authority, being female, and even "acting white." At the same time, the threat of deportation and the promise of wages and public services gave new stakes to long-held moral norms.

By contrast, Vista and Escondido haphazardly targeted immigrants, passing laws that made it easier for police to arrest them. Respondents in North County regularly saw or heard of police stopping migrants in public places, often by race, and turning them over to ICE.[5] Hostile police fed off migrants' isolation: it was hard to get around North County without driving, so police used traffic stops to ask for migrants' papers. Local employers also operated with impunity, browbeating workers by threatening to call police or ICE. In this context, respondents saw state practices as *arbitrary*. Instead of believing that police and bureaucrats differentiated among migrants by behavior, they suggested that the local state labeled *all* unauthorized migrants *bad*, making it unpredictable who might be subject to harassment or deportation.

These modes of control encouraged contrasting feelings of belonging. The conditional mode gave migrants hope. Respondents in Los Angeles believed that as long as they were good, police would overlook their legal status and employers would treat them well. Many trusted the state to intervene in labor abuse. Conditional treatment also lent a sense of order to immigration enforcement, making it appear that individuals invited deportation or police mistreatment by acting badly. This logic of individual responsibility mitigated respondents' fear of deportation and gave many of them a sense of control, even freedom. Nevertheless, when police violated good/bad categories—such as at moments they acted more haphazardly—hope gave way to alienation.

Meanwhile, arbitrary control left migrants feeling alienated. Uncertain of when, where, and whom police might deport, respondents in North County San Diego felt powerless and afraid. Most avoided public services. They were scared of employers as well. In turn, they resigned themselves to perpetual exclusion. Few wanted to stay in the United States. As in Los Angeles, however, these experiences were not universal. Those who felt relatively protected—such as women and the few individuals with legal residency—expressed somewhat less disaffection.

Finally, both conditional and arbitrary control used ideas about gender for legitimacy. In Los Angeles migrants tended to believe that state agents tied support to deferent, feminine behavior and punishment to criminal, masculine behavior. For instance, LA police promoted U visas, nonimmigrant visas for victims of crime, for women who suffered domestic violence. In so doing, however, they framed women as victims and men as abusers. Such police protection—combined with LA employers' preference for women—compounded women's sense of escape from Partida. Women in Los Angeles, especially, felt they belonged. While men from Partida also expressed a sense of inclusion, many were ambivalent. In North County San Diego, by contrast, immigrants were treated as masculine criminal threats regardless of their sex. Women did not feel they could count on more support than men. Instead, arbitrary control redoubled their suffering. Afraid of the police, women like Lupita relied on their husbands for information and protection. They found little recourse to escape male domination. Instead, they endured gender violence, reinforcing their cynicism toward the United States.

CONDITIONAL CONTROL IN LOS ANGELES

In Los Angeles County life as an undocumented migrant was mixed. Los Angeles had a huge immigrant population and deported more people than most cities in the United States.[6] The Los Angeles Police Department and county sheriffs were also notorious for their brutality, backing programs such as Secure Communities and 287(g). At the same time, police and public servants were eager to maintain good relations with the large Latino community. Los Angeles had long been a nucleus of Mexican immigrants' and Chicanos' rights. In the 1990s in particular, the city was home to innovative social movements, as pro-immigrant organizations joined with unions, churches, and left-wing academics to defend the rights of janitors, gardeners, domestic workers, and garment sewers.[7] In the first decade of the 2000s these organizations helped spark a nationwide movement for immigrants' rights. As federal laws grew harsher toward immigrants, people in Los Angeles pushed back. Officials like mayors, sheriffs, and police chiefs responded by lauding immigrants' virtue, denouncing police-ICE collaboration, and opposing legislation that criminalized unauthorized immigration.[8]

Pro-immigrant activism also helped contain local immigration enforcement. In 1979 Los Angeles was one of the first U.S. cities to declare itself an immigrant "sanctuary." Passing a policy known as Special Order 40, which is still in effect today, the city prohibited local police from reporting undocumented immigrants to ICE until after they had been convicted of a crime.[9] Thus, Los Angeles became a prototype for sanctuary cities nationwide. Los Angeles County also sought to contain the expansion of federal immigration control. For instance, in 2001 Los Angeles County sheriff Leroy Baca adopted the 287(g) program to target the city's gangs. Most of the Los Angeles County Board of Supervisors opposed. Ultimately, they compromised, accepting 287(g) (and later Secure Communities) on the condition that police and sheriffs not ask people's legal status until after criminal conviction.[10] Similarly, when the federal government made Secure Communities mandatory, the Los Angeles police chief advocated restraint in turning migrants over to ICE. Likewise, while California law enabled police to impound the cars of unlicensed drivers (i.e., all undocumented migrants prior to 2015), Los Angeles took a lax approach to the policy, often refusing to enforce it altogether.[11]

LA police also conducted outreach to distinguish themselves from ICE.[12] In Los Angeles and Huntington Park, they disseminated "know your rights" flyers and radio announcements, informing residents that immigration control was separate from regular law enforcement. Police programs also urged ("good") migrants to report other ("bad") migrants whom they suspected of crimes. In particular, under the 1994 Violence against Women Act, police encouraged victims of domestic violence to help law enforcement prosecute and deport their abusers, in exchange for U visas.

Service providers also affirmed immigrants' work ethic, humility, and values, insisting that migrants deserved support. Because unauthorized immigrants were not allowed driver's licenses in California until 2015, Los Angeles County promoted Mexican consular identification cards as an alternate form of identification. Consular IDs enabled migrants to get library cards, business licenses, and bank accounts. They also helped migrants enter public buildings, register children for school, and access continuing education. Respondents from Partida were able to do things like attend free adult schools to study English or computer literacy. Universities, hospitals, and other institutions also helped migrants skirt legal eligibility requirements and obtain education or care. Combined with deportation, this local support gave migrants a hybrid experience of control.

The Two-Faced State

Elvia and Inés Aguilar were sisters, both about four foot ten, with jet-black hair that hung to their waists. They left Partida to escape their father's abuse and had lived in Los Angeles for more than twenty years. Both were garment workers, out of work in the months I spent in Los Angeles, so we often met up on weekdays to eat and talk. One brilliant LA afternoon, I asked them to take me to their favorite restaurant, my treat. They chose a nearby enchilada joint, and Elvia volunteered to drive her beat-up Honda, her glasses peeking barely over the wheel. Not two blocks from her house, a police car sat parked in the road. Elvia was unfazed. Despite her unauthorized status, she had called the police on more than one occasion, even inviting them inside her home. When she first got married, she recalled, "[My husband] wanted to hit me one time, but I didn't let him. I called the police. I said, 'I told you that I can't be a submissive, silly woman like the ones that let men hit them, that let men manipulate them. No,' I said. Then they took him to jail . . . and he changed; he realized I couldn't be a woman like the ones from the pueblo." For Elvia, police were allies.

A few minutes later we stopped at Inés's apartment and stumbled into their brother Álvaro asleep on the doorstep. He roused a bit to meet me, breathing liquor into the LA sunshine. Chagrined, his sisters shooed me inside. "If I were his wife I would have ended that [behavior] long ago,"

Inés snapped. Elvia added, "We have no tolerance for badness." Another of their brothers had acted similarly, eventually getting himself "kicked out [of the United States]," even though he was one of Partida's few migrants with legal permanent residency. Inés explained, "All he did was drink. Then, the government arrested him. He was drinking, so he got deported."

The Aguilar sisters' stories illustrate the two different faces that LA respondents saw in the state. On one hand, they felt that *if* they were good, they could access police protection and public services. Like the Aguilars, Gloria Chávez, a mother in her late forties, believed she received food stamps for her five U.S.-born children *because* she worked hard. In the United States, she insisted, "If you need something—and you *really need it*,—the government is there for you." But Gloria also qualified her appreciation. She went on, "When I started working, I immediately went back and told them, 'I started working again; now I can support my family, and thank you for your help.'" In Gloria's mind, she earned public assistance by committing to self-sufficiency. Likewise, Juan Serrano told me that by working hard and achieving outstanding grades, he convinced a community-college dean to help him get a state-level grant (AB-540) and continue his education. For such migrants state services appeared to be a reward. As long as they worked hard and avoided government dependence, they could seek support without qualms.

On the other hand, 90 percent of respondents in Los Angeles saw deportation as a response to bad behavior. Like Elvia and Inés, most informants had acquaintances or family members who had been deported. Nevertheless, nearly every time they mentioned a fellow migrant's expulsion, they invoked laziness, drinking, drug abuse, or domestic violence. In my six months of observations, Álvaro Aguilar was one of perhaps two or three migrants from Partida I ever saw drinking heavily. Likewise, statistics show that less than half of deportees have ever committed a crime. Nevertheless, LA respondents echoed hostile, public stigmas that labeled deportees as criminals. Perhaps surprisingly, even deportees I met in Partida linked their expulsions to bad behavior. For example, Mario Vargas, a lanky forty-two-year-old, was deported on drug charges in 2009. Hanging out in the village square, he presented his deportation as if by way of introduction. He told me, "Oh, I lived in LA for twenty years. I miss it, especially my two sons. But I can never go back. I did something really bad." Women, meanwhile, often hinted that deported (male) family members had "gotten what they deserved." By implying that such men brought deportation on themselves, women made sense of—and distanced themselves from—that threat.

In addition, migrants also extrapolated the criminal/law-abiding binary to other arenas, including hard work, femininity, and racial assimilation. Some even implied that social acceptance hinged on acting "white." For example, Patricio Lara had been in the United States twenty years and worked as cook. He told me,

> I always felt at home here because I worked here, and I like life here. Now when I go back to Mexico, I feel strange, I feel different. . . . I think I'm one of those people they call "coconuts," white on the inside, brown on the outside. [Abigail: Why?] Because that's how I am. That's how I like to be. Maybe 40 percent I think I'm white inside and outside maybe 60 percent. [Abigail: Which are the white parts of you?] Well, for example—I'm, well, I don't like to make noise in my neighborhood here, because of my neighbors. . . . When we go out to a restaurant to eat, I tell them [my children] don't make noise, because other people aren't going to like it.

While it is not entirely clear how Patricio came to see whiteness as good, he reinforced his sense of belonging by distancing himself from his Mexican roots and practicing behaviors, like being quiet, which he saw as white. These actions made him *feel* both white and at home.

Conversely, some respondents linked exclusion to acting "Mexican" or "Indian." Blanca Martínez, for instance, suggested that to take advantage of opportunities in the United States, immigrants had to leave their indigenous roots behind. "If you don't try to learn things," she told me, "you're just going to be a submissive little Indian *[indio]* that doesn't know anything, that doesn't learn—just enclosed in yourself. With so many opportunities in life, if you don't know how to take advantage of them, the years pass you by." Blanca had once overheard a white woman on the bus blaming "Mexicans" for making a mess of Los Angeles. Though Blanca felt offended at first, eventually, she too began to frame recent migrants as dirty, lazy, and "bringing in bad attitudes." Thus, she drew racial boundaries between her own actions and the "Indian" or "Mexican" behavior of other (bad) migrants. If immigrants acted "American" (or white), such narratives implied, they might have more opportunities. Migrants from

Partida probably held such moral distinctions before coming to the United States. But police capacity was far greater in Los Angeles than in rural Mexico. Migrants' unauthorized status therefore *linked* their existing moral categories to the apparently binary practices of the state.

Good versus Bad at Work

Los Angeles's conditional control reverberated at work. Like almost two-thirds of migrants from Partida, Julia Chávez worked in Los Angeles's $24.3 billion apparel industry, sewing jeans for brands like Guess, Levi's, Lucky, and American Apparel.[13] In good years Julia could earn up to $25,000. Often she made less. She had no rest breaks, no overtime, no leave, no sick pay, and no guaranteed minimum wage. Nevertheless, thanks to Los Angeles's unions and immigrant movement, Julia and her counterparts from Partida received more labor protections than undocumented immigrants almost anywhere else in the United States.[14] In the 1990s, the Justice for Janitors Campaign; the domestic workers' movement; and organizing by the Service Employees International Union (SEIU) and the Union of Needletrades, Industrial, and Textile Employees (UNITE) had pushed Los Angeles to extend labor rights into sectors heavily staffed by undocumented immigrants. By 2000 Los Angeles had a living-wage ordinance and laws holding manufacturers liable for their subcontractors' labor violations. In particular, the LA Division of Occupational Safety and Health began inspecting garment factories.[15] The Labor Commission also instituted a protocol to expedite unauthorized workers' minimum wage and overtime claims, broadcasting "know your rights" information in Spanish at their workplaces. Meanwhile, LA workers' centers and nonprofits offered orientation and support to workers like housekeepers—including a third of those from Partida—who fell outside traditional labor laws.[16]

As a result, LA employers had limited recourse to coercion. Instead, as I mention in chapter 3, they often used good/bad binaries as well, encouraging migrants to compete with one another and rewarding faster workers by giving them easier tasks, more jobs, or access to materials that could speed up their work. Though migrants from Partida rarely felt threatened, piece rates encouraged them to race for speed and avoid taking breaks.

Many took pride in how intensely they worked and how rapidly they could pound out garments, drawing admiration from coworkers. For instance, several people in the LA community talked about how—in the Jenco factories in the 1990s—young migrants from Partida worked like "animals." They remembered how other workers used to marvel, "the folks from Oaxaca just got here, the ones from Partida." Juan Serrano was one. Though Juan was proud of his hard work and had sewed garments for almost a decade, he also remembered, "People fought for the work and took it from one another—because there are cloths that are softer and you can do it faster, and among ourselves we'd be fighting. The managers loved it, [saying], 'Look, people even go get their own fabric' [instead of waiting for managers to deliver it]." As scholars have long pointed out, labor control does not always work through threats. Consent can even be more efficient, relying on hierarchies such as good/bad binaries to divide workers and obscure the bosses' control.[17]

When I asked Julia Chávez about work, she echoed the same divisions. Unlike most undocumented immigrants, Julia trusted state agents and was unafraid to make labor claims.[18] She and many others from Partida kept the local labor commissioner's card in their wallets, so they could call and complain in case of mistreatment. When I asked if Julia would be willing to report a violation, she replied,

> I would go to the labor commissioner if I had bad problems, because that's what it's there for, right? To help hardworking people. Because we [immigrants] really are hardworking. As long as we work, I think they [the government] are going to treat us well. But if someone depends on the government, then they blame us, saying that Latinos just feed off the government and all that.

In Julia's mind, state agencies judged not only migrants' legal behavior but also their merits as workers, offering services and enforcement in exchange for hard work.

Other migrants hinted that hard work might also be a means to legalization. Blanca Martínez, for example, had moved to Oaxaca City as a young woman and then to California, where she found a housekeeping job in a "palace" in Beverly Hills. I met Blanca in early 2011 at her meticulously kept home in South Los Angeles. She had cleaned the same house for more than twenty-five years. Eventually, her employers helped her apply for legal authorization. Fiddling with lace on her tablecloth, Blanca argued, "They liked my work a lot. I dedicated myself to my work, and they saw good things in me and thought that I had a right to get papers. So they helped me." To her, legal residency could be compensation for dedicated, dutiful service.

"Here There Is Freedom"

Conditional control gave migrants a sense of hope. Unlike other undocumented immigrants, respondents in Los Angeles tended to trust the police. One day, Andrea Campos's twenty-two-year-old son, Gabriel, was driving her to work when a police officer pulled him over for running a stop sign. Both Andrea and Gabriel were undocumented and unlicensed. Nevertheless, Andrea leaned over to the police officer, explained that her son was law abiding and hardworking, and convinced the officer not to detain him. In our interview a few months later, Andrea explained, "I see discrimination elsewhere, like they say there are laws that discriminate against people just for their skin color in Arizona, but I've never had problems. . . . [Police discrimination] doesn't affect me much." She added that the United States offered opportunities; it was just a question of whether migrants decided to take them. When I asked Andrea if she would ever go back to Mexico for rights or peace of mind, she quickly replied, "No. I like it here, and I want to stay here for the rest of my life. My mother says, 'You have to come back.' But I wouldn't go. Only to visit; not to live."

Los Angeles's conditional mode of control enabled migrants to feel they belonged. Respondents like Andrea felt they had some influence over their fates—or what many of them called "freedom." Good/bad contrasts made enforcement seem logical rather than arbitrary. When I asked if migrants felt targeted by race or legal status, most of them said no. They expressed relatively little fear of deportation. Like Andrea, they demonstrated this trust by interacting openly with police and service providers. I saw many migrants from Partida drive; visit hospitals, schools, and state agencies; and talk to police (practices unheard of in North County San Diego). More than half of interviewees had attended public adult schools, learning English, computer repair, or other skills that helped them find jobs. At least three attended community college and earned bachelor's degrees. Trust gave them access to mobility, police protection, education, and services.

Conditional control also conveyed a logic of individual responsibility, making migrants feel they could *choose* to be good or bad. In reality, migrants' legal status left them little choice except to be good. Nevertheless, two-thirds of LA-based interviewees told me they felt free in the United States. Bruno Torres, a portly fifty-three-year-old parking attendant, explained,

> [In the United States] there's freedom; you can do what you want. You want to work? Work. You want to stay in the street? Stay in the street! Ask for charity, ask for what you can, but don't [complain]—and now you're in the street like a vagrant. But if you want to study, the schools are right there.... [The United States] gives you the opportunity to be the person you want. For instance, if I want to improve, I can take classes, make my mind work and all that.

By pinning deportation on bad behavior, respondents could take credit for working hard and distance themselves from risk. Many felt that migrants could either act good and reap rewards or act bad and be punished; they (and not the U.S. state) were answerable for their fates.

Many respondents also blamed other migrants for inviting government mistreatment. When I visited Blanca Martínez, we often talked about the recent escalation in policing and deportation. Gazing out over her chain-link fence, where two young men were blasting music, Blanca reflected,

> Right now, yes, things [police actions] have gotten a little [worse]—and it's because of the bad people who come here with other intentions, with another way—the evildoers who have arrived, and, well, that's the truth. Just as we hardworking people have come with the desire to get ahead, they have come too.... There are many people that have gotten ahead working [se ha superado], but people have also come with other intentions and another way of living. Maybe that's what they learned in their country, but they come, and they do that here. It makes me sad because this country has been so generous in having us here.

In this discussion, as in many we had, Blanca blamed "evildoers" for inviting mistreatment, while holding U.S. citizens and the state in high regard.[19] She included both people she knew personally—like her brother or the youth across the street—and the anonymous "lazy," "criminal" immigrants of public stereotypes. At the same time, Blanca insisted that the United States was generous: "the country of opportunity, the country where if you come to work and you work hard, you can accomplish your dreams." Blanca emphasized her own hard work and self-sufficiency, especially from government benefits. Migrants abused the system, she felt, rather than the reverse. Thus, respondents like Blanca deflected accountability for deportation away from the U.S. government and onto other migrants.

Despite their unauthorized status, many migrants in Los Angeles appreciated the United States. Bernardo Cruz, a construction worker in his midfifties, explicitly credited the U.S. *government* with granting him access to fairly paid work. Sitting in his apartment over *pozole* (corn stew), he recounted,

> I came here to find freedom. This country has offered and continues offering freedom of expression, freedom to work. . . . Or that as a worker you earn what you deserve; you're free to ask for what your effort is worth. . . . Here, as an immigrant, God gave me—or *the government gave me*—the freedom to have what I hadn't had either in Mexico City or in my pueblo. Thank God for this freedom to earn for my effort, for my work [my emphasis].

Perhaps surprisingly, Bernardo linked freedom not only to appreciation for the United States but also to *work*. Rather than viewing the U.S. government as discriminatory, he appreciated it for giving him opportunities.

Gloria Chávez, who lived with her five children and two grandchildren in a rent-controlled apartment in Echo Park, also valued the United States. In the United States, she told me, state agents offered "a lot of support, not like in my country [Mexico], where there are poor people who have nothing to eat, and it doesn't matter to the government at all." Like Bernardo, Gloria associated freedom with economic opportunity, explaining, "There is freedom here. This is a country where there is freedom. [Abigail: What do you mean by freedom?] The freedom to progress. Anyone who wants to can progress. There is also freedom here to work in what you want. . . . I really liked coming to this country, really, there's a way to move up in the world here; there's something for the future."

Though Gloria's husband wanted to buy land in Mexico, she told him without hesitation,

> No. I came here to stay. . . . I am not going with you. The door is open if you want to go back to Mexico, but I'm not going back there anymore. . . . I've been living here for so many years that now I feel like it's my second home. When I go back to my pueblo, it would be pretty for a week or two, to see my family, but once that's over I have to come back here.

For Gloria, economic opportunities mitigated political exclusion. Instead of pining for her country of birth, Gloria identified with Los Angeles. For migrants like her, Los Angeles offered not only services but also a comparatively welcoming, pro-immigrant context.[20] At least five of those from Partida called the United States their *patria* (homeland). Others said the United States had welcomed or "adopted" them and that they "loved it" or "felt at home."

Combining appreciation for the United States with the desire to escape Partida, most migrants in Los Angeles wanted to stay. Undocumented status notwithstanding, more than 85 percent settled permanently in the United States. Only 10 percent expected to return to their homeland, compared to about 34 percent of noncitizens nationwide, including legal residents.[21] Hoping for inclusion, they set their sights on a future in the United States.

The State between Women and Men

Women felt especially privileged by conditional control. In Los Angeles, as nationwide, more than 90 percent of deportees were men. Women were far less likely than men to be stopped by LA police. On the contrary, LA police gave them some protection, especially from household abuse. Factory and service employers also differentiated by gender, recruiting female workers and showing preferential treatment to women.[22] As a result, women tended to feel the most favorably toward their adopted home.

Not surprisingly, women in Los Angeles showed more faith in police and felt more free than men. As the story of Elvia and Inés Aguilar suggests, women distanced themselves from deportation by associating it with their male counterparts' laziness, drinking, or violence (reinforcing harmful stereotypes). Trusting state agents to differentiate between good and bad, several women also called the police to help them confront domestic abuse. Nationwide, only about 15 percent of unauthorized victims report domestic violence.[23] By contrast, of thirteen women in Los Angeles who told me they had been beaten at home, seven reported it to the police (54 percent). Several women from Partida also pursued U visas, allowing them to obtain legal asylum if they helped police prosecute their assailants.[24]

For many women, wages and work reinforced the feeling of "progress." For a while, for instance, Mariela Olvera's husband beat her. Unlike many of Partida's migrants, Mariela had married in the village before moving to Los Angeles. Once she got to the United States and earned money, however, Mariela began to push back. She explained,

> For me, it was better to be here [in the United States], because here I had my job—I worked, and I had my own money. If I wanted something, I bought it for myself, and in the pueblo I didn't know how to work [i.e., didn't have work]. . . . When I found out that I could have what I wanted by my own sweat, that's when I started to change. . . . [I told him] "I paid the rent, I paid the grocery store, I paid my bills, and I bought this without you; now I've proven that I can." That's how I stopped letting him treat me that way.

But Mariela's sense of empowerment did not come from work alone. Employment had this effect *only* because she felt privileged in the workplace (thanks to gendered norms) and could live without fear of police. In North County San Diego, where women worked similar jobs, most faced even *more* abuse than they had back in Mexico.

Women in Los Angeles often credited the United States for their household empowerment, reinforcing their sense of escape. Thanks to work and state support, female respondents argued that living in the United States had helped them "modernize" their gender relationships. A full 84 percent said they felt liberated in the United States. For instance, Estrella Gómez, a bright-eyed thirty-three-year-old with bouncing curly hair, spent a decade working as a nanny in Los Angeles before returning to Partida in 2010 to attend to her father's store. She longed for California. The United States offered her an opportunity, she said, to "be more civilized, take the blindfold off my eyes, and not be around people like my father who are so stuck in the mind." Some of those who had originally come to the United States for wages also started to build new cross-border comparisons after they arrived. For instance, Valentina Zamora explained that, while she came to California for money, over time she began to believe, "Here, women are worth a lot—a whole lot. Back in the pueblo there is machismo, but not here." Likewise, when I joked with Gloria that perhaps I'd marry a Oaxacan, she quipped, "No more men from there! You've seen that in Mexico the men are really *machistas*."

In contrast, Latino men were more targeted by LA police, for everything from traffic violations to domestic violence. They were also less favored for garment and domestic work.[25] While women could recur to police for support, their male counterparts tended to feel like objects of control. Some men shared women's senses of freedom, but others were more ambivalent. For instance, Wilfredo Rojas said his wife enjoyed the United States and wanted to stay. By contrast, he added, "I feel trapped here. There [in Mexico], you have more freedom. Here it's just to work and back home again, over and over again. . . . One day I want to go back there." Though Wilfredo arrived in Los Angeles in 1988 and had lived there most of his life, he still did not feel it was home.

Other men resented U.S. police for supporting women. For instance, Pancho Franco, a longtime migrant who had since returned to the village, quipped, "Women win in LA. You know—they just call 911, and the dude goes straight to jail." Similarly, Víctor Rangel believed U.S. police pursued men unfairly, for actions he saw as trivial. He told me,

[In the United States] women have—the government really respects women. You can't put a hand on them, or give a woman a pinch, because she sues you, and the punishment is bad. So there you can't really tell a woman what to do. If you discover that she's doing something bad, well, you have to put up with it. . . . And a lot of women abuse the system, thanks to the rules they have there. Because [women] know [police] defend them a lot, so maybe they get together with another man—and of course, well, the husband—it's his honor, right?

Such men felt that women and state agents teamed up against them. While some credited the United States with giving them opportunities, others believed they lost autonomy in the United States. They felt unfairly framed as criminals from whom their female counterparts needed protection. Thus, conditional control positioned U.S. state agents *between* migrant women and men.[26]

Breaks in the Good/Bad Logic

Nevertheless, the link between policing and behavior in Los Angeles was tenuous. Migrants' lived experiences and social relationships proved more ambiguous than the good/bad narrative that many attributed to the state. When the correspondence between treatment and behavior faltered, so did migrants' feelings of belonging. In the 2010s, for instance, police began to target some LA respondents despite their good behavior. Men, in particular, felt they faced unfair punishments, such as being stopped by police even when they followed the law, or working as hard as they could only to find they were blocked from promotions or raises. While some men continued to identify as good, others grew disillusioned.

For instance, Alejandro Campos was a thirty-four-year-old immigrant who came to Los Angeles in 1991, learned English, and started his own business in digital photography. He took pictures of weddings, *quinceañeras* (fifteenth-birthday festivals), and other local events. Alejandro never drank alcohol. He drove carefully. During the fifteen years he worked in LA garment factories, he often "tried to break records for speed," on the faith that hard work would earn him social mobility. Then, between 2009 and 2011, police impounded Alejandro's car four times, undermining his trust in conditional enforcement. By the time we met, Alejandro had started to see LA policing as contradictory. Sitting in his third-story apartment, packing up photography equipment so he could return to Partida, Alejandro reflected, "You [migrants] can do a lot here, but you get sick of the treatment. Just for driving, what happens? They take your car. Though you drive carefully, you never drink, you never do that, and suddenly you hit a checkpoint and 'boom,' you're out." As Alejandro faced ever more arbitrary treatment, he also started to associate policing with racial discrimination, undermining his faith in the promise of U.S. freedom. He added, "[Police] know very well which section of the city they're in, because they don't do it in Beverly Hills, where all the people go out nice and drunk; they do it where there are all Latinos."

Similar clashes struck Alejandro's friend Juan Serrano. A gregarious, sleekly dressed man in his midthirties, Juan first worked cleaning windows. He then moved into garment factories and eventually found a scholarship to college, getting a bachelor's degree in international business. Yet because Juan was unauthorized, he could not find better jobs. He became cynical, reflecting that while he used to think of garment jobs as "good work":

> It wasn't actually that good, right? Seventy, eighty dollars to work from 6:00 A.M. to 5:00 in the afternoon, working to earn that, and it was pretty killer—it was really, really hard, because you had to be seated all day, right? ... Then I started to learn how international business works, and I came to the conclusion that I didn't want to work for those companies, that I don't want to get into that. That's when I started to say, "To hell with this." I was working with this system that was manipulating me, using me.... [I thought], "I'm not going to play the game that they are playing, because a game functions because we play it." ... I don't like the United States. I don't like the system. There is no freedom there.

When Juan hit this ceiling, he grew disillusioned about the rewards to hard work. He dismissed good/bad comparisons as a tool of corporate control and questioned the freedom he once associated with the United States. For good/bad categories to elicit belonging, migrants must trust the state's conditionality. When policing was arbitrary, their perceptions of both work and state agents changed, giving way to alienation.

ARBITRARY CONTROL IN NORTH COUNTY SAN DIEGO

North County San Diego was less hospitable. For one, San Diego was ground zero for the militarization of the Mexican border in the 1990s and the first decade of the 2000s.[27] Because towns like Vista and Escondido were within a hundred miles of the U.S.-Mexico line, the Border Patrol operated freely there. San Diego was also one of the first places ICE and the Border Patrol collaborated directly with local police.

In addition, Escondido, Vista, and nearby towns were also hotbeds of anti-immigrant advocacy. In the 1980s the Ku Klux Klan revived in San Diego County against immigrants, becoming one of the strongest KKK chapters in the country. Later, anti-immigrant groups like the Minuteman Project and Americans for Immigration Reform supplanted the Klan, while sustaining its violent, white-supremacist character.[28] In the 1990s and the first decade of the 2000s, the Minutemen regularly staged anti-immigrant demonstrations in Vista and Escondido, with signs that read, for instance, "Go back to Mexico," "We don't want you here," or "Illegals go home." Even though Vista and Escondido were nearly 50 percent Latino by 2010, most Latinos lacked voting rights. Republicans still dominated local politics. Local officials also positioned themselves against immigrants. For instance, former Escondido police chief Jim Maher labeled migrants criminals, declaring, "America has enough of its own criminals. We really don't need criminals from another country, and that's what our goal is—to remove them."[29]

In the first decade of the 2000s Escondido and Vista also created a series of restrictive policies targeting the undocumented. Escondido banned residents from renting property to unauthorized immigrants.[30] It prohibited street parking in Latino neighborhoods and created other ordinances to protect what officials saw as the local quality of life. Similarly, Vista adopted resolutions to prevent people from hiring day laborers, most of whom were undocumented. Girded by anti-immigrant demonstrators, both cities blocked the Mexican consulate from distributing identification cards that might give migrants access to banks or services.

North County San Diego was also one of the first places in the country to formalize police participation in immigration enforcement, above and beyond federal mandates. In 1994 the San Diego Police Department created a joint special unit with the Border Patrol, authorizing police to hold detainees and turn them over to Border Patrol prior to criminal conviction.[31] In May 2009 San Diego County was the first jurisdiction in California to implement the Secure Communities program, deputizing police to detain "criminal aliens." Escondido, Vista, and other nearby cities also expanded their own policing of immigrants. For instance, in 2010, Escondido became the only city in the United States to place federal immigration agents *inside* the police department, through a special agreement it made with ICE.[32]

More informally, North County police used their regular duties to detain undocumented migrants and turn them over to ICE. Traffic enforcement offered a particular point of attack. North County San Diego is spread out and has limited public transit. Therefore, prior to 2015 migrants had little alternative but to drive without licenses. During my fieldwork, Escondido had instituted a network of checkpoints ostensibly aimed at stopping drunk drivers. Yet most of their stops were at hours like 9:00 A.M., and 90 percent of those detained were undocumented.[33] At such stops, police either turned migrants over to ICE or impounded their vehicles for thirty days, fining the owners around $1,000—an entire month's wages—to recover a car.[34] North County police were also known to stop migrants haphazardly, in pharmacies, supermarkets, and the streets of Latino neighborhoods. Respondents reported being detained for violations such as driving without a seatbelt or riding a bicycle on the sidewalk. Police would reportedly even check migrants' legal status when responding to domestic-violence calls.[35] In surveys among migrants from Retorno to North County, 39 percent of those stopped were detained (compared to 3 percent of legal residents nationwide), and 23 percent were deported.[36]

At the same time, services in North County San Diego were limited. According to the Immigration Advocates Network (2017), Los Angeles had thirty-one registered immigrant–legal advocacy NGOs, while North County had three. Even where migrants did have rights to state support, many were afraid to engage with service providers at all.

"Nos Pescan" (They Fish for Us)

Marcelo Sánchez, whose family I got to know during the months I spent in Vista, lived in North County San Diego on and off from the age of fifteen. Now fifty-two, he worked in a hot-tub factory and lived with his wife and son in a one-story house in Vista. But when Marcelo first arrived in the 1980s, he—along with ten thousand to fourteen thousand other farmworkers—lived outside, near the farms where they picked tomatoes. Given the high cost of housing in San Diego County, the demand for farmworkers, and the lack of available land, migrant homelessness far surpassed other agricultural areas in the state.[37] One day Marcelo showed me around the hillsides where he and his friends had camped. To sleep, he demonstrated, they dug out ditches among the trees and covered them with foraged plastic. By day they worked in the fields; by night they came back, played basketball, and drank a beer for dinner—if money sufficed. The scene—poignantly described in Leo Chavez's (1998) anthropology of San Diego farmworkers—included almost everyone from Retorno.

Their homelessness made them targets for immigration control. When Marcelo lived in the canyons, he recalled, "La migra used to treat us badly. They were mean, as if they wanted to hit us all the time—always really hard, scaring us so that we would return to Mexico." His friend Mateo Herrera, who had lived in the hills as well, added,

> We were really pursued. Every two weeks or twenty days they would come, and if not they would follow us at night. And they could find you easily! Because you just walked up to sleep in the hillside—where we made our little homes—and they would follow our footpaths and come to take us out at night, while we were sleeping. . . . When we would try to go down to the supermarket, they could pick us out by our black hair. Like, I remember one day they took me off the bus here in the transit center . . . right here [in Vista].

As soon as migrants from Retorno entered the United States, they felt targeted by race (their "black hair"), as well as scared and abused.

Twenty-five years later Patricia Sosa told a similar story. Also fifty-two, Patricia had come to the United States in 1995 on her husband's insistence, her three children in tow. When I asked Patricia about her perceptions of Vista police, she shook her head. Last week, she told me, "They [police] deported two friends from my hometown, women. They had been here forever. . . . They were on their way to work, in the van, and the police stopped them and called la migra, and right there they took them away." Patricia invoked similar moral categories to those in Los Angeles, associating goodness with working, being female, and living for a long time in the United States. Yet instead of believing police differentiated between immigrants based on those characteristics, she underscored that her friends had been deported *despite* being good.

Marcelo's and Patricia's stories show how—from the time migrants from Retorno first arrived in North County through the 2010s—they felt targeted *arbitrarily*. They believed state agents discriminated not by migrants' behavior but by legal status and race. Dozens described being pulled over for reasons like failing to stop at stop signs, having cracked windshields, or "suspicious driving." Others watched friends detained in public places. In surveys 29 percent of respondents had friends or family detained by police, and two-thirds of those had been stopped on the street. For instance, twenty-nine-year-old Rubén Ramos recalled that one day when he was on a public bus to high school, one of his friends got detained. Wiping tears from his eyes, Rubén recalled, "They sent him straight to Tijuana with his backpack and books and all." When I asked Rubén why, he replied, "For political reasons [i.e., local anti-immigrant politics], bad luck." Hugo Lara, a construction worker in his fifties, added, "A lot of times the police wander around in places like bars, dance halls—public places where people drink. So it's just a matter of [them] waiting, and when people [migrants] go out, *nos pescan* (they fish for us)."

While respondents saw themselves as good, they did not believe police made such distinctions. Many offered examples of people deported "without reason." For instance, forty-year-old Carolina Díaz complained, "The police take away lots of cars, and if you don't have a license or papers they kick you out. I've seen it lots of times when I'm on the way to work. . . . They don't care if migrants need work." While such comments sustained the good/bad frame and emphasis on hard work of those in Los Angeles, migrants from Retorno used the good/bad distinctions to underscore the *il*logic and *un*predictability of North County enforcement. In these respondents' minds the United States *projected* criminality onto migrants, meting out punishments even without a crime. Few of them observed rewards to being good. Thus, José Luis Salazar, a thirty-two-year-old deportee whom I interviewed back in Retorno, lamented, "Because eight or ten or twenty other people—fellow Mexicans—end up committing big mistakes, big crimes there [in the United States], we all pay. . . . Because of other people that behave badly there, innocent people pay." At once, José Luis blamed "bad" people and highlighted the injustice of current control.

Migrants in North County also felt targeted because they were Mexican. Studies show that when police are involved in immigration control, as in North County, they almost always engage in racial profiling.[38] Respondents confirmed this view. Some commented that as indigenous people (who tend to be darker skinned than other Mexicans), they had it even worse than their mestizo peers. For instance, Rafael González had recently been stopped by police. He explained, "You see, one looks [I look] really Mexican, dark skinned and short—almost as if my flag is right here." Basilio Ramos agreed. He argued, "The political current that has taken hold in Escondido is definitely that of the racists, and there, effectively, they can detain you by your racial profile. . . . They want the cheap labor force, but they don't want to see their neighborhoods, their areas, the cities, start to populate with ever more migrants." With local enforcement based on race instead of behavior, migrants in North County never knew if they would be next.

The Weight of Threat at Work

Arbitrary treatment colored the workplace as well. By the time of my fieldwork, only 15 percent of Retorno's migrants remained in agriculture, while 85 percent held jobs in factories, construction, and housekeeping, just like those from Partida. Both faced unstable employment, under- and nonpayment of wages, denials of rest breaks, and long hours without overtime pay. Yet their experiences at work were shaped by the local mode of control.

In 2011 the city councils of Escondido and nearby Oceanside took what was then an extreme position by mandating that all businesses use a federal system called E-Verify, which allows employers to check workers' documentation status online.[39] At the same time, these cities extended few labor protections to undocumented immigrants. Informal workers faced particular harassment, as police did regular sweeps of day laborers and imposed fines on anyone caught hiring them.[40]

In this context, many respondents argued that employers treated migrants like "slaves." Forced to move to Vista by her husband in the early 1990s, Dolores Muñoz had worked in factories for more than seventeen years. She described,

> In each [factory] the treatment is the same. . . . If someone speaks up, they fire him—or they say that they'll call immigration control on him. And once, yes, immigration control did come to the factory, and people were so afraid that a lot of people ran. . . . As illegals [sic], we lived through abuse in the factories. Through so much humiliation . . . At one point, I started to work in a factory where they printed T-shirts. Likewise, the manager of that factory

used to scream horribly at us *(nos gritaba horrores)*. That he wanted the work done, "But now, but faster. If you want, and if not, the door is big enough for you to get out." In that company, they also made a lot of people cry; there was a lot of abuse of people—too much. [Abigail: Was the abuse physical or verbal?] Verbal, but they were shouts as if we were—it's like remembering in the years when they had black people working in this country, like the slaves. That's how they have us. . . . Here, as an immigrant in this country, you can never enjoy the little you have. You're always like a slave, like a slave.

North County's political context gave employers tools for intimidation. Amid anti-immigrant policing and few state controls, they reverted to force.

Employers used the hostile context to browbeat workers. Respondents remembered that managers in North County often threatened to call the police on migrants or invite ICE to conduct I-9 audits, checking their social security numbers. Some had even brought ICE agents into the workplace dressed in the guise of civilian police. Other bosses degraded migrants using racial slurs, such as "Indians," "little Oaxacans," "dirty," or "pigs."[41] When workers in one factory attempted to unionize, the managers promised to check the documents of anyone who joined.

As a result, migrants experienced work as an interminable grind. Paloma Pacheco, who spent several years picking tomatoes and cucumbers, told me that on the farms, "I just cried and cried, Abigail, because there are foremen that—they don't care. They have no feelings. It doesn't matter to them—they're just saying, 'Hurry up! We have to finish! We have to send these boxes of tomatoes or cucumbers!' And they don't care. They have no feelings—as if they're more with the boss than with the worker." Marcelo Sánchez's wife, Teresa Estrada, added that in her two decades in Vista, "I have worked ceaselessly, without stop—and with little kids too. . . . All the jobs were bad! Because it's hard, really—ay, no!—quick, like a race. Ay, no! For me, they were all bad." Rather than feeling free at work, migrants from Retorno felt trapped.

"There Is No Freedom Here"

Arbitrary policing left migrants terrified, cynical, and estranged. I arrived at Ricardo and Salomé Garza's home in Vista one warm Saturday evening in 2010. The street bustled with boxy white trucks selling fruit out the back and tight-jeaned teenage girls, laughing and leaning over the second-story railings. Inside the Garzas' apartment, their nine-year-old daughter, Mari, sat squished between her three siblings on the bed, engrossed in a school worksheet. The TV sprayed black and white. The signal cost too much, Salomé admitted sheepishly. In the 1990s Ricardo had picked strawberries in Vista, coming and going from Retorno alone while his wife stayed in the village. Then, in 2001 he brought Salomé and their two (then) toddlers. Brushing off his dusty black jeans, Ricardo glanced at his children and sighed. "We bet it all for them," he said, but "I don't know what we will be able to give them."

Ricardo's thought halted when a siren screamed outside. While police didn't usually come in, Salomé told me, "They're always out there. So we're afraid to leave." Though Salomé gave birth to two additional children in the United States, she admitted, "I've only seen a doctor twice in my life; I'm too scared." A few hours later, just after 9:00 P.M., I made my way back to my car. The street was dead. No music. No bustle. Just one white car, shining its headlights in my eyes, hovering while I fumbled for directions home. Then I saw the floodlights and realized it was an unmarked police car, watching me in the dark. Living there, respondents said, they felt perpetually excluded, like temporary visitors, eking out a living in a land that was not theirs. Ricardo added, "We want to go back [to Retorno], but— well, here we are."

Even though most people from Retorno had been in California over a decade, they did not believe they owned their own fates. Paloma Pacheco, for one, had worked in Vista for almost eighteen years. Her three children were U.S.-born citizens, and she did not want to leave. Yet she felt helpless. As her children played at our feet in a gaping, empty coffee shop, she murmured, "I know I am not doing anything wrong. But immigration [control] is out here each day, and one day they're going to find me, and then they'll find me guilty of being illegal here, and I'm gone to Mexico. They're just going to take me; they're not going to ask 'Would you like to go?'"

Unable to predict who would be caught and expelled, migrants from Retorno lived in fear. In surveys 67 percent said they were afraid to drive a car, 64 percent to walk in public, 37 percent to go to the hospital, 36 percent to take public transit, and 36 percent to go to work.[42] Roberto

Gutiérrez, a thirty-two-year-old construction worker, linked this fear to what he called "not knowing." "There is always, always fear," he explained. "[You think] 'Who knows when the police will stop me, when they will find out that I don't have papers, when la migra will stop me.'" Indeed, almost every time I went somewhere with migrants during my five months in Vista and Escondido—whether to a child's school or a festival—informants asked me to drive. Many gave me their keys the first time we met. I saw fear in public as well. I remember the day I invited José Ortíz, a twenty-four-year-old warehouse worker, to meet me at a Starbucks, where large windows opened up to the palm-lined street. Just after we sat down, José darted under the table. It took me a few long seconds to realize a police car had passed. He explained, "When you don't have papers you go around with that feeling of anxiety all the time. Going out to work or on the freeway, or arriving at stores. It's a stress you feel everywhere."

Respondents in North County were also afraid to use services. Dulce Ochoa met me in the oversized T-shirt she used to clean houses, which made her look thin and worn. She was a soft-spoken woman in her mid-forties, and her dark eyes blazed with the weight of her twenty years undocumented, trying to make ends meet. A few years after Dulce arrived in California, she gave birth to her youngest daughter. The entire time, she admitted, she was afraid. She recalled, "When I had my daughter, they gave her MediCal [state health insurance]. I think that's good, but it scared me too, because I said, 'Maybe it's a trap—or they're doing something mean to us.' . . . I was afraid, really, really afraid." Even hospitals were uncertain ground. Dulce never knew when she might be exposed. Others admitted that they didn't feel safe going to the police or the courthouse, even when faced with a crime. As one put it, "You can't trust that nothing will happen."[43]

Fear kept migrants immobilized. As one thirty-eight-year-old woman said, "You can't go out. Even to go grocery shopping. They [the police] hit us; they treat us really badly; they put us in jail. You're trapped." Afraid of driving, migrants stayed close to home. When I asked respondents to lunch (my custom when inviting someone for an interview), those in North County often hesitated. Most had never been to a restaurant nearby, let alone to the beach, just twenty miles west. Only two people I met in North County had ever been to Los Angeles. Not only were their social networks concentrated nearby, but the checkpoint between San Diego and Los Angeles blocked their passage. Instead of moving, they stayed isolated.

Camila Mejía illustrates the alienation such respondents felt in the United States. Throughout our one-hour interview, Camila cried and cried. Smoothing her long, black braids, she explained that, for her, life in the United States was filled with pressure and stress. Though Camila had been ambivalent, her husband, Rafael González, insisted she cross the border in 2001. On the first attempt, Camila was detained. Today she feared leaving her house. Like Alma Sandoval, all she saw in the United States were racist people, discrimination, and government control. She wanted to go home. Choking back sobs, Camila reflected, "Right now I don't want to be here [in the United States] at all—I feel horrible here. . . . I think that life is nicer there, and there's no pressure or anything like here. . . . It's nicer there because life is calmer. The only reason to be here is because there's no work there." Her dream, she added, was to go back to Mexico.

Many others told me, "There is no freedom here." Of thirty-seven interviewees who had lived in North County, all but three used the word "suffering" to characterize their experiences in the United States. Unprompted, more than a third said they felt "like slaves." As Lupita Suárez put it, "When I came, I regretted it because I saw how people lived here—how people got up early to work, got home late—leaving their children with other people, and then all afternoon rushing around." Basilio Ramos added, "I don't think there's any good environment for migrants. Working in the United States will never be very calm, very pleasant. In reality you go to the United States—before and now and probably later—to a place where hostility may not take a physical form, may not take the form of direct aggression, but you know it's there. If the boss hires you, if he gives you work, the truth is that it's because he needs you. But he doesn't want you." Arbitrary policing left such migrants feeling pressured and excluded, with few stakes in the game.

Like Camila Mejía, 89 percent of respondents in North County hoped to return to Mexico. In the initial days of Retorno-U.S. migration, men had circulated between the village and the United States. Some of the earliest ones got legal permanent-resident status in 1986 (through the Immigration Reform and Control Act, IRCA). Perhaps surprisingly, however, they continued the circular pattern, using their newfound legal status to move more freely.[44] Many more undocumented migrants also arrived. By the peak of Retorno's U.S. migration in 1993, only 22 percent of its migrants had settled in the United States. Some, like Lupita, contrasted Retorno with the United States, suggesting, "The thing I like best about my hometown is the freedom. You don't have that pressure." Similarly, even though Dora López had legal permanent-resident status, she told me, "I'm planning to go back and live in my pueblo. Everything's fine here, but there's so much pressure, and in my pueblo, I feel happy; I feel calm." Such migrants considered their village an alternative to the stress and confinement they faced in California. Even though Retorno had once excluded them, its migrants came to see Mexico as open to change, as I show in chapters 4–5. Comparing the United States and Mexico, they repeated a common refrain: "U.S., country that screws you; Mexico, country of freedom" (Estados Unidos, país de la chingada; México, país de la libertad).

After September 11, 2001, however, intensified U.S. border enforcement made it harder for migrants to come and go. In the first decade of the 2000s, the United States dramatically expanded border control, increasing the rate of deaths at the border and the cost of a smuggler. As of 2010 migrants had to pay more than US$5,000 per person to cross, a third of their annual income. They responded by staying longer in the United States.[45] While 89 percent of those surveyed wanted to leave California, only 8 percent planned to go back that year. Basilio Ramos was one who went back. I interviewed Basilio at his home in Retorno, and when I asked why his adult, undocumented children did not return as well, he reflected, "Here in the village there's little hope of supporting your children . . . so my children decided they're better off staying in the United States, that things will still be better there. With things as they are currently [economically], it will be better to stay—to fight with immigration control, to fight with the police, to fight with the racists, but there they will stay." Circulating, as Basilio had done when his children were young, was no longer a feasible option. Others feared losing their families. Ensconced on an old couch in Oceanside beside the husband who used to beat her, Griselda García explained, "I'm fed up with this country. The only reason I can't leave is because my sons are still here. They need me." Griselda stayed for her children. But her heart and mind returned to Mexico.

Some of those in North County planned to stay until they could earn enough money to go back for good. Camila, for instance, longed to spend Christmas with her mother in Retorno. Instead, she stayed in the United States, hoping that she could eventually pay for a house in Retorno and move back permanently. Luisa Ramos, likewise, planned to work in North County until she "broke down." She told me, "I know that at my age [late forties], my body can't work much longer. My body will no longer function, and if that happened, well, I would go there [to Retorno], and I wouldn't come back anymore." Even those who wanted to stay in California, like Paloma, felt resigned to deportation. Though Paloma's children were U.S.-born, she told me, "At some point, you [migrants] have to return to your country. So, right now, I'm thinking that I'll work really hard, save what I can, so that the day they come throw me out, I'll have a little savings and a place to land." Trapped, respondents lived in a precarious state of "mental exit," working in California while pinning their hopes on return.

The State against Women and Men

Arbitrary control also made women vulnerable. One day I knocked at Paloma's house in Temecula, California, twenty-five miles northeast of her relatives in Vista. Her husband opened the door brusquely, brushing past me without a hello. Paloma had been vivacious and chatty each time I saw her in public. This time, she looked up from the sofa, her face soaked with tears. Scooping up her fussy two-year-old, she begged me to drive her to the supermarket two miles away. In the car she brought out pictures of her bruised face and asked me to confirm that this was abuse. She knew it, she added, but was afraid to report her husband. He had legal permanent residency and she did not. He had threatened that if she "messed with him," he would get her deported, cutting her off from her children. She was unsure how seriously to take this threat. She reflected, "I hope they wouldn't take away my children, but he used to threaten me like that, that if something happened he would take away my children." She couldn't turn to family members, she added. Her brothers lived forty-five minutes away, and she had no car to reach them. Wary of police, she looked to the sky, sighing, "Please, God, come. Come help me." With limited access to family or the state, Paloma felt she must turn to God.

Like Paloma, more than 90 percent of women from Retorno followed their husbands or fathers to the United States. As of 2011 women still represented less than a third of U.S. migrants from Retorno. Because they crossed after men, some couples were mixed-status, the husband having obtained legal residency through IRCA and the wife remaining unauthorized or waiting for papers through her husband. Men who did have visas controlled a key gateway to documentation for their wives and children. Even when a husband requested papers on his wife's behalf, women often had to wait decades for approval.[46] Meanwhile, some men did not request papers for their wives at all. As Cecilia Menjívar and Olivia Salcido (2002) show, such status differences can increase abuse. In mixed-status marriages, 77 percent of Latina women experienced intimate partner violence, compared to 49 percent in same-status marriages. In 69 percent of those mixed-status cases, the man had failed to file a visa petition on his wife's behalf, despite her eligibility. Like Paloma, at least half of the women I interviewed in North County told me they had suffered domestic violence. In contrast to their counterparts in Los Angeles, not one had called the police or applied for a U visa.

Fear reinforced women's dependence on men. In North County's arbitrary context, women did not trust the police. So they stayed locked inside, waiting for their husbands to tell them when and where it was safe to leave. Fear also made some men more controlling of their daughters and wives. Ana Rivera, who went to Vista for a few years with her father when she was eighteen, remembered that she wanted to work in elder care, but her father would not let her leave his sight. So she ended up working beside him—for lower pay—in the fields. "I did whatever he did," she explained, "because he was very jealous [controlling] and would not let me leave the house—partly because of immigration control—but I went wherever he did."

Other women hesitated to report abuse because they relied on their husbands for money. In 1994 Dolores, then thirty-four years old, joined her husband, Saúl Bernal, in Vista, where he had been working for several years. Dolores wanted to stay in Retorno with her parents and her three children. Yet Saúl got jealous of a lover she had in the village. He threatened to stop sending money unless Dolores came to the United States. Having built her own life in Retorno, Dolores found moving to North

County San Diego to be an enormous shock. When she arrived, Saúl beat her so loudly that a neighbor called the police. Yet Dolores refused to turn him in. She was afraid to lose his salary, which was critical to their children's livelihoods and their capacity to one day go home. She described,

> Someone called the police, and I had gone outside to cry. When I saw the police car arrive, they asked me if I was okay and I said "Yes." . . . I told them, "I twisted my ankle, but I'm fine." When they asked if anyone hit me, I said "No, it's fine." [Abigail: Why didn't you want to tell the police?] I was afraid they would do something to him. . . . He was the only one working . . . and for fear that they would put him in jail, and he'd end up without work. That's what made me afraid. . . . So I didn't denounce him, and we spent years like that. He continued; he never changed.

If Dolores wanted to keep her family alive, or make enough money to return home, she could not risk her husband's detention. She went on, "In the United States I came to live a life of abuse. I lived in poverty in Retorno, but in the United States I came to suffer even more." She added that coming to California was "very, very sad for me. . . . I never imagined myself here."

Though scholars often presume that domestic violence among migrants reflects residual machismo from Mexico, I show that in North County San Diego, fear laid the groundwork for suffering. A full 90 percent of women respondents from Retorno held paying jobs, traditionally seen as the lever of women's empowerment.[47] Nevertheless, under arbitrary control, more than two-thirds said they *lost* household autonomy. In contrast to those in Los Angeles, they rejected the idea that coming to the United States represented "modernization." They felt that the state was *against* both women and men.

Avoiding Alienation

As in any group, there were exceptions within this trend. Single or divorced women, migrants with better jobs, and those with legal permanent resident status tended to feel less fear. Although 90 percent of women migrants from Retorno lived with their husbands, those who were able to migrate alone or live by themselves found more autonomy. Yesica

Márquez, for instance, was a forty-six-year-old single woman from an upper-class family in Retorno. She came to California on her own, after getting a nursing degree in Mexico City. In Vista she used her training to find work in elder care. She came to feel, "In the good jobs [like mine], it [the United States] is not that much work; only in the factories. . . . Life here is safer, calmer—or at least calm compared to the stress with which you live in Mexico City." Yesica also thought of the United States as home. Chattering away over tacos, she told me that these days traditional foods from Retorno tasted soggy to her. "My body doesn't tolerate this stuff anymore," she joked. Instead, she said, she had adapted to California. Whereas women had to cook and clean in the village, she added, in the United States, "Sure, you work and you have chores too, but the difference is that if you aren't married, you can come home and lie down, no problem! *[Laughs.]*" Yesica's class status and education gave her financial stability, while living alone made domestic life easier. These unusual circumstances helped her to feel she belonged.

Other women gained peace when they left their abusive husbands. Isabel López had come to the United States with a husband who beat her. Eventually, however, she left him, learned her own way around, and started a business selling Tupperware door-to-door. Today, she felt, she made an adequate income and was comfortable in the United States. Similarly, twenty-two-year-old Felisa Montes, who arrived on her own just five years before our interview, suggested that as long as one was single, "It's easier for a woman to be in the United States than a man, because we're not as visible to immigration control, or at least that's what they say. A man is more persecuted—because they're the ones that do the little mischievous things. Or maybe because of the way they dress—that's why they're always running after them. And a woman, no." To the extent women could avoid relying on men, they enjoyed some preferential treatment, similar to those in Los Angeles.

Class privilege also helped. Even though most migrants from Retorno were poor, a few, like Yesica Márquez, came from Retorno's elite and initially migrated to Mexico City rather than Mexican farms. While most such migrants remained in Mexico, the few who did cross the border used their degrees and class status to find relatively comfortable work, such as in individual care. Finally, it should go without saying that migrants who were able to get legal status in the United States eventually came to feel more settled and at home. In 1986, for instance, Marcelo Sánchez's employers helped him get legal permanent-resident status as a seasonal agricultural worker through the U.S. Immigration Reform and Control Act. Even though Marcelo's wife and children remained undocumented, he now moved about Vista with confidence—and little fear for his own deportation.

THE IMPORTANCE OF LOCAL CONTROL

This chapter reveals how local level policies, policing, labor practices, and public services mediate "illegality," shaping whether immigrants feel appreciative or cynical toward the United States. I call these practices *modes of control*. In both Los Angeles and North County, state agents used force. Both also relied on moral, racial, and gendered distinctions, marking migrants either good or bad. Migrants' understandings of police and state services depended on the application of these norms in practice. When migrants associated police actions with their own moral behavior, deportation appeared predictable, giving them a sense of control. When coercion violated migrants' moral categories, they felt powerless. In turn, local laws and police practices reverberated at work and among women and men.

In Los Angeles migrants saw state treatment as conditional. They believed police and public services distinguished between immigrants based on behavior.[48] Most associated services with hard work and deportation with criminality. While their lived experiences did not necessarily break into such neat divisions, good and bad categories gave many a sense of control. Migrants felt comparatively little fear. They appreciated that Los Angeles offered them services and jobs. In turn, many adopted Los Angeles as home. However, good/bad binaries also had the unintended consequence of legitimating an exclusionary regime, deflecting blame for deportation onto individual choices instead of the state. Even though most respondents in Los Angeles felt grateful to the United States, they remained excluded from substantive rights.

By contrast, migrants in North County San Diego perceived state actions as arbitrary, assuming police and bureaucrats drew lines against them by race and legal status. While police were present in Los Angeles as well, they acted less predictably in North County. As a result, most unauthorized migrants from Retorno felt unfairly marked as bad. Similar to immigrants studied in North County San Diego by Leo Chavez (1998) in the 1980s, as well as more recent rural migrants described by Seth Holmes (2013) and Leah Schmalzbauer (2014), they felt estranged from the United States, and most of them lived in fear.

The relationship between gender and migration also hinged on the local mode of control. Women felt more liberated in Los Angeles because they were protected by police and privileged at service and factory jobs, as compared to Latino men. By contrast, in North County San Diego, arbitrary policing magnified women's reliance on men, giving them little protection from domestic abuse. These domestic inequities reflected not just the "sticky" patriarchy of Retorno, or the families' failure to assimilate to U.S. gender norms, but instead the household-level fallout of fear, isolation, and absent state support. Women endured more violence when they did not trust state agents to help.

Conditional and arbitrary control were not independent; rather, they played off each other and sometimes overlapped. For instance, LA police officers' willingness to overlook migrants' legal status appeared as a reward only in *relation* to the threat of deportation, in Los Angeles and elsewhere. Both modes of control could also shift over time. Thus, migrants' feelings of belonging in Los Angeles slipped into alienation at moments when ICE or local police grew more arbitrary. Local state treatment varied *within* each locale as well, by gender, class, and legal status. In places and among groups who felt directly targeted, such as men, the state seemed more arbitrary, regardless of place. By contrast, those who believed they were spared—including most migrants in Los Angeles but also independent women and those with legal authorization in North County San Diego—were more likely to feel a sense of belonging.

These U.S. modes of control interacted with the legacies people from Partida and Retorno brought into the United States. On one hand, conditional and arbitrary treatment exacerbated the distinctions between the two groups. For instance, Los Angeles's support helped women who had escaped from Partida feel even more free. Meanwhile, fear in North County San Diego exacerbated the agonies faced by women from Retorno.

Yet U.S. contexts also had impacts of their own, revealed in the ways they *changed* migrants' attitudes. For instance, some men migrants' sense of belonging in Los Angeles encouraged them to distance themselves from the egalitarian history that had given them advantages back in Partida. Likewise, conditions in North County San Diego helped compel people who had been pushed out of Retorno by debt to eventually want to go home. In the following chapter I examine how these feelings of inclusion and alienation sparked distinct political attitudes and activism toward the United States.

3 Stoicism and Striving in the Face of Exclusion

Blanca Martínez hoped that acting "good" would earn her a chance to belong. I often visited Blanca at her ranch house in South Los Angeles. She kept the furniture spotless and covered with lace, and she usually greeted me with a plate of fresh fruit. For more than twenty years, she had worked twelve-hour days cleaning houses in Beverly Hills. Only once in three decades had she taken public support. Her toddler had hit his head and was bleeding badly, but when Blanca got to the hospital, she was turned away from the emergency room because she had no insurance or money to pay. Hospital staff encouraged Blanca to sign up for MediCal (state health insurance), which automatically came with food stamps and welfare. Blanca accepted the health coverage, but only to heal her child's wound. Despite the state bureaucrats' encouragement, she refused the other services. She explained, "I felt that it was not fair, that I could work. And even though I didn't have any money, I had a lot of pride in not wanting to abuse the government, because for me doing that is an abuse if you can work." Other than that one instance, she pronounced, "In the time I've been here I have never gone on strike or asked for food stamps or tried to get things that the government gives out to people, even with my son. . . . I don't like to take those things." By working hard and avoiding strikes, food stamps, or any entitlements, Blanca distinguished herself from immigrants she marked "bad."

Politically, Blanca proved her goodness by declaring appreciation for the United States. In 2006 several of her fellow migrants from Partida joined Los Angeles's marches for immigrants' rights. But Blanca dismissed such marches as counterproductive. She was particularly critical of protestors who carried Mexican flags or expressed ethnic pride. She insisted, "If they want the support of this country, they should carry the American flag, feel proud of living in this country that has welcomed them." Protests caused problems, she argued, adding, "[The bad elements] end up hurting the ones who are protesting in good faith. And since I have never been in a union or any of that, well, I wasn't in any protests or fighting against any injustice, because I have never been a victim of injustice, as far as I'm concerned. I have always been treated well." Blanca's counterparts marched because they believed in the promise of inclusion. Blanca embraced this prospect, but she also saw belonging as a prescription. If immigrants worked hard enough, learned English, and refused to depend on government services, she hoped, they could show they deserved to stay.

In North County San Diego, by contrast, respondents often denounced the U.S. treatment of immigrants as hostile, racist, and unfair. Basilio Ramos had lived in California almost as long as Blanca, working in North County from the early 1980s until 2010, when he gave up and went back to Retorno. He took a far dimmer view of the United States. In an interview conducted by one of my fellow members of the UCSD Mexican Migration Field Research Program in 2011, he reflected,

> Above all, [U.S. politicians] are in support of their country. They're not supporting immigrants. No, not at all. . . . Just like anyone else, [immigrants] need medical services, but no more than one or a few. Then [politicians] take that to say we're people who live off the system, lazy people, that we're people prone to drug trafficking, that we're undesirable, that we're ignorant, that we're small, or brown, that—racist things. . . . In practice, they agree with the most racist sectors, the most backward sectors of [the United States]. . . . Even if American laws are fair on the surface, below—to put it that way because it's not always visible—there is that rejection, those feelings of viewing other people like inferiors, like children, so "If we have to exploit them, well, let's exploit them. And if we have to use them, then use them."

Instead of denouncing other immigrants for causing trouble, Basilio criticized the U.S. government for *stereotyping* migrants as dependent, lazy, and criminal. Rather than using such racial scripts to distinguish himself, he rejected them for reinforcing exclusion and exploitation.

Basilio's cynicism fed a politics of withdrawal. In the late 1980s and early 1990s, Basilio and several fellow migrants from Retorno protested the persecution they faced in North County. They formed an organization called the Popular Committee of the People of Retorno (PCPR), staging marches, holding meetings, and garnering attention from the press. As local policing intensified, however, they grew resigned to exclusion. Even though they condemned the intensification of immigration control, most gave up fighting for rights in the United States. Basilio's only option, he explained, was to hold out until he could escape the hostility of U.S. life. In the meantime, as Mexican political parties sought migrants' support, he shifted his advocacy toward the sending side.

THE POLITICAL INCORPORATION OF
THE UNDOCUMENTED

This chapter explores how different modes of control—and different historical pathways—shape migrants' strategies of political incorporation in the United States. While undocumented immigrants cannot vote or hold elected office, there is a vibrant debate about whether U.S. exclusion makes them cynical or spurs them to fight to belong.[1] Blanca, Basilio, and their communities make it clear that there is no single form of undocumented activism. Exclusionary national laws cannot explain why some migrants protest while others internalize state norms, and still others resign themselves to exclusion. This chapter untangles such variations by digging deeper into how particular, local experiences of "illegality" shape migrants' collective identities, their attitudes about U.S. laws, and their actions (or silence) for immigrants' rights. In so doing, I build on research emphasizing the importance of place in shaping social mobilization.[2]

In Los Angeles, I argue, conditional control fueled a politics of belonging, meaning that migrants actively worked to earn inclusion in the United States. This strategy entailed two, seemingly contrasting, approaches to activism. On one hand, a third of respondents joined marches for immigrants' rights. Perhaps counterintuitively, these migrants' faith in the United States inspired them to protest: they trusted the United States to recognize their hard work by granting them legal rights. On the other hand, two-thirds of respondents avoided protests, to prove they respected the United States. While public services, police protection, and stable jobs gave migrants hope, they also created a strategic playing field in which incorporation hinged on being seen as deserving. Whether or not respondents like Blanca truly approved of U.S. laws, they internalized state norms of hard work and political deference. (Scholars refer to the naturalization of such subordinate status as "symbolic violence.")[3] In the civic arena they either dismissed marches as disruptive or insisted on "carrying the American flag." At work they avoided unions or public dependence, taking pride in their own fortitude. Good/bad binaries also pitted migrants against one another. Indeed, many migrants in Los Angeles conducted what sociologists Michèle Lamont and Virág Molnár (2002) call "boundary work," drawing sharp lines between their own good behavior and the transgressions of "other" migrants. Nevertheless, when good behavior failed to earn the promised rewards, migrants grew disaffected and cynical, like their neighbors in North County San Diego.

In North County arbitrary treatment provoked a politics of withdrawal. Uncertain about when they might be deported, respondents from Retorno felt little hope for inclusion. In contrast to those in Los Angeles, they impugned U.S. treatment as unfair and illegitimate. In the 1980s and 1990s several of them fought against abuse. Over time, however, despair dampened their protests. As enforcement grew harsher, migrants in North County became resigned to perpetual exclusion. They were also afraid. By the time of my fieldwork, most had withdrawn from contentious politics on the U.S. side. In politics almost none attended protests for immigrants' rights. At work most took a "grin and bear it" mentality toward their bosses' abuse. Even though Retorno had once excluded them, they came to see Mexico as more dynamic than the United States. So they set their sights on the promise of return and turned their efforts toward changing Mexico (as discussed in chapter 4). In this case early protests *were* the exception. By 2010 almost everyone had given up on activism in the United States.

These cases highlight how advocacy is driven not only by grievances but also by hope. Common knowledge suggests that people join protests to express dissent. Yet, ironically, though respondents in Los Angeles had more stable jobs, faced less police persecution, and generally appreciated the United States more than their counterparts in North County, they were more likely to march for immigrants' rights. Often the people who protested expressed the *greatest* sense of belonging in the United States. While those in North County San Diego tended to feel more cynical and alienated, almost none of them marched. At the same time, hope could also dissuade migrants from protests by giving them a stake in the game. As Blanca's story illustrates, many migrants who saw a promise of inclusion embraced state norms of good behavior, self-sufficiency, and political deference in order to prove they belonged.

Gender also mediated migrants' politics. In Los Angeles good/bad categories inflamed a gendered divide. Having left Partida to escape paternal abuse, some women saw little choice but to pursue inclusion in the United States. As discussed in chapter 2, LA employers and police often treated women preferentially, making them particularly likely to think they could earn rewards for being good. The combination of hope and a lack of cross-border choices may help explain why women predominated in Los Angeles's immigration protests more broadly. At the same time, some women from Partida also turned against their male counterparts, feminizing good behavior. By contrast, men in Los Angeles were more likely to feel degraded by police and employers, undermining their faith that formal inclusion was possible. Meanwhile, women in North County San Diego were at the vanguard not of protest but instead of forbearance. There the combination of fear and male domination cut women off from politics. As women saw their hometown evolve, they also held out hope of returning to Mexico, encouraging some to stay stoic in the face of domestic abuse.

THE STRATEGY OF BELONGING IN LOS ANGELES

LA migrants saw integration not only as a promise but also as a prescription. Conditional control gave them a stake in meeting perceived norms of behavior. Yet good/bad contrasts also encouraged migrants to regulate themselves according to standards of the state. In addition, they pitted migrants against one another, dividing women and men.

Carrying the American Flag

Santiago Morales worked as a high-end butler for Los Angeles's rich and famous, and he took great pride in his job. A vocal leader of Partida's community in Los Angeles, Santiago had slicked-back hair that belied his forty-six years. He delighted in telling stories about his pueblo. He also regularly declared his love for his "adopted nation." Though Santiago was suspicious of me at first, we quickly became friends. They day I conducted his interview, we met in Koreatown, talking for hours over numerous rounds of beer.

Santiago had marched for immigrants' rights more than once. He participated, he explained, because "I love the United States. I feel like a patriot." But he had strong feelings about the "right" way to become part of his second home. He explained,

> I have gone to the [immigrants' rights] marches, but I am an enemy when I see a Mexican flag in American territory; I don't like that. I reject that idea of a reconquest.[4] I am an enemy of that. . . . For me they're carrying the wrong flag. . . . I don't like it 100 percent. If they listened to me, I would give them some tips. I'd say, "Why are you marching in favor of amnesty in the center of Los Angeles, if we don't win anything? Let's go to Sacramento [the state capital]. You're going to go to Sacramento in an organized way without affecting any third parties. Let's demonstrate that we want to be part of the mechanism called the United States."

Even though Santiago attended protests, he drew sharp lines between his own pro-U.S. advocacy and the contentious approach of protestors who criticized the United States. He worried that by marching in Los Angeles and failing to work with the system (such as with legislators in the state capital), migrants drew negative attention. He underscored the strategic importance of using formal political channels. His attitude exemplifies the ambivalent politics of many similar migrants, who hoped to belong *if* they did things "right."

In 2006 more than 3.5 million people across the United States marched for immigrants' rights, roughly 650,000 of them in Los Angeles (thanks to Los Angeles's coalition of immigrant networks, NGOs, social movements, day-labor centers, unions, churches, and Spanish-language radio). More than a third of interviewees from Partida joined these protests. Given that undocumented immigrants have so few political rights, this level of civic engagement is astounding. They protested because they believed the United States might grant them legal inclusion.

Those who marched were motivated by faith, hope, and a desire to belong. They felt their hard work had earned them the same opportunities as U.S. citizens. For instance, Julia Chávez said she protested in 2006 because "I was inspired for the migrants who can't have papers, because there are so many hardworking people who deserve to have them—more than anything, the students or the children of people like us. They need, at least, to have residency." For respondents like Julia, legalization represented the logical extension of Los Angeles's support for migrants the city marked good. Felipe Contreras, a line chef, also thought his diligence had earned him inclusion. Though Felipe refused to join a union to advocate for labor rights, he *did* march for immigrants' legalization. After hearing about protests on the radio in 2006, cooks at his restaurant decided to close the kitchen and join the march. Among his friends, he recalled, "Everyone woke up [politically], and everyone wanted to participate." When I asked why he marched, Felipe explained, "Because—I am an [undocumented] immigrant too, and I would like to have a [driver's] license." Echoing surveys of other immigrant marchers, these respondents identified with the United States and trusted that their adopted nation would reward their hard work.[5]

Surprisingly, faith in the U.S. government also motivated some respondents to engage in electoral politics. It may seem odd that unauthorized migrants would mobilize voters or call senators and congressional representatives, when they could not vote. Nevertheless, some did. In 2001, for instance, Alejandro Campos canvased for California State Senate candidate Gil Cedillo, who later gained fame for advocating driver's licenses for unauthorized immigrants; writing the California DREAM Act, a state assembly bill that granted financial aid to undocumented students; and urging California to boycott Arizona's SB1070 law, which allowed police to detain immigrants for "looking" undocumented. Alejandro was a twenty-five-year-old garment worker at the time, and idealistic. One afternoon, as I sat on his black leather couch, he told me, "You wouldn't believe how much I supported Gil Cedillo, the [state] senator Gil Cedillo. What wouldn't I support? I would walk around here and there; I would skip work to help the campaign and all that." Alejandro's activism, he emphasized, was driven by hope.

Other respondents argued that working through formal channels—*instead* of protests—was the most effective way to bring change. Ramona Vega, for instance, told me, "I don't think we need so many marches. We could call the politicians on the phone, send them letters, emails." Andrea Campos shared a similar view. Though she joined the LA protests in 2006, she now considered marching too contentious. She explained, "I don't think that [marching] is the correct way to ask for things. We [immigrants] demand a lot, and I think it's better to do it other ways. That's why nothing happened [after the 2006 marches], because that was not the proper way to ask the government and senators for something, right? . . . I don't think it's a good idea to march. It's better to call the senators on the phone. Better to write letters." Los Angeles's conditional context made these migrants believe that advocating within the system might, in fact, yield change.

People like Santiago, Alejandro, and Andrea also distinguished their own disciplined approach to civic advocacy from that of their rabble-rousing counterparts. Among immigrants' rights activists in the United States, there has long been contention around whether to carry Mexican flags, which represent migrants' ethnic heritage, or U.S. flags, which symbolize their commitment to integration.[6] In 2006 organizers of the immigrants' rights marches encouraged migrants to carry U.S. flags and wear white, strategically framing themselves as good, law-abiding workers, families, and neighbors. This good-immigrant display was intended to resonate with the U.S. public and indeed garnered more popular support than prior protests invoking ethnic rhetoric.[7] My interviews suggest that the good-immigrant frame also helped mobilize migrants themselves, echoing their own day-to-day strategies of presenting themselves as good.

Respondents in Los Angeles insisted that *if* migrants protested, they must display a desire for inclusion rather than critique U.S. laws. Lingering over a coffee in Echo Park, forty-five-year-old Epifanio Cruz proudly presented me with a manila folder filled with essays he had written for his English class at a local adult school about "becoming American." When I asked what he thought of immigrants' rights protests, Epifanio argued that marchers should demonstrate their commitment to U.S. assimilation. He explained,

> If I am going to go to a protest, I am going to fight for something [legalization]. But what do you think comes out? They come out with their Mexican flags, with their Central American flags, or whatever, and that is not okay. You have to go [to] protests and fight for migrants, so what are you going to carry? I think it has to be the flag of the United States or to speak English or to change yourself—to start to adapt to this country. . . . That way it will get more attention. It's better that way, because they're going to see it over there in Washington, where the important politicians are, and [think] "What do you think? They carry our flag; they care that they are here." You want something, so you have to adapt to the system. . . . You can't just go to the marches, and whenever the opportunity comes [for legalization] you take it. If the opportunity comes and you don't speak English, you don't have a good character like a citizen, and you're going around lost, how can you ask for solutions? . . . You hang yourself all on your own *[te ahorcas solo]*.

For Epifanio, showing Americanness was critical to earning public approval. Becoming "American" meant intentionally behaving like a citizen: learning English, assimilating culturally, and minimizing one's Mexican roots, as symbolized by the flags. In conjunction, Epifanio blamed those who criticized U.S. policies or failed to pursue such inclusion for undermining *themselves*.

At the same time, the politics of belonging was politically indeterminate. While migrants' feelings of deservingness encouraged some of them to protest, they also encouraged civic compliance. As a whole Partida's migrants remained ambivalent about marches. While a third attended protests, two-thirds refused to march at all. The latter distinguished their own behavior from that of protestors, highlighting how they contributed to the United States and stayed quiet. For instance, Epifanio's cousin Bernardo Cruz never joined a protest. A thin, soft-spoken grandfather, he had silvery hair and worked in construction, a job he'd held for years. When I asked why he didn't march, Bernardo replied,

> I don't like to go to protests because being a protestor in a place you don't belong—I don't like that. Why am I going to go make a lot of noise where it's not my home? It's not my city. . . . As an immigrant, I start thinking, and

I ask myself, "What am *I* contributing to this nation?" What am I contributing? Well, being a good worker, paying my taxes, not owing the government anything, and obeying—respecting the laws. That's all for me.

For Bernardo, immigrants had a duty, perhaps above and beyond citizens, to work hard and contribute to the United States rather than make demands.

These political distinctions sowed divisions. Those who stayed quiet, like Bernardo and Blanca, worried that protests provoked crackdown. They feared that marches might blur the lines between good and bad—the very same lines that gave them a sense of control and let them avoid the fear the undocumented felt in other parts of the United States. They also blamed their activist counterparts for inviting hostility against migrants as a whole. Ramiro Valdez, a thirty-seven-year-old warehouse worker, for instance, said, "People [migrants] scream and go out to the streets. But, I think it's a lot of noise—and for what? No, I think the most important thing is to be humble." Similarly, Ramona Vega reflected, "In marches there are always clashes and that sort of thing. So the politicians end up seeing us badly—as if the people who don't have papers are causing problems." Thus, Los Angeles's conditional mode of control pitted migrants against one another, eliciting particular rancor for those who criticized the existing regime.

Some respondents in Los Angeles went so far as to argue that the United States should grant legal status *only* to those who worked hard, did not drink, or established their desire to belong.[8] For example, fifty-six-year-old Isidro Fuentes told me he favored legalization only for immigrants who demonstrated hard work and self-sufficiency. He reflected, "[Work] is what people need, and the [U.S.] government should give us immigration reform so we have an opportunity to work. But they shouldn't give papers to the people that don't deserve it." Julia also saw legalization as a promise specific to those who worked. She underscored that she never used government assistance: "We [my husband and I] have everything we have thanks to our work. . . . But there are also tricky people who abuse [the system]." While Julia had marched so that workers like her could get rights, she wasn't sure if the "tricky people" deserved the same. Bruno Torres, meanwhile, suggested, "The more difficult they make the laws for

immigrants who do illegal things, the better." Such proclamations acquiesced in (others') deportation, reiterating some U.S. politicians' claims
that only *certain* migrants deserved to stay.

"I'm Proud of My Work"

Work was a second key area where migrants showed they were worthy.
Andrea Campos, who was forty-nine and had worked in garment factories
since the late 1980s, described facing labor abuses, locked bathrooms,
nonpayment of wages, unpaid overtime, and summary firings, all of which
she was aware violated U.S. labor laws. Andrea had gone to the LA labor
commissioner to seek enforcement against such violations. Now, she
added, "The foremen stay quiet. They don't say anything to me now,
because I don't let them yell at me anymore." Nevertheless, Andrea also
insisted that she had *earned* the labor commissioner's support by working
tirelessly. She then criticized other immigrants' shoddy practices and
"anger" about labor conditions. As we stood in her kitchen, adding chilies
to a steaming soup, she told me,

> I like doing my work well. There are people that, no matter what, just pass
> it [a garment] through and throw it down; they don't pay attention to if it's
> well done. They just want to earn money. But I've always thought that's bad;
> I undo mistakes even if it takes me a little while. I'm proud of my work. I tell
> my children that when I go to work it's like it was a party; I dress up, I'm
> happy, and nothing about going and being angry. . . . Sometimes people say,
> "Why are you so dressed up? If you're coming to work in the dust, and you're
> coming to do work." But I tell them, "My work is like I was at a party, and I
> love my work because that feeds me." . . . That's what I tell my kids: you have
> to be like that; you have to love your work.

To Andrea, being a good worker entailed toiling happily and with pride
rather than objecting to dusty, backbreaking conditions.

For migrants like Andrea, hard work was both a ticket to support in the
workplace and an antidote to deportability. "Honorable" hard work is a
core value shared by most Mexican migrants, even before they move to the
United States and even when they live in repressive contexts like North
County San Diego.[9] Other scholars have observed that many migrants
take pride in having a stronger work ethic than working-class U.S. citizens,

particularly African Americans, "lazy" (poor) whites, and other wage workers.[10] I argue that in Los Angeles hard work also became a point of distinction among migrants, as they contrasted their diligence with their counterparts' tendency to "complain."

Like in politics, the implications were mixed. On one hand, Andrea and her peers believed the state would enforce their labor rights. This faith enabled them to advocate for decent treatment, even when they lacked legal status. For instance, Ramona Vega, who sewed jeans for American Apparel and had worked in factories for twenty-five years, explained, "Sometimes they [bosses] want to fire us and find someone new, and we don't let them. We tell them that we can go file a complaint there at the labor commissioner, and they back down." Ramona did not hesitate to approach state officials if she was denied rest breaks, overtime pay, or other lawful entitlements. In this way migrants' own actions helped extend state reach into the factories, blocking employers from using excessive force. At the same time, migrants took pride in working hard. Even when they did not face employer coercion, they pushed *themselves* to work faster or better. Alejandro Campos, for instance, recalled how he would sew eight hundred pairs of pants a day. "By 6:00 P.M. your arms were burning, gone," he remembered. Yet, out of pride, he worked on.

For most migrants in Los Angeles, being a good worker also implied refusing to join unions or fight existing work environments and wages, except through formal means. More than half of informants in Los Angeles encountered unions at work, particularly at large factories like Guess Jeans, where there were significant organizing campaigns in the late 1990s. Given the decline of U.S. unions in the past several decades and the long-standing tensions between unions and unauthorized workers, this was a far higher rate of exposure than among immigrants elsewhere in the United States.[11] Nevertheless, only one interviewee in Los Angeles—a lawful permanent resident who had arrived in the mid-1980s and worked as a trucker since the 1990s—had joined a union.

Respondents rejected unions because they believed it was strategic to cooperate with their employers. Scholars often presume that migrants avoid unions out of fear, which they did in North County San Diego.[12] In Los Angeles, however, respondents were less afraid. Instead, at least five said they disliked unions because they saw work as a meritocracy, in which

migrants should (and implicitly could) earn good wages through diligence. Felipe Contreras, who was thirty-four and had spent many years
staffing an Italian restaurant, suggested that immigrants should *earn*
raises rather than struggle. When a union attempted to recruit him at
work, he refused to join, telling the organizers, "There is no reason to force
the owners [to pay us more]. If you want to work hard, and if you think
you deserve a raise, well, show it with your actions. . . . This boss gave me
an opportunity, and I feel really thankful. . . . That, to me, is a privilege. I
can't betray this person because he gave me something great." Having a
job at all, Felipe implied, was a reward he earned through hard work.

Carmen Rojas also contrasted union members' sense of entitlement
with her own compliance in the factories. The unions, she argued, "come
to get us fired for going on strike or [make us] lose our jobs—or demand
wages that are higher than what we deserve to be paid—because there are
people that come and say they want to earn a lot more than what they
really need." Carmen distinguished her own acceptance of existing wages
from such resistance, adding, "The day I started work, I told my boss,
'Well, the minimum is good for me.' Because to be honest, for someone to
pay you by the hour [instead of piece rate] in any factory right now, they
don't do that. . . . So I felt grateful to him because the truth is that when I
arrived at his factory I didn't have enough experience to demand more." In
light of the competition for low-wage work, Carmen felt lucky to have a
job at all. She trusted that being deferent would pay out in the long run, by
keeping her employed.

Such respondents separated themselves not only from workers who
protested but also from other migrants who did not work hard enough or
who depended on the government. Santiago, for instance, boasted endlessly about the work ethic of his *paisanos* (fellow migrants) from Partida.
When Santiago's bosses asked him to organize their sumptuous dinner
parties, for instance, he insisted on bringing only cooks, servers, and
attendants from Partida, because they "knew how to work." Santiago also
turned against immigrants who depended on the state. He proclaimed, "I
am an enemy of the people who screw with the system. I am an enemy of
the people who live off of food stamps without needing it. I understand
that there are people who need it, and we have to help the person who
needs it, who doesn't screw with it. But the guy who has a nicer car than

mine—a neighbor we had used to have a $45,000 truck, and his wife was living off welfare—okay, hello?"

Even though respondents valued the public support available to them in Los Angeles, many of them also vilified people who used such services, blaming them for failing to be self-sufficient and for drawing scorn to immigrants as a whole. Ramona, for instance, told me,

> We [my husband and I] always worked hard. We never asked for MediCal for our children, nothing from the government, no type of help. We always worked. . . . There are many people—we know of people who have possibilities—that is, they don't need MediCal or the support checks, but they do it anyway. They even own property; I don't know how they do it. No, there are many who only come for that, to take advantage, to take things from the government—to take things from the contributors, and the workers are the ones who pay. And people build themselves houses [back in Mexico], and they live off that. We know of several of them. . . . We never liked that. We have to give an example to our children that they should not live off the government; they have to work.

Despite Los Angeles's relatively accessible public institutions, respondents like Ramona and Blanca took pride in refusing their services.

Sometimes working hard extended to being hard on themselves, and migrants internalized the very abuse they would not tolerate from employers. I first met Paula Solís, a garment worker and mother of three young children, in 2010 in a deserted Jamba Juice across from the factories near downtown Los Angeles. She spoke Spanish in the soft clip of native Zapotec and admitted that she had hesitated to meet up with me, since her teenage daughter was suspicious of the strange voice at the end of the phone. As Paula told me about her job, I asked whether working in the garment factories was tiresome. Showing off the fabric she had recently sewn for Orbit 7, she replied, "No, I don't get bored. I like being busy. I spend all my time working. . . . I'd rather be busy than get bored." In later interviews Paula juxtaposed her forbearance with that of less willing workers:

> I don't like to cause problems. For example, a lot of people, when they tell them, "You're going to do this," say, "Aw, I don't want to do that; I don't like doing that. I don't like that. I won't do that. I don't know how to do that."

I never say that. I always like to learn more. . . . I don't like to reject work. If it's a hard job, I like other people to see that, yes, I can do it. . . . It doesn't matter, sometimes I'm sick, I have a cold, I don't feel well, but I don't like to stay home. I would rather be at work.

Paula took pride in her industriousness. She knew that hard work helped ensure her ongoing employment. And she underscored her willingness to do difficult jobs. Nevertheless, her pride also came to her detriment.

The day we first met, Paula had sniffled with what appeared to be a cold. As we grew closer over the coming year, she learned that she had a rare form of sinus cancer—almost certainly attributable to the toxic dust that came off the fabric in the factories, where windows were often sealed closed. Nevertheless, Paula continued working for months, disinclined to tarnish her good-worker status. As we talked on the phone one day, she explained that she had worked through hunger to buy her girls diapers, and she would work through this. I was one of the few people Paula knew who owned a car and spoke fluent English, so I sometimes took her to the nearby public hospital. As Paula's tumor grew ever more visible, pushing aside her nose and left eye, I urged the doctors to speed up her treatment. Yet Paula hushed me, insisting that she deserved only what was offered, because she was a "guest in the house." She had left Partida fleeing her father's abuse. Keeping her head down and working, she hoped, might secure a better future as Americans for her little girls. A year later, having worked her whole life, Paula was dead.

The Ambivalence of Women's Empowerment

Compared to men, women in Los Angeles were especially likely to adopt such strategies of belonging, including both marching and striving to show good behavior. Preferred by police and employers, as discussed in chapter 2, women tended to feel more faith than men in U.S. treatment. They also had fewer alternatives back in Mexico. Paula, for instance, no longer wanted to live with the violence she had seen as a girl. Her sister Irene had been badly beaten when she married, so Paula never considered returning. This lack of choices gave women like Paula even more stakes in U.S. inclusion.

For such women, associating the United States with empowerment had contradictory implications. Sociologists Ruth Milkman and Veronica Terriquez (2012) show that Latina women were "out front" in the immigrants' rights marches in Los Angeles and tend to be more politically mobilized than their male counterparts in general. This chapter suggests that such political mobilization may reflect women's particular investment in the United States. Thanks to the combination of their own histories and the gender-differentiated treatment they experienced in Los Angeles, women from Partida often trusted the United States more than men did. Yet women's appreciation for Los Angeles also echoed public narratives that framed immigration as empowering to women, despite the ongoing exclusion of the undocumented. When women's gratitude for the United States did not come with marches or demands, it may have legitimated their own disenfranchisement.

Gender dimensions within good/bad divisions also spurred women to push themselves at work and even turn against men. At work managers sometimes pitted women against men, pushing them to compete for speed. Carmen, for instance, remembered that when she sewed for a subcontractor of Guess Jeans, at the behest of the bosses,

> we used to have competitions with the men. For example, we might be ten workers, five men and five women, and we [women] would say to one another, "Look at that guy; they brought him a cart with five bands of cloth. Let's see what time they finish it, and we're going to see what time we ladies finish," and it would make the men so mad, seeing that we finished first. We [women] always beat them. . . . There were men that got really mad. They used to say, "But why can you women do so much and we can't?"

Thus men and women competed to produce and earn piece rates. Most of the time, according to Carmen, women won. Such gendered games of speed encouraged workers to sew harder and faster, even though they were protected by labor laws.

Likewise, while local police helped protect women from abuse, they also stipulated that victims of domestic violence prove their hard work and frame their male counterparts as criminal, derelict, or undeserving, reinforcing public stereotypes. To get U visas women had to demonstrate that they were economically self-sufficient contributors to U.S. society.[13]

They also had to cooperate with law enforcement to identify and prove the case against men who had beat them. Therefore, survivors' access to legal status hinged on actively impugning their male peers. Symbolically, the stipulations also signaled to women that they should play a gendered, racialized role as hardworking victims, while contributing to the villainization of immigrant men.

In contrast, men's feelings of emasculation in Los Angeles—both at work and by police—often drove them to more contentious forms of dissent. Although men made up half the workforce in the factories, many felt they were *treated* like women.[14] For instance, Manuel Rosas began working in the garment sector when he arrived in Los Angeles in 1991, at the age of sixteen. Right away, he resented the work. He recalled, "When I saw the sewing machine, I thought, I'm not going to do this. Sewing—that's for women. It was a struggle; it hurt my back, my waist, because I was used to running around here and there, working as a carpenter, and I wanted to do construction, to lift heavy things." This lens stayed with Manuel, who later became a vocal advocate against dehumanizing labor conditions. Likewise, Juan Serrano, who initially worked cleaning homes, said that the feminization of household labor made work feel more arduous. He explained, "[The work] was a kick in the butt *[laughs]*. I said, 'No, I'm not going to sweep like this, if I don't even sweep in my own house, if at home I don't even wash dishes. How am I going to do this here?' They made me wash the bathrooms, and it made me furious.'" The feminization of work degraded Juan as a man. In later years, this sense of emasculation helped fuel Juan's critiques of labor conditions, driving him to fight for fair wages at the factories and eventually to give up and go back to Mexico.

The Fragility of Hope

While many migrants in Los Angeles adopted a politics of belonging, their strategies varied over time and relation to the individual treatment they received in California. When civic participation and hard work yielded few changes in rights, some lost their faith that the United States would give them support.

Just as hope encouraged migrants to protest and act good, political defeats fueled cynicism. While several respondents marched in 2006, many later lost hope that such protests could change U.S. laws. Juan, for instance, explained that in the first decade of the 2000s, he "joined every immigration protest." By 2010, however, he was so disenchanted that he gave up on the United States. He went on, "I saw migration reform die, saw the DREAM Act die, and then I lost hope. I said, 'I need to leave here [the United States] forever.'" As Juan lost heart, he stopped viewing the U.S. government as legitimate. Forsaking political advocacy in the United States, as well as good behavior, he returned to Mexico for relief.

Other respondents emphasized that their faith was fragile. In interviews, many described the 2006 immigrants' rights marches as the moment when they had the *most* hope for inclusion. Felipe, for instance, explained that since joining the marches in 2006, he had never protested again. The faith he had at the time—that marching might result in legalization—was now gone. He reflected, "For all the noise you make, I don't think they pay attention. We're not—in spite of being a big crowd—we don't have so much power to change the government here. . . . Here, the only opportunity you have is to marry someone or to get papers through family members." Alejandro also lost hope that civic engagement would yield political change. Although Alejandro had advocated for immigrants' rights and campaigned for Gil Cedillo, he recalled,

> Later I started to realize that it's all to help himself when he needs to mobilize people . . . and then I stopped believing so much . . . and I realized that politicians here are sometimes the worst of liars. But the people—Latinos—believe in that, believe deeply in the news. But sooner or later you realize, and thanks to the Internet, I started to open my eyes. . . . I have gone out to protests, but now I just feel like, "what for?" Politics is the same everywhere. They make a lot of promises, but it never comes to pass.

When Alejandro's hope diminished, he stopped participating in politics. He also criticized his own, earlier trust in the United States, along with that of other Latinos. Under such conditions, migrants grew skeptical of the promises that had kept them marching without rights, and working hard, even as real wages declined. As they delinked good behavior from substantive rewards, they disengaged. A subset even returned to Partida. While good behavior and peaceful protest were products of hope, distrust fueled resignation.

THE STRATEGY OF WITHDRAWAL IN
NORTH COUNTY SAN DIEGO

In contrast to their counterparts in Los Angeles, respondents in North County San Diego saw U.S. immigration enforcement as *il*legitimate. Because the local mode of arbitrary control posed a general threat to migrants, it unified them.[15] Initially, it also pushed them to demand better treatment in the United States. But the combination of fear and cynicism eventually led migrants from Retorno to give up on U.S. politics. Believing Mexico was more open to their influence, they held out for the promise of return. Women were especially isolated from political advocacy and stoic in the household, awaiting their chance to go home.

From Struggle to Stoicism

In the fall of 1988, white residents of Vista, California, brutally beat an immigrant from Oaxaca. In the doorway of a store just across from Rancho Romero, where several migrants from Retorno were workers, they tied the man up and mocked him. For many early migrants from Retorno, that assault was the tipping point. As described in chapter 2, migrants had lived by the fields in the 1980s and 1990s, cut off from society by the police, who would hunt them and beat them, following their "black hair." So Basilio Ramos, Arturo Molina, Domingo García, and a few others from Retorno got together to fight back. They gathered more than two hundred people to protest the abuse, right there in front of the store. They marched, Arturo explained,

> to show the city and society how badly migrants were treated. They had accused this guy of stealing something, and they tied him up like so, in the doorway of the store, and they put a paper bag on his head and funny eyes, and it was a denigration of his person, right? His rights—and that was enough—to protest the action . . . and that was our first action, enough to say, "We have to defend migrants."

In North County San Diego this was the first time undocumented immigrants took to the streets.[16] They protested less from hope than from a sense of injustice.

Such protests built on migrants' legacies of advocacy within Mexico.[17] Before Basilio, Arturo, and other migrants from Retorno arrived in the United States, they had worked on farms in Sinaloa and Baja California (as discussed in chapter 1). There, in the 1970s, students aligned with the Mexican Communist and Socialist Parties began to organize labor strikes, laying the foundations for what would become Mexico's major farmworkers' unions.[18] Basilio, Domingo, and other young men from Retorno, then teenagers toiling with their parents in the fields, quickly radicalized. They started to work as organizers, galvanizing as many as sixteen thousand farmworkers at a time to strike, halt the harvests, and demand wage increases, along with better water, lodging, and schools. Given the scale of these protests, nearly every farmworking migrant from Retorno got embroiled in the fights. Migrants then linked these struggles—and their communist-inspired critique—to the exclusion they faced in the United States.

In the early 1990s, building on that first protests and their earlier activism in Mexico, these migrants formed an organization they called the Popular Committee of the People of Retorno (PCPR). The group waged political battles *both* in their hometown and for immigrants in the United States. Domingo García, a former organizer in Sinaloa and outspoken migrant advocate, became its first president. At the time most of Retorno's migrants circulated between their village and California. When I asked Domingo what the PCPR's goals were, he said that migrants were fighting on two fronts:

> It [the PCPR] had to do with a lot of things, right? Things there [in the United States]—the question of immigration, the question of defending the accused in court, defending people, looking for legal help. The question of lodging too. And seeing how to defend ourselves from la migra. But also the people who were on their way [to the United States] and faced extortion at the border or on the way. The question of the bodies when a fellow migrant would die. All of that, right? There were various people who lost wire transfers. We had to see how [to deal with that]. And abuse by the Mexican police. Various things. We were already involved in fights at the level of both countries.

Rampant violations of human and labor rights drove migrants' struggles in the United States. At the same time, these struggles stretched across place, tying the abuses the migrants faced in California to their ongoing battles in Retorno and Mexican fields. So, as the PCPR fought for migrants' rights, it also challenged the domination of the PRI in Retorno and Mexico.[19] (I examine the Mexican side of these struggles in chapter 4.)

In the early 1990s, however, things in North County got worse. Then-governor Pete Wilson began to push for increased border enforcement in the San Diego region, expanding the presence of the Border Patrol. State voters also passed Proposition 187, which would have blocked immigrants from public services had it not been held up in court. Once again migrants from Retorno fought back. They demanded protection from Mexican gangsters and an end to border extortion. They insisted on more security in the canyons where they camped, asking for housing programs and a stop to local police abuse. Juan Lita, one of the leaders of those protests, described the migrants' motivation in an interview with Laura Velasco Ortiz:

> Among all of us, we started to talk about our situation because we used to live in the canyons in really awful conditions. For me, that killed me, that I could live in such a subhuman way. . . . At the time we started to hear news about Pete Wilson's racist policies. So we had a meeting in the canyon, and we wrote a letter to the media about our opposition to those policies.[20] We argued that it was not possible that immigrants—in this case, Mixtecs— were the people causing crimes because we couldn't even go down out of the hills because immigration would catch us. We were so isolated. (2005a, 179)

As Juan emphasized, migrants' protests were driven by their feelings of dehumanization and their critiques of state mistreatment. This time migrants from Retorno also looked to the *Mexican* government for protection against abuses they faced in the United States. They protested at Mexican consulates, demanding help with everything from pressuring the U.S. government for immigrants' rights to obtaining identification cards. They found that even though they lived in the United States, government agents from Mexico were more responsive to their needs than those in North County San Diego.

Migrants' grievances in North County also built solidarity among them, in contrast to the divisions forged in Los Angeles. On the sending side, Mexican state policies had historically set neighboring villages against one another, as discussed in chapter 1. In California, however, Mixtec migrants began to develop a sense of cross-village solidarity that they had not had in Oaxaca.[21] As Rogelio Méndez described to Laura Velasco Ortiz, "Among the hills and the canyons we would run into people we knew. 'Where do you live?' 'Well, in that gulch.' 'You?' 'Over there [in the same gulch].' That's how we started meeting up, and we started organizing" (2005a, 177). Juan Lita, also interviewed by Velasco Ortiz, added,

> Often, when people get to the United States there is more solidarity. It's a peculiarity we have as Mixtecs and people from Retorno. Here we get more unified. . . . I went to the United States and there I linked up with the people from my hometown. . . . And from there [the first protest] we saw that our problems went beyond just us as migrants from Retorno. We couldn't do anything if we just stayed focused on our own community, organizing at the level of our village. It became necessary to be broader, to look at the question of Mixtecs [as a whole] (178–79).

One might expect living in the United States to weaken migrants' identification with one another and with Mexico, as it did in Los Angeles. In North County, however, migrants realized they needed unity to confront their common plight.

The visibility of migrants' actions also expanded their alliances. As people from Retorno began to protest North County mistreatment, immigrants from other nearby villages reached out in shared dissent. Soon the PCPR decided to form a coalition with other hometown associations. Domingo García, who led this process, explained, "In California, we made it bigger. It stopped being just about Retorno and no one else. We had to see that we had fights to wage as migrants. [Abigail: Why did you feel you had to open it up more?] It was a necessity. And because people from other communities came to see us." Thus, dissent drew migrants together.

In 1992 the PCPR joined with other Oaxacan migrant organizations to form a new transnational, indigenous, immigrant association called the Frente Indígena Oaxaqueño Binacional (FIOB; Oaxacan Indigenous Binational Front). Inspired by broader decolonial and indigenous struggles in the Americas, they inaugurated the new organization on the five-hundred-year anniversary of Columbus's arrival and the colonization of the Americas.[22] They chose the name *Frente* (Front) to imply a coalition around a common cause.[23] For those from Retorno, the FIOB largely supplanted the PCPR. The FIOB had two goals: "to defend migrants' human rights and help in the democratic transition of the country of Mexico."[24] First, it would fight the mistreatment of migrants in California. Second, it would pressure Mexico to open up to party competition, punish corruption, and redistribute resources to indigenous pueblos (as I detail in chapters 4–5). Nevertheless, in the face of repression, hopelessness, and fear, migrants' efforts to protest U.S. mistreatment eventually gave way to a politics of withdrawal.

By the time of my fieldwork in 2009–12, migrants in North County San Diego had grown surprisingly resigned. Despite their ongoing feelings of dissent and their history of activism, most felt disillusioned. Arbitrary local treatment gave them little faith in the fairness of the U.S. legal process or their prospects for changing immigration laws. Unpredictable detentions and deportations also inhibited their efforts to organize. Migrants like Basilio Ramos and Juan Lita, who had once pursued a binational political agenda, began to focus more narrowly on Mexico, where they felt they had more of an impact. Though most stayed in California— too wary to cross back and forth—they pinned their hopes on return. In the meantime, they withdrew from U.S. advocacy, grinning and bearing it for the promised escape. In economic terms scholars describe this focus on Mexico as a "dual frame of reference."[25] Theorists argue that undocumented migrants accept low wages in the United States because they plan to go home and exchange their dollars for Mexican pesos. Here the dual frame of reference was also political: migrants' plans to return enabled them to tolerate legal exclusion while in the United States.

In Vista's civic arena only two respondents had attended an immigrants' rights protests since the early 1990s. Their reticence was not a sign of approval for the United States; on the contrary, nearly every single respondent from Retorno objected to arbitrary immigration control. But as North County enforcement grew more ubiquitous and unpredictable in the first decade of the 2000s, many felt hopeless about their ability to gain legal inclusion. For instance, Dolores Muñoz, one of two respondents who *had* attended an immigration protest, reflected that when she marched in 2006, there were only a few thousand people participating in Vista.[26] Most of the immigrant-advocacy organizations were based in Los Angeles, she noted, and to an undocumented migrant with no driver's license, Los Angeles might as well be the moon. Dolores quickly lost faith. She explained, "Yes, I went to the protests when they had them in Vista, but they never listen to us. We can cry louder and louder, but they will never hear."

Basilio added that though the PCPR and FIOB began as political-advocacy organizations in California, they lost motivation when nothing happened. Even though the FIOB attracted important attention from U.S. philanthropists, such support depoliticized its work. Basilio reflected, "It turned out that in the United States we ended up doing what we didn't want . . . giving out food, giving out blankets to migrants. [Abigail: What did you want?] Well, a political movement. But that has no place when there's not some motivation . . . and that's what happened with [our organization]; we were focused on the idea of a political movement, and nothing happened." As Basilio hinted, they lost the will to resist.

Migrants' orientation to Mexico also reinforced their disengagement in the United States. Initially, the FIOB was politically active toward both countries. Yet their efforts yielded more fruit in Mexico. In the late 1980s and 1990s, as I describe in chapter 4, Mexican opposition political parties began seeking migrants as allies. Even though Retorno's migrants had long been excluded in Mexico, they began to feel they could now be heard. Over time organizers like Basilio, Domingo, and Arturo either returned to Mexico or shifted their advocacy to homeland issues, mobilizing from afar. Basilio believed that their efforts in North County fizzled because "our lens was focused on Mexican society. . . . So we said, 'Why are we going to do that [fight for rights in the United States], if instead what we have to do is change our own politics, change our people?' See, what we have to do to is change Mexico, that is, change Mexico from over there [the United States]. That was—in reality, that still is [the goal]."

Younger and more recent migrants were even more cynical. They had watched their peers detained, harassed, or deported with little provocation. Most felt powerless to avoid police mistreatment. Even though they denounced U.S. aggression and racism, they had little faith in their collective capacity to push for, let alone attain, legal authorization. While their predecessors had mobilized politically, they explained, such advocacy would not be feasible for them. Now, they told me, "You can't do that." When I asked Paloma, a mother in her thirties, if she hoped for immigration reform, she responded, "Well, we can die hoping, but you see, there is nothing. . . . Those hopes are almost stupid—for an undocumented Mexican to say, 'I'm *not* going back to Mexico.'" As for their subjection to harassment and deportation, some told me, "*Así es la vida* [That's life]."

José Ortíz, for instance, was a twenty-four-year-old wage worker who stacked pallets in a cement room for fourteen hours a day. He had lived in the United States for almost a decade and resented its hostile treatment. Yet when I asked if he would advocate for immigration reform, he replied, "So many of us would like immigration reform, but the truth is, I have never been in any organization or anything. . . . The reason is that my main goal is to go back [to Mexico]. The truth, for me, is that I don't have any motivation in the United States. I'm leaving. There [in Retorno], I feel free." Not only did José translate his economic prospects back to Mexico, thinking about how the money he made could help him start a tire-repair shop back home, but he also held out for *political* freedom on the sending side. His focus on return left him without motivation to march for better treatment. In the first decade of the 2000s, circulation from Retorno diminished. Nevertheless, the *idea* that life in the United States was temporary continued to discourage migrants from defying the regime that held them in its sway. While they were in California, this orientation kept them stoic about economic exploitation, political exclusion, and even domestic abuse. Coercion not only scared migrants out of marching, it also alienated them from the promise of integration. Withdrawn, migrants shunted their engagement to the Mexican side.

Scared into Silence at Work

Migrants also stayed silent about their treatment at work. They tended to face more abuse at work than their counterparts in Los Angeles, and, as described in chapter 2, many felt treated unfairly. Nevertheless, not one had joined a union. Basilio, who held jobs in a range of farms and factories over the course of his thirty years in the United States, argued that workers in North County were afraid to make a wrong move, in both labor and the streets. He explained,

It's very common that in the factories, in the workers' centers, they hire illegal *[sic]* workers. And there, well, it's not the same—the stress isn't the
same. The person with papers will never worry about anything, when each
year—or each cycle—they [employers] ask people for papers, for social
security numbers. But the guy who has borrowed papers or false papers,
well, he's there with Jesus in his mouth [i.e., biting his tongue].

With bosses regularly checking documents and threatening to call immigration control, undocumented workers in North County were afraid to
complain. They tolerated abusive conditions not just to prove their deservingness, but because they were afraid.

Migrants' focus on Mexico also inhibited unionization. In the early
1990s the United Farm Workers (UFW) started a campaign to recruit
Mixtec migrants in California, including those from Retorno. Organizers
went out into the fields, trying to drum up support among tomato pickers.
They failed. Arturo Molina, who joined the UFW as an organizer, reflected,

There were some farms where we mobilized people, but they weren't really
big mobilizations, because the laws here [in the United States] are different. . . . In this country it's more difficult. There are certain laws, and, in addition, they [growers] don't even let you enter onto the farms to organize. . . .
Lately, if they see you with a camera or that sort of thing, they won't let you
in. There's security. . . . Organizing is harder, even though we tell workers
their rights; sometimes they're undocumented, and what they want is a job.
Even though they give them less than $5.00 an hour, they want a job.

Employers' use of intensive security on the farms (and possibly even
police) made it difficult to organize. At the same time, migrants remained
focused on having a job at all, so they could make enough money to go
home. Unions, they worried, would hamper their efforts to return.

Migrants' alienation from the United States also gave unions less
appeal. For instance, I asked Basilio why the UFW campaign had been
unsuccessful, when these migrants had founded the PCPR and the FIOB.
He replied that even though migrants were angry about their treatment in
the United States and politically active vis-à-vis their village, "We didn't
have a union life as such. Our movement was more communitarian—more
social, but not union. . . . When we got together at the farms [where
migrants worked], it was to see if we could put doors on the church [back
home]." He added,

If we [organizers] arrived with our story that we wanted them to join Cesar Chavez's movement [the UFW], well, they would complain, and it wouldn't work. [Abigail: Why didn't they want to join? Because they were afraid, because they didn't have papers, because they thought the union was corrupt, or what?] They didn't know anything about Cesar Chavez; union organizing in the United States had no interest for them. [Abigail: They just didn't see reasons to do it?] No, and after a little while, it failed. The union funded some projects—our [FIOB] offices and that—but we couldn't do it. . . . For us—in the unions—we were not going to do anything.

While migrants resented employers' discrimination and exploitation, they remained estranged. In contrast to those in Los Angeles, they felt little investment in fighting for better conditions in the United States. On the premise that their time in the California was limited, they stayed out of unions, tolerating low wages and labor abuse.

How Women Held Out for Home

For many women the situation was even worse. In North County, women's uncertainty about immigration control left them vulnerable to men at home. In turn, household inequities constrained their engagement in politics. When Paloma Pacheco first came to the United States in the 1990s, she liked to participate in fund-raisers and meetings run by the PCPR and the FIOB. Then Paloma got married. As described in chapter 2, her husband beat her and threatened to have her deported. He also blocked her from attending political events. She described, "I used to like to participate in [civic] events. Now I would like to be involved, to be part of things. . . . But it is one of those things that I can't decide for myself. He [my husband] always has to decide for me or give me permission to do something or not. He doesn't let me feel free." Thus, Paloma's dependence on her husband—and her fear of repercussions if she defied him—stymied her political mobilization. Faced with such situations, women tended to engage in politics in roles subservient to their husbands, coming to meetings only to serve food or do support tasks, if at all. Women also represented less than a third of Retorno's migrants in North County. As a result, they rarely played a central part in political meetings among that community in the United States.

Holding out to someday escape to Mexico encouraged women to endure household abuse. As described in chapter 2, for example, Dolores was beaten by her husband, but she refused to turn him in. She preferred to withstand his abuse, so both could make the money they needed to go home to their children. Likewise, fifty-two-year-old Dora López planned to stay in California only until she and her husband paid their debts. When her husband beat her, Dora's employer—for whom she worked as a housekeeper—attempted to intervene. Yet Dora stopped him. She recounted,

> I got a job in Riverside [California], but each week my bosses would bring me here to Vista where he [my husband] was. Two times my husband beat me really badly. . . . He hit the side of my cheek, and I couldn't eat for three days. So one time I came with my boss, and the man, Mr. Smith, said, "I am going to put him in jail because I don't like people like that." But I said, "No, sir, I came to work to help him out a little bit, but I'm leaving—just let it be—I'm leaving." "Okay, right," [he said], and the man didn't get involved.

The sooner they paid their debts, Dora explained, the sooner she could go back to Retorno. Instead of using the state against their male counterparts like those in Los Angeles, such women strategically focused on going home. Their form of politics was to "vote with their feet": to leave.

When the topic of domestic violence arose with men in North County, they were generally matter-of-fact about the abuses that women described. Most had grown up watching their fathers batter their mothers and responded little when nother migrants mentioned they had injured their wives. For instance, though Marcelo did not directly mention beating his wife, he talked almost jokingly of browbeating her into coming to the United States—and with a bit more chagrin about his decades of alcohol abuse once she arrived. Likewise, as I talked with Griselda García one day in her living room, she gestured at her husband, who was sitting feet away on the couch, and mentioned how badly he used to abuse her. In answer, he sat and nodded, sipping a glass of water. Perhaps more noteworthy is that men in North County did *not* express the same sense of threat or emasculation as those in Los Angeles. They did not see the United States as a place where women "won," or men lost their honor. Without intervention from U.S. police, and likely under intense personal stress, many perpetuated the household abuse they'd faced as children themselves.

In North County the exceptions to the rule—the men and women who *were* invested in changing the United States—had mostly lost hope by the time my fieldwork began. Whereas migrants' enchantment with the United States varied in Los Angeles, in North County San Diego disillusionment stifled hope. Though men did not face the same household control as women, they too felt powerless in the face of workplace and state coercion. Even people like Basilio and Domingo, who had once been major organizers, gave up and went home.

CONTAINING DEFIANCE?

This chapter traced how conditional and arbitrary control shape migrants' strategies toward the United States. In both Los Angeles and North County San Diego, migrants' attitudes, collective identities, and protests reflected their efforts to navigate exclusion. Yet undocumented immigrants did not adopt a single, common mode of politics but instead took piecemeal approaches, specific to the local opportunities available. They also built on legacies they brought in from Mexico, including their family structures and histories of homeland advocacy. In Los Angeles conditional control led most migrants to perform belonging. In North County San Diego arbitrary enforcement encouraged emotional withdrawal.

The politics of belonging appeared more promising than withdrawal for bringing substantive change. When migrants believed inclusion was possible (albeit only for a subset of the undocumented), many were willing to voice their political demands. Ironically, respondents were *more* likely to join marches in Los Angeles, where they arguably had fewer grievances, than in North County, where conditions were worse. Upending common perceptions of political protests, these marchers focused on their appreciation for—and desire to be included in—the United States. Their willingness to express these demands may have helped hold local state agents to their promises to support "good" immigrants. Nearly a decade later, even though the federal government had not passed comprehensive immigration reform, California had begun to adopt a slew of pro-immigrant laws. Nevertheless, encouraging migrants to embrace the United States was not an unmitigated good.

Migrants' hope for rewards in Los Angeles, from wages to legalization, also encouraged them to perform according to the perceived norms of the United States and to distinguish themselves from those who acted "bad." To the extent migrants embraced a logic of individual responsibility, they self-regulated. Though some of them protested for rights, others kept silent, hoping their deference would prove they deserved inclusion. Many internalized the idea that uncomplaining hard work was a ticket to membership, even going so far as to tolerate sickness and substandard conditions or wages. They also deflected blame onto their counterparts, undermining unity and obscuring the backdrop of threat behind the good/bad regime. Nevertheless, both hope and good behavior were tenuous. When migrants did not receive the expected rewards for hard work or deference, they grew disaffected, shifting toward a politics of withdrawal.

Migrants in North County San Diego *also* performed as good workers, tolerating low wages and keeping quiet about their political exclusion. Yet the mechanism was different, as were the implications for Mexico and the United States. In North County immigrants avoided protests not due to identification with the regime but out of fear and disillusionment. Similar to unauthorized migrants surveyed by other scholars, they described U.S. treatment as illegitimate and hypocritical.[27] At first, these critiques sparked outspoken dissent. Over time, however, expanded enforcement dampened their activism. Instead, migrants' alienation encouraged them to turn attention to Mexico, muddling the common assumption that migrants assimilate over time. Even though circulation grew ever more difficult, migrants suppressed their anger, waiting to return home. Despite their critiques of employers and the U.S. state, fear and the focus on Mexico discouraged them from challenging the oppressions they faced.

The chapter also shows how women can end up at the extremes of political action or silence. In Los Angeles, and likely other places the state provided support, services were especially strong for women, giving them hope and motivating them to play leading advocacy roles. At the same time, gendered state and employer protections also pitted women against men and made them especially likely to actively conform to state norms (itself a form of politics). In North County San Diego, and places where immigrants were more under threat, women faced dual burdens of fear and household abuse, often blocking them from engaging in politics, even if they felt critical of the regime. Women's isolation under arbitrary policing pushed them, in particular, to hold out for home.

Ironically, both the strategy of belonging and the strategy of withdrawal may have contained political defiance, helping reinforce the modes of control in their respective cities. In Los Angeles migrants' efforts to act good restricted their protests to a subset of so-called proper behavior and deepened lines of difference among them. In San Diego, despite migrants' feelings of dissent and unity, their focus on Mexico kept them stoic. Arguably, each mode of control imposed its own form of legally sanctioned violence. In Los Angeles migrants took to heart the idea that they did not deserve better wages or were "guests in the house," keeping them marginalized. In North County physical threats imposed fear, suppressing migrants' voices. Both modes of control also drew lines of difference that intertwined with gender and race: Los Angeles distinguished *which* immigrants were deserving, while North County marked the unauthorized in general as less deserving than citizens. Thus, conditional and arbitrary control imposed distinct yet complementary forms of regulation.

At the same time, both strategies of politics also left contradictions brewing. Migrants in Los Angeles sought to hold the U.S. government to its promises. Yet the federal government repeatedly crushed their hopes, expanding detention and deportation and leaving respondents increasingly disillusioned. Likewise, those in North County turned their critical consciousness toward Mexico. Yet even as they did so, their transnational relationships were cut off by growing border enforcement, leaving a dangerous combination of disengagement and trapped dissent. In both cases, as I explore in chapter 4, migrants' U.S.-side political actions developed in *relation* to their hometowns, shaping the character of their cross-border engagement.

4 Cross-Border Fights, Rifts, and Ties

One afternoon during my fieldwork, I joined a small group of migrants from Partida for a meeting at the Mexican consulate in Los Angeles. Carmen Rojas and her compatriots Renata Salazar and Concha Hernández—the current leading officers of Partida's hometown association (HTA)—were preparing to solicit matching funds for a project they had launched to rebuild Partida's primary school. As we walked down the hallway of the four-story building, their heels clicked against the glistening floor. Fifth-grade education be damned, the women meticulously copied down details about a Mexican government grant from the 3x1 Program for Migrants. The program encouraged emigrants to invest in hometown development by offering "three for one," with the Mexican federal, state, and municipal governments matching the funds raised by HTAs. By the time my fieldwork closed in 2012, the women had raised over US$40,000 and gotten the grant, securing a combined US$166,000 to rebuild the village school.

Two things made their actions surprising: first, like most respondents in Los Angeles, Carmen, Renata, and Concha did not plan to return to Mexico. On the contrary, they regularly described Partida as "backward." Second, even though people in Partida often appealed for support, 80 percent of its emigrants in Los Angeles refused to give the village their money or time. Though Partida remained communal, migrants had set out as individuals, many of them to escape. Distancing themselves from Mexico helped affirm that they belonged in the United States.

Interestingly, the 20 percent of migrants who did participate in Partida's HTA often used the organization to demonstrate their own "progress," compared to friends and family still living in Mexico.[1] They questioned Partida's collective governance. They sought to instill new household cleaning habits, better education, and more environmental protections. They also insisted on women's inclusion in politics. Thus, migrants presented themselves not only as good immigrants to the United States but also as advanced and American compared to the hometown they had left behind. I refer to this approach as *polarized* transnationalism.

Migrants from Retorno to North County San Diego also built a hometown association. But in contrast to their counterparts in Los Angeles, people like Alma Sandoval and Basilio Ramos thought of their HTA as a tool for transnational *solidarity*. They rejected the assumption that the United States was the site of progress. Instead, they looked to their village to escape the fear, isolation, and abuse they faced in California. Though they appeared withdrawn toward the United States, they channeled their critiques of U.S. life into cross-border action. They used the HTA to build alliances with their hometown counterparts, other indigenous migrant organizations, and opposition political parties. In particular, when the Partido de la Revolución Democrática (PRD; Party of the Democratic Revolution) began reaching out to migrants to fight the PRI, they signed on. Even though Retorno had been profoundly unequal when migrants left, they hoped they could change the village by demanding public resources and democratic control. Thus the migrants mobilized on the PRD's behalf, while the party helped expand their demands for rights and resources beyond Retorno to hometowns across the state of Oaxaca. These migrants' transnational actions also drew women into leadership roles. Yet in this case, perhaps surprisingly, women became politicized on the Mexican side. As migrant men sought allies in the village, they looked to women whose husbands were away in the United States. Soon women such as Alma Sandoval were leading marches and political committees and fighting for state support. As these women gained standing in

Retorno, migrants and nonmigrants began to think of their hometown—
not the United States—as the site of gendered freedoms.

THE POLITICS OF MIGRANTS' CROSS-BORDER ACTION

Immigrants' efforts to navigate U.S. control did not end in the United
States. Migrants from Partida and Retorno also responded to U.S. exclusion through their interactions with Mexico. Their transnational practices
varied, reflecting the legacies of their hometowns, the modes of control
they faced in Los Angeles and North County, and the shifting political
dynamics on the Mexican side. In this chapter I examine how migrants
related to their hometowns, how they engaged with broader Mexican politics, where they hoped for progress, and where they included women.

In the 1990s and the first decade of the 2000s, as migrants confronted
exclusion in the United States, new spaces opened up for them to participate in Mexican politics. For most of the twentieth century, the PRI had
ruled Mexico as a one-party state. In the 1980s, however, economic crises
and falling wages fueled dissent, driving poor people, in particular, to
align with communist and socialist critiques.[2] In 1987 a politician named
Cuauhtémoc Cárdenas split off from the PRI to form a new leftist opposition party, which would become the PRD. Cárdenas ran for president in
1988, demanding transparency and reinvigorating Mexico's electoral
process. To bolster his campaign, he reached out to Mexican emigrants in
the United States, encouraging them to fund-raise and press friends in
Mexico to vote.[3] Other parties later joined the fray, including the Catholic,
probusiness Partido Acción Nacional (PAN; National Action Party), which
finally defeated the PRI and took the presidency in 2000.

Though the PRI won the vote against Cárdenas and retained control in
the state of Oaxaca, in particular, until 2010, democratic opposition forced
PRI leaders to recognize migrants' political and economic power. After
Cárdenas's campaign, the PRI, PAN, and other parties also began wooing
emigrants to play long-distance roles in Mexican politics. Beginning in the
1990s, for instance, the PRI created an expanded network of consulates
and programs for emigrants, hoping to channel remittances and political
sway back to Mexico.[4] When PAN candidate Vicente Fox was elected

president in 2000, he too made emigrant engagement central to his agenda. He legalized dual nationality, so emigrants could vote starting in 2006. He also created several programs to support U.S. migrants and encourage them to form associations (these programs included the Presidential Office for Mexicans Abroad, the Institute of Mexicans Abroad, and the 3x1 Program).[5] Such efforts made emigrants a new cornerstone of Mexican politics.

Hometown associations—voluntary civic organizations created by emigrants from a common place of origin—played a central role in this process. Typically, HTAs fund-raise to provide social welfare in their home communities.[6] By 2008 there were approximately a thousand Mexican hometown associations in the United States.[7] Some HTAs also formed coalitions, like the Council of Mexican Federations in North America, a group of sixteen organizations promoting migrant engagement in both the United States and Mexico. In Los Angeles such federations collaborated with immigrants' rights organizations and even with the then LA mayor Antonio Villaraigosa to draw attention to immigrants' concerns in the United States. They also pushed for rights in Mexico by emphasizing their economic contributions.[8]

One of the earliest and largest coalitions of HTAs was the Frente Indígena Oaxaqueño Binacional (FIOB; Oaxacan Indigenous Binacional Front), established by migrants from Retorno and nearby hometowns, as described in chapter 3. Founded in 1992, on the five-hundredth anniversary of the colonization of the Americas, the FIOB used indigenous identity to mobilize migrants against U.S. and Mexican state abuse. In contrast to most HTAs, which were village-specific, the FIOB did not just send money home. Rather, they promoted a radical agenda, demanding decolonization and the "right not to migrate."[9]

Beyond HTAs and migrant coalitions, many emigrants from Mexico lead what scholars call "transnational lives."[10] Roger Waldinger (2013), for instance, shows that 70 percent of migrants call home monthly or more, 52 percent send remittances each year, and 33 percent travel at least once every two years. Typically, scholars trace such transnational practices to cultural nostalgia or ethnic identity. Some add that migrants can also form HTAs to build cohesion and a sense of belonging in foreign contexts.[11] Others such as Luin Goldring (2003) add that HTAs can give migrant men, in particular, a vehicle to reclaim lost patriarchal status or feel economically privileged in relation to those back home. Finally, a few scholars note that migrants can also practice "reactive transnationalism," turning to their homelands to cope with discrimination or negative experiences on the receiving end.[12] Nevertheless, most studies of migrant transnationalism say surprisingly little about the impacts of U.S. exclusion.

This chapter fills that gap, demonstrating how migrants' political pathways shape their engagement in HTAs. I focus, in particular, on the transnational implications of different U.S. modes of control. As other scholars show, HTAs are not always cohesive; they can also be a site of contention among members of a migrant community.[13] I add that HTAs also give migrants a forum through which to respond to both U.S. "illegality" and Mexican democratization. Therefore, migrants' transnational involvement, cohesion, and contention reflect not just their cultural attachments but also their reactions to the unique kinds of exclusion they face as undocumented migrants in the United States.

Emigrants' transnational practices (or lack thereof) extended their U.S.-side politics. In Los Angeles migrants from Partida reinforced the binary notion of good immigrants versus bad immigrants by drawing a second contrast between the United States and Mexico. More than 80 percent of respondents in Los Angeles distanced themselves from Partida. Nevertheless, in the early 1980s some of the village's first migrants formed an HTA. One of their goals was to help one another get established in Los Angeles. They also wanted to pass their feelings of progress on to those remaining in the village. Therefore, they started to fund-raise for sanitation, better schools, and so on. This stance grew more complex in the 1990s. As ever more people left Partida, those remaining began to demand that migrants contribute to the hometown's collective government.[14] The villagers threatened to block migrants from coming back, should they refuse to help. Thus, the HTA took a third role: it began to enforce the hometown's demands, with migrants who were sympathetic to the village tracking who else contributed or not. Even as these migrants fund-raised, however, they continued to put pressure on Partida to change its collective governance. Focused on making Partida more *like* the United States, they also remained aloof from political shifts occurring in Mexico. By abandoning or trying to change their counterparts in the village, in short, migrants in Los Angeles marked their difference from the hometown, reinforced their belonging in the United States, and fueled transnational *polarization.*

In North County San Diego, meanwhile, migrants' U.S.-side with-drawal promoted transnational *solidarity.* Despondent about their pros-pects for U.S. inclusion, migrants sought hope in Mexico. Combined with the separation of nuclear families between Retorno and California, migrants' desire to return encouraged them to maintain close transna-tional ties. In particular, a group of migrants from Retorno began collabo-rating with those in the hometown to overthrow village elites and democ-ratize local leadership. This cross-border advocacy then drew the attention of the dissident PRD, amplifying the migrants' political sway in Mexico. In turn, the people of Retorno joined with those of nearby villages to form the FIOB, connect to the PRD, and demand resources from the Mexican state. Even though Retorno's hierarchy had driven migrants out, they found they had more power to effect change in Mexico than in the hostile terrain of North County San Diego. Rejecting the United States, they remitted dissent.

This chapter also highlights how women's political participation inter-twines with transnational advocacy. Interestingly, both HTAs acted as levers of gender equity. Transnational engagement was not divided simply by sex, as other scholars suggest, with men feeling greater nostalgia for Mexican *machismo.*[15] Nor could "social remittances" alone be credited for women's empowerment.[16] Rather, women mobilized in the places where local politics created the best opportunities to work for change. These openings for women varied with local modes of control. In Los Angeles, as described in chapters 2–3, women got particular support from service providers and police, creating a distinct divide between their suffering in the village and their empowerment in the United States. Women migrants used their HTA to demonstrate these gains to men back home. They also used the organization to press for similar changes on the sending side.

By contrast, in North County San Diego arbitrary control made wom-en's suffering even worse than in the pueblo, and both men *and* women sought refuge in Mexico. Several women returned to Retorno or stayed in the village instead of moving to California at all. In turn, men realized that to change the hometown, they needed to organize women on the sending side. As I detail further in chapter 5, women were especially important to Retorno's resistance as the Mexican government started tying state funds to women's participation. In what follows I trace how each U.S. mode of control combined with hometown legacies to shape migrants' cross-border actions, including the goals of their organizations, the HTAs' involvement in Mexican politics, and men and women's distinct engagement in transnational life.

POLARIZED TRANSNATIONALISM FROM LOS ANGELES

In Los Angeles the combination of independent youth migration and conditional enforcement polarized migrants from their counterparts in Mexico. Most migrants cut ties to their hometown. Others formed an HTA to help one another integrate into the United States or send back U.S. ideas to Partida. They took pride in the economic and gendered accomplishments they had made in the United States. Nevertheless, many people still in Partida rejected these efforts at modernization, driving wedges between migrants and those in Mexico.

An HTA with the Goal of Integration

In the early 1980s, long before most of Partida's migrants arrived in Los Angeles, a dozen early arrivals started a hometown association.[17] Blanca Martínez was among them. She explained that when the group first got together,

> we had the idea that we had to support one another because people were going to keep arriving. [We thought], "We have to give them a chance in the first few months—so they can work, pay off their debt, and contribute to us [cooperar] afterward." And that's how we started to give one another mutual aid [apoyarnos mutuamente] . . . and to help one another, in case someone got sick. If someone died, we would send the body back home to their parents. . . . [We thought], "It's good to be united because if you have an emergency or something, the organization helps."

As more migrants arrived, the HTA gave them a safety net in California. It supported them through sickness, death, and family emergencies. Since few people from Partida had health insurance, the organization filled in. For instance, after a member was diagnosed with cancer, the organization hosted a series of dances, raising $10,000 to help pay his medical bills. Likewise, when a recently arrived migrant got shot, the group pooled their money so he could buy food. Some even proposed to create a "house of Partida" in Los Angeles that could welcome incoming migrants and serve as a base for social activities (though it never came to fruition).

In this way Partida's migrants extended the long-standing practices of mutual aid that had given them an advantage from the moment their migration pathway began.[18] Indeed, HTA members adopted indigenous concepts like cargos (civic posts), tequios (communal labor), and *cooperación* (monetary contributions), which had been core to Partida's collective governance. Santiago Morales was one of the organization's figureheads, often serving as emcee for its LA events. One afternoon we ate donuts and talked about novels at a restaurant in Huntington Park. Santiago argued that indigenous traditions gave Partida's HTA strength. He boasted,

> This organization has existed for thirty years because it's had its own base. In this organization you start from below [as in the village]. First, you're going to be a representative *[vocal]* and then treasurer or secretary and finally president. So there it has its base. It's organic. What happens is that we have this tradition. In the Sierra we were never conquered. So we never [lost that]. . . . As long as we still practice tequio, we cannot dissolve.

While Santiago took pride in his indigenous heritage, he wanted to *use* this legacy to better integrate into the United States. Partida's migrants formed their HTA in the first place, he added, precisely because "[our] people suffer discrimination by race in Oaxaca—discrimination within Mexico—and when you get to a foreign country [the United States] you suffer that discrimination [too], so being Oaxacan is a huge struggle. In the years when I arrived here, my fellow migrants were still embarrassed to say they were from Oaxaca, and even more to say that they spoke the Zapotec language." Perhaps ironically, the HTA insulated migrants from such exclusion by extending indigenous traditions to the United States.

Forming an association also helped migrants from Partida build social ties in Los Angeles. Raquel Moreno, another early organizer of the community's HTA, remembered, "Back in the day we were lonely. There were very few of us, and we used to get together to eat and hang out. That's how we formed the organization." Belonging to the HTA made migrants feel like "part of something." Juan Serrano added that even though he arrived in Los Angeles later, in the mid-1990s, he felt similarly. He joined the HTA, he explained, because "more than anything the connection you have to the community and your friends. And they would have parties—I don't know. You would see everyone there, and you'd do it. More than anything because you felt like part of a community again. And that's a community that's here too, right?" Such respondents insisted that in building connections with others from their hometown, their goal was not to return to Partida—as in some HTAs—but to establish themselves in Los Angeles.

The "Reluctants"

Even as some migrants from Partida formed an HTA, most felt deeply ambivalent toward their hometown. For instance, Epifanio Cruz, a forty-five-year-old legal permanent resident in Los Angeles, worked fixing computers. Like many women migrants, he had left Parida to escape his father's abuse. One day I met Epifanio at a café in Echo Park. I had just seen a photo he posted on Facebook, in which he appeared wrapped in a checkered blanket and locked in the jail below Partida's town hall. I had a hunch about what was going on. Starting in the 1980s growing numbers of young people left Partida, promising never to return. Their departure deprived the hometown of staff for its many public posts, degrading its communal structure, described in chapter 1. In response, those remaining in the village began to insist that migrants send them money and perform cargos in Los Angeles, through the HTA. In the late 1980s people in Partida also voted to require each migrant to donate a hundred dollars a year.

If migrants failed to provide support, the village threatened what anthropologist Tad Mutersbaugh (2002) calls "civic death." They decided that migrants who did not contribute were "not allowed to return to the village in good standing, either to visit or to live." The punishments ranged from jail time, to cutting off the water and electricity from the houses migrants left behind in Partida, to permanent expulsion. To enforce these demands the village asked the HTA to serve as its proxy in Los Angeles.

While enforcing hometown requests had not been migrants' original goal, pressure from Partida gave them little choice but to comply. Even though most of Partida's migrants wanted to stay in Los Angeles, those who participated in the HTA were loath to give up *all* ties to their families back home. So the leaders of that organization began to collect other migrants' hundred-dollar "taxes" and track the time each person contributed to fund-raisers and the HTA. When a migrant returned to visit Partida without having met these demands, villagers locked him in jail. Epifanio would stay in his cell until he paid the taxes he had missed.

Epifanio was incensed. He complained that the people still in Partida were stubborn, rigid *(necio)*, unfair, and "uncivilized." Though Epifanio had participated in Partida's HTA during his early years in the United States, after a decade in California he grew distant. He reflected, "I started realizing that we must end that custom of giving service, of giving tequio each year. I tell them, 'In this day and age, who wants to give a year of service for free?' . . . And then donate money, just to throw it away on the village festival. [The HTA] is just a waste of time." When Epifanio returned to Partida in 2010 to check on aging relatives, he faced the consequences.

Partida categorized people like Epifanio as *renuentes* (reluctants). These migrants did not participate in the hometown association or send money to the village government (though roughly 35 percent still sent individual remittances to their families). While it might seem surprising that undocumented immigrants would risk "civic death" back home, given the perils of deportation, Partida considered more than 80 percent of its migrants "reluctants."[19] The migrants, meanwhile, explained that not only did they have demanding jobs and children (and little time to spare), but they also lacked the motivation to maintain ties with their village. For instance, Jorge Marín, a migrant who refused to join the organization, reflected, "What am I going to go [to HTA meetings] for—not me. I'm not interested in Partida. I'm not interested in that. . . . I wouldn't even go back there if I was crazy." Guillermo Reyna, who felt just as hostile, added that Partida's demands had reinforced migrants' disinterest: "We're really discouraged, because of the things the pueblo has imposed on us. . . . Now when we go to the pueblo, they look badly at us, right? No, we're better off not going anymore. . . . I don't have anything there anymore; why am I going to contribute?" People like Guillermo felt they no longer had stakes in their hometown.

While these reluctants were aware that they could be excommunicated from Partida—and such exclusion was especially risky for the 72 percent who were undocumented—few believed they would return to the village. As described in chapter 1, most of Partida's migrants left Mexico alone, before marriage, in search of a "better life." These emigrants also followed a linear pattern, with nearly three-quarters settling in the United States on their very first trip. Separation was rare among spouses from Partida. Therefore, many migrants felt emotionally removed from the village. As Renata Salazar, who was president of the HTA during my fieldwork, explained to me, she didn't have close ties to the pueblo, because "my whole family is here [in Los Angeles]."

At the same time, distancing themselves from the village also formed part of migrants' strategy to belong in Los Angeles. Respondents described their own migration trajectories as opportunities to "get ahead" *(avanzar)*, "make progress" *(progresar)*, and even "overcome themselves" *(superarse)*. As they did, they mapped historical progress onto the geographic divide between Mexico and the United States. They associated Partida with the life they had left behind. Guillermo put it this way:

> Lots of people [migrants] don't want to be *comuneros* [formal members of the community] anymore . . . because they don't want the responsibility to continue—to have to be, for example, president of the landholdings, treasurer, secretary. They don't want to be on the supervisory board. They don't want to participate anymore because these are people—they're young people that don't want the responsibility anymore. They live in the present.

When I told emigrants like Guillermo that I had lived in Partida, they often joked about how "closed" the village was or wondered how I could tolerate engaging with its suspicious and protective community government. While one might expect Partida's migrants to wax nostalgic about their communal legacy, the obligation to participate in the home community also clashed with their efforts to belong in Los Angeles.

The Organization for the Improvement of Partida

Nevertheless, about 20 percent of migrants from Partida did participate in the community's HTA. As if to explicitly link emigration to modernization, they named their association the Organization for the Improvement of Partida (OIP). Santiago illustrated their attitudes. When I first met Santiago, he was emceeing a baptism party of over a hundred people, for a baby born to two young migrants from Partida. Eduardo Chávez, who was then acting president of the OIP, introduced Santiago as *el famoso* (the famous): among migrants from Partida, Santiago had a reputation as a "godfather" type. Yet he looked more fresh and clean-cut than I expected. As Santiago stood at the microphone, a young man passed with a broom. Here in California, Santiago joked, guys had to do the sweeping.

Later that night, Santiago talked at length about the importance of indigenous identity. "For me," he explained, "serving the community is a passion, and thanks to the career I chose [as a high-end butler], it allows me to play that role." He pulled out his iPhone, swiping through photos from Partida: his aging mother; a child riding a horse; and plastic bags that littered the side of the road. Though Santiago waxed nostalgic, he never thought about going back. On the contrary, he told me, pointing to the image of trash, he wanted to hold workshops for the young people. There were hardly any trees left in Partida, he said, and he wanted to ask the children where the pine trees were, to teach them to value nature.[20] He continued, "The first thing that caught my attention [in the picture] was that there is no sign prohibiting litter. I told them, 'Damn Indians, you have to write a sign.' You have to tell people in a way they understand." While Santiago used the word "Indians" facetiously, the racial undertones still colored his relationship to Partida, as if he had become white, while they remained stuck in their ethnic past. "I want my people to wake up," he went on, to "modernize" the village: "not to take it away, just to improve it." In short, he wanted the Organization for the Improvement of Partida to "improve" the village, just as its name implied.

Santiago loved Partida, and he and his brother Lorenzo had led dozens of five-digit fund-raisers supporting the village. But its demands made him mad. He argued, "Today it makes me sad because [the OIP] has become political [contentious]. We were stronger when [participation] was voluntary; the strength of goodwill is the best weapon we could have." He added, "Once we [migrants] get here [to the United States], we break free of all the bad things. The negative things that come from the pueblo get buried, and we are more powerful." Migrants had modernized traditional community service, he felt, by "breaking free" of precisely the kind of obligations the village insisted they meet. At one point Partida's government demanded migrants *return* to serve cargos. Santiago was incensed. Mobilizing migrants in Oaxaca City, Mexico City, and Los Angeles, he hired a bus to go to Partida and protest. At the village town hall, the migrants brokered a deal. They would support Partida's government, but only by sending the money to hire replacements. They would not come back.

When I asked Santiago about Partida's demand that migrants serve cargos, he replied,

> This policy is what has held them back. Why? It doesn't allow us to advance.... People have to leave their work here [in the United States], their family here, their reason for being, their trucks, their horses, their donkeys, their fleas—everything. And then they return for twelve months to do a cargo.... That's turning backward! ... If they [the villagers] do that, they themselves will force the OIP to disappear.

Not only did Santiago disagree with his hometown counterparts, labeling them as backward, but he also wielded the OIP's fund-raising as a threat. If the villagers insisted, he warned, they would lose this crucial source of support.

Instead of making migrants return, Santiago argued, Partida should replace collective obligations with modern technology and individual responsibility. He gave the example of the night guards who kept watch at Partida's church and school:

> Why the devil do those poor Christians have to go sleep there! Let's put a camera and an alarm on the church, and who the hell is going to enter? They say, "Damn Santiago is really Americanized [*Norteamericanizado*], that maniac." But it's not a stupid idea. Same thing in the schools: camera and alarm, and if something happens we'll all leap up when we hear the alarm.... And why the devil do I have to be on the school committee if I don't have a child there? ... I say if your kid is there, you do it.

For Santiago, dismantling community-service obligations represented a key component of Partida's improvement.

Santiago embodied the ambivalence of many migrants who participated in Partida's HTA. On one hand, they felt loath to lose contact with their families or roots. Respondents were proud of the HTA's capacity to send money. The OIP regularly raised up to US$30,000, sponsoring a new potable water tank, building public restrooms, paving roads, and rebuilding the church and town hall in Partida. In 2011 the HTA's contributions nearly matched Partida's annual operating budget, helping to redo the local primary school, expand its multimedia classroom, put a roof over the gym, and reconstruct the children's bathrooms. On the other hand, migrants disdained the village's demands, including their own role as enforcers. They wanted to end the very traditions that villagers hoped to sustain. Making claims on racial and temporal terms, they framed the hometown as "backward."[21]

Many other migrants in Los Angeles fought to "modernize" Partida as well. Blanca Martínez, for instance, said she was inspired to fund-raise for Partida after visiting the village, shortly after she had first come to the United States:

> I went to visit my pueblo, and all the tragedy, the need there is in the pueblo for many things, made me think, "We have to do something. I want to do something in the village. There are so many needs, and look at how the paths are all dirt, filled with mud." . . . I told my brother-in-law, "Even though you're poor, even though it's a dirt floor, throw some water on it, sweep it, pick up the trash, clean the plates, and this will be a paradise if you know how to care for it." But they leave everything a mess. They let the animals make a mess, and they could have the animals locked up and clean. . . . I said, "I've been poor too, and I like to keep things neat and clean."

While Blanca lamented Partida's poverty, she also blamed villagers for being messy and disorganized. She responded by trying to teach them "new ways to work." She went on, "It's a question of talking with people, giving them classes. Teach them and they'll learn. . . . I like to help people to learn things, trades." It made Blanca feel good to share the little money she'd made in housekeeping with those who had less. She went on, "Through all these years I've been really blessed. . . . So I think that helping people is giving back a little bit of what life has given me." By teaching desirable U.S. habits, Blanca both helped the pueblo and reinforced her own distance and "progress."

The OIP as a whole also resisted "returning to" cargos. Like Santiago, Alejandro Campos argued that the best "motor" of emigrant participation was the goodness of people's hearts. When Alejandro became OIP president in 2008, he challenged Partida's demands. For many years, HTA donations had gone to the village fiesta, the annual festival in honor of Partida's patron saint. Though migrants bought liquor and food for this festival, they got little credit with those in the village. From now on, Alejandro decided, the HTA would give only to visible projects on which they could put their name and claim. He remembered,

> We thought to ourselves, "Okay, we always give $5,000, $10,000 dollars for the fiesta, but no one reports it, and where does that money go? Let's not give money to the fiestas anymore. No one even knows that we contributed. . . . Instead, let's gather all our money together and do big works that we can see the benefit of." . . . Since then, we [the OIP] haven't sent money for the fiestas, only for public works—a water tank and now the school.

Under Alejandro's leadership, the OIP began placing a plaque on each project it sponsored. Works like the water tank in Partida, donated by the OIP in 2009, now bear signs, reading, "This project was done thanks to the devotion and dedication of the people who make up and support the Organization for the Improvement of Partida living in Los Angeles, California."

Migrants' views about their village also extended to a broader cynicism about Mexico and Mexican politics as a whole. In another study Rafael Alarcón, Luis Escala, and Olga Odgers (2016) found that Mexican migrants living in Los Angeles rarely expressed positive opinions about Mexico. Regardless of political party, they associated Mexico with corruption, poverty, violence, and an incapacity to govern. Even though migrants' fund-raising gave them access to Mexican politicians, they tended to declare themselves apolitical. The OIP was no exception. In 2001 the OIP joined a coalition with other hometown associations, including the FIOB—the organization formed by migrants from Retorno and many other Mixtec and Zapotecs in the early 1990s. Now, however, that federation was dormant. Santiago explained, "We learned not to [collaborate with them]." According to Santiago, organizations such as the FIOB had sold out by seeking government money. They were too focused on wooing parties to gain power for their cause. By contrast, the OIP declined to participate in the democratic process in Mexico, rejecting such efforts as "too political." In Santiago's mind, "The problem for the Mixtecos was that they looked for funding from the outside, from the government, while this organization [the OIP] sustains itself on its own." The OIP had kept up its philanthropy, Santiago argued, precisely because it stayed away from politics and built its own financial base.

In short, migrants joined the OIP not to engage in Mexican politics or make practical investments in a future return but to share their successful integration into the United States.[22] At the same time, they also clashed with the village, distancing themselves and dismissing those remaining as "behind." Thus, they reinforced the divide between those in Mexico and those in the United States.

A Proving Ground for Women

For women migrants the OIP was also a platform to show newfound power. During my fieldwork Partida continued to exclude women from voting and was governed exclusively by men. Not one female migrant I knew of returned to the village, unless she had a sick family member, aging parents, or children left behind. Nevertheless, Partida required migrant women— particularly those not married to a man from the pueblo—to pay fifty dollars per year (half of men's "tax") and serve in the HTA. One might assume that female migrants would feel little love lost for Partida's machismo and leave the HTA to men. Instead, they used the organization to fight back.

The first time I visited Raquel Moreno at her Huntington Park apartment, she was wearing a smoking red dress and grilling an equally smoking heap of barbecue meat. As she cooked flanks of steak, we talked about her experience in the Organization for the Improvement of Partida. Raquel had come to Los Angeles in the mid-1980s, when her mother insisted she leave the village. With Blanca, she'd been one of the founding members of the OIP in Los Angeles. Raquel joined, she explained, because she wanted to spend time with other migrants—as well as support her family back home. She didn't mind the long hours the women spent cooking mole sauce and tortillas to sell as they fund-raised. But she resented when those hard-earned dollars went to the village men: some of the very same individuals who had beaten the women of Partida, excluded them from civic affairs, and driven them out.

In the early years of Partida-U.S. migration, women made up the majority in the OIP. They decided to protest the all-male town government by sending their funds somewhere else. While men migrants like Santiago insisted that the money the OIP raised was for the pueblo, Raquel, Blanca, and other women replied, "No, we do not want to support the village government, because the government in the pueblo uses the men—and the single mothers, the single women, the widows—for public labor." Just as men did public service on behalf of their families in Partida, the village forced women heads of households to do the same. But village leaders often gave women the most hated public tasks, like serving food and alcohol to mocking, drunken men at the village fiestas, late into the night. In the face of such treatment, women like Raquel rejected the cargo system altogether. Instead, migrant women said, they would send their money to the church, the other main institution in Partida. Raquel recalled thinking, "We don't want it [our money] to go to the village political leaders because that's all men. Better it goes to the church."

Women also confronted migrant men within the HTA. Describing the tensions between male and female migrants, Raquel went on, "We come from a pueblo where machismo has triumphed. So if [women] propose ideas here [in the United States], the men don't want to accept it. [They say], 'No. Just because we're here, women aren't going to tell us what to do.'" By the late 1990s women had fund-raised over US$20,000. Men like Santiago demanded that they hand it over to Partida's town government, to fund the annual festival. But the women refused. In their minds the fiesta gave men in the village an excuse to get drunk on the migrants' dime. They told migrant men, "You men don't contribute; you don't do much. Instead, we women are just going to send this money for the church. . . . We don't want to work with you if you're going to try to control things." Then, for a few years, Raquel, Blanca, and the other women created a separate HTA, without the men. Blanca explained,

> We were willing to help them work for the town government, but not [give the men] all that money. Through thick and thin, we had worked hard for that money. The sleepless nights when there was a dance [fund-raiser], and we had to go wash a mountain of dishes afterward, or having to go around selling tickets, holding raffles. . . . It was as if someone had made a beautiful cake, and the cake has gotten so big, and someone else comes and says,

"I want that cake." . . . So all the women who didn't want to give up the money signed a statement saying we would not keep working with [the men]. . . . There were eighteen of us who signed, I think—basically those of us who started all of this, who were always the ones who worked the hardest.

Proud of their work and committed to gender equity, the women refused to submit to the demands of men, in either Partida or the United States.

Though these clashes occurred in the late 1980s and early 1990s, similar tensions echoed again in my fieldwork. In 2011, in the words of one male migrant, Carmen, Renata, and Concha "took over power" in the Organization for the Improvement of Partida. In a dramatic spring meeting, they denounced the organization's male leaders—particularly then-president Eduardo Chávez—for mishandling collective funds. They insisted that the HTA replace these men with more "responsible" (women) leaders. Eduardo reacted by accusing his female counterparts, particularly Renata, who was then HTA secretary, of causing the mistakes. Renata was incensed, and she phoned me to vent:

Don't think I'm going to accept this because I'm a woman! Don't think that because I'm a woman I'm going to let [Eduardo] blame me for his mistakes. I'm not just going to lie down and let him walk all over me! He doesn't know me! I am a household head. I am the one who supports my family. . . . Just because I'm a woman, I'm not going to say, "Okay, it's my fault. I did it." Imagine accepting or letting him do that to me—blame me for something he did. How would I look in front of everyone? Bad!

Together, the women convinced the HTA to oust Eduardo and other male leaders and install an all-female cast instead: Renata as president, Carmen as secretary, and Concha as treasurer. Migrant men reacted by insulting them, calling them "girls" or "damn old ladies." Nevertheless, by 2012 these female leaders had won their 3x1 grant from the Mexican consulate and raised more than US$160,000 to rebuild Partida's school.

By leading the HTA these women proved themselves to men. Carmen, for instance, had been hesitant to join the organization at first. When she came to Los Angeles, she thought of the OIP as men's domain. Now, however, Carmen felt empowered. Once she joined the organization, she explained, "I understood that we women had to go too, that women can do it. Like right now we're three women that are in the [HTA] leadership! *[Laughs.]*" When I asked if Carmen faced gender discrimination as OIP secretary, she replied,

> Not so far, because we [women] know how to defend ourselves. We're demonstrating that we can do it. Even more with this 3x1 project, though it's taken a ton of time, and it's broken our heads into pieces trying to fill out that paperwork that we don't know how to do. But we're getting there; we're getting there. Imagine, Abigail, if we win this 3x1 money—no, better said: if we prove that we're going to do this project, to rebuild the primary school that's fifty years old, and then it gets rebuilt? If we accomplish this project, it's going to be a great luxury we'll give ourselves: to show that we women are capable, first. Second, that you can reach new heights when you want to, when you struggle for it. . . . As always, there are men who think that women can't speak up, that women can't express their opinions. But no, there we are.

Thus, Renata, Carmen, Concha, and the other women confronted men, using their financial leverage to push for gender equity in both Los Angeles and the village. Proving their mettle made them proud.

Participation as Insurance

There were also exceptions to the trend of migrant-hometown polarization. In particular, a subset of interviewees joined the OIP for "insurance." Even though respondents planned to stay in Los Angeles, most were undocumented. So they kept up ties in the pueblo, in case U.S. inclusion failed to work out. Some of the migrants may also have planned to return to other parts of Mexico, where there were not such stringent demands. But since most people's closest contacts were still in Partida, the village remained their point of reference—and possible return.

Luz Hernández, a single mother, offers one example. In 2011 Luz was nominated to organize and cook for all OIP fund-raisers. The position was a ton of work, requiring her to walk long distances to the sites of fund-raisers, get up at 4:00 or 5:00 A.M. to cook, and stay late into the night to clean. Luz looked thin and often had circles under her eyes. Her teenage daughter, Marla, complained that her mother was never home, leaving the girl alone in their apartment to fend for herself. Luz accepted the cargo, however, because "I didn't want them [the hometown government] to bother me if I have to go back there or to make me pay [old migrant 'taxes']—because if I don't pay [and I want to go back], then they're going to call me and charge me the money for many years [that I missed]." Though Luz liked the United States and didn't plan to return to Partida, she figured, "you never know." Luz also hoped that Marla—a U.S. citizen—might get to visit the village. She went on, "I started to go [to the HTA] for my daughter—for me and for her—because she would like to go to the pueblo. . . . So I started because I don't want them [the village government] to bother my daughter." If Luz maintained the connection, Marla could go back to visit and learn of her family and roots.

Others kept ties to Partida in case they wanted to retire there or escape the pressures of work in the United States. Though Carmen often extolled the benefits of Los Angeles, she thought she might eventually retire to Partida. When I asked why, she replied,

> For me the pueblo is tranquility. This country of America is very nice. Thank God, it gives us everything we need [economically]. But it's a lot of stress, a lot of running around, a lot of pressure. . . . I like the United States, I like it, but as I say, I might like to end up there [in Partida] in my old age. . . . I would like to return one day if God lets me. I want to go live in my mother's house—the little house she has there. . . . I would return, and if one day my son wants to come with me, he's welcome. Actually, I'd like him to go there, so he gets to know it, so he becomes familiar with my family and gets to know my pueblo.

Despite Carmen's love for the United States, sustaining contact with the village offered a "retirement plan" as well as cultural ties for her son. So, when her fellow migrants insisted she join the HTA, Carmen figured, "Either I do it now, or I'll have to do it later. Anyway, let it all be for my pueblo. It's for the love of my pueblo." Like Santiago, she was ambivalent, torn between feelings of progress and stress, of praise for California and tenderness for her village.

Even in a welcoming context like Los Angeles, life could be draining for those without papers. Carmen's friend Maribel Parra added, "I want to go back; I'm tired of working all the time. I don't want life to be like this. . . . There are some benefits that people who have papers get, who are already citizens and all that—so that when they retire they get their pension. But many of us cannot have those things. . . . So you think, 'What's the point?'" To keep her options open, Maribel stayed in the HTA, sustaining her links to home.

SOLIDARY TRANSNATIONALISM FROM NORTH COUNTY SAN DIEGO

In contrast to their counterparts in Los Angeles, migrants from Retorno used their hometown association to build cross-border unity. As discussed in chapters 2–3, most felt alienated from the United States. Many also sustained thick ties with family members back in the pueblo. Therefore, the organizations they built—including the Popular Committee of the People of Retorno (their original HTA) and later the FIOB, which replaced it— sought to address both the abuses they faced as farmworkers in California and their ongoing marginality in Mexico. In the 1990s migrants' organizing helped connect them to rising opposition parties in Mexico, amplifying their sense of voice in their homeland just as enforcement stifled their protests in the United States. Whereas Partida's migrants thought of their hometown as "stuck in the past," those from Retorno made their pueblo dynamic, framing it instead as their hope for the future. Mobilizing across borders, they also drew women into politics on the Mexican side.

The Popular Committee of the People of Retorno

Retorno's HTA—the Popular Committee of the People of Retorno (PCPR)—first emerged as migrants' answer to their history of exclusion in Mexico. As described in chapter 3, most of the migrants who founded the organization had been involved in labor strikes in Sinaloa in the 1970s and 1980s. Leaders of these strikes, including Basilio Ramos, Domingo García, and Arturo Molina, also received training from the Mexican Communist Party and the Unified Socialist Party of Mexico, who sought out farmworkers and taught them communist ideology and strategy. Basilio recalled that in these sessions, "We talked about Marxism, about the proletariat. We talked about the bourgeoisie and all that. At that moment we were interested in national political issues. . . . At the most general level our goal was that the PRI—the party that for years and years had governed Mexico—that it was the moment to get rid of it." As these organizers protested, several of them—including Basilio and Domingo—were beaten, abused, or killed by mercenaries of the growers and Mexican state. As Michael Kearney (1998) shows, this repression pushed the Mixtec leaders to adopt an ethnic identity as "Us the Mixtecs" versus the growers. Thus, migrants tied their indigenous identity and class solidarity to the fight against PRI domination in Mexico.

In the 1970s and 1980s, as these migrants circulated between Sinaloa and Retorno, they began to link their subordination as farmworkers to the inequities they'd faced in the hometown. Looking out over Retorno one hot afternoon in 2011, Basilio reflected,

> Sinaloa opened our panorama. There, it was another thing; there, there really was a bourgeoisie. But we brought that back to this social sphere. . . . We twisted that [communist critique] to what was going on here. . . . For example, we used to call anyone who owned things here "rich" and compare them with the bourgeoisie. . . . [We thought] that we had to take out the PRI, to form a leftist party that would really push for democracy in Retorno and in all of Mexico.

With this mindset, young migrants from Retorno got together to form a hometown association that would advocate for democratization in Retorno, even before they moved to the United States.[23] Emphasizing their grassroots leftist origins, they named their organization the Popular Committee of the People of Retorno.[24] In contrast to most HTAs, which fund-raised to send donations to their home villages, this committee aimed to transform Retorno, socially and politically.

In the 1980s the PCPR began pushing to check Retorno's inequality. By fund-raising and keeping detailed records of their money, migrant members of the organization demonstrated that the caciques (political bosses) who had kept a stranglehold on village leadership—particularly the Coronado family—had pocketed more than 50 percent of the funds recently designated for a new village secondary school. At the same time, their allies held meetings in the village. They organized, as one put it, to "stop putting up with these types of people." Then, one day in 1982 or

1983, the rebels amassed outside Retorno's town hall and blocked the two-decade PRI secretary Dario Coronado from going inside. As Basilio said to a UCSD interviewer, "Led by this group of young pioneers who were about twenty years old, they overthrew a PRI government. They kicked them out of the town hall, and the pueblo refused to recognize them, driven by these guys. From there forward, people lost respect for the PRI."

Not to be easily defeated, the PRI in Retorno fought back. In the 1980s and 1990s, local PRI sympathizers drew on the party's vast funds and patronage networks to rebuild their power and discredit the migrants and their allies. As economic crises hit Mexico in the 1980s, most of the migrants who had been activists during their seasonal stays in Retorno had to move on to the United States to make ends meet. When they left, their power in the village diffused. Nevertheless, the Coronado family was gone. These early PCPR actions also showed migrants that it was possible to change their hometown, even from afar.

When migrants moved on to California, they reestablished the PCPR in North County San Diego, as described in chapter 3. While these migrants considered the PCPR a hometown association, their focus was not charity for the village, so much as sustaining the struggles they had started in Sinaloa and Retorno. Throughout the 1990s most of Retorno's migrants circulated back and forth between the village and the United States. As they did, they began to link their ongoing battles in Mexico with the day-to-day abuses they faced as undocumented Mexican migrants in California. As Basilio put it, "When we got to the United States, many of the same people went who had already been in [the struggle in] the village, and we thought, 'Well, if we already did this in one place [Sinaloa] and another [Retorno], then we have to do it in the United States.'" Thus, the organization was born with a dual goal. On one hand, they confronted the mistreatment of migrant workers; on the other, they fought for change in their hometown.[25]

Cross-Border Cohesion

Unlike in Partida, the people living in Retorno never demanded that migrants participate. On the contrary, Retorno's landowners had long barred the poor from local politics, keeping the spoils of PRI patronage for themselves. When poor families emigrated, elites made new pretexts to block them from voting in local elections or taking on cargos, claiming, for instance, that those who lived abroad had not resided in the village for long enough or done adequate service to "earn" leadership posts. As the PRI revived in Retorno in the late 1980s, its representatives insisted that unless people had lived consistently in the village, they could not vote, let alone hold local leadership posts.[26] In this case local leaders were more concerned about migrants' incursion than the possibility of abandonment.

In contrast to migrants from Partida, meanwhile, most of those from Retorno sustained close relationships in their village. By the time Marcelo Sánchez married his wife, Teresa Estrada, in 1982, for instance, he had already made his first few trips to Vista. While Teresa stayed in Retorno, Marcelo came and went more than a dozen times, through the birth of their daughter in 1986 and son in 1989. Eventually, in 1996, Marcelo raised enough money to bring his wife and children across through the desert, all of them undocumented. Yet he never stopped dreaming of going home. When I met Marcelo, he had been living in Vista (on and off) for more than thirty years. Still, he talked incessantly of his house in Retorno. He had spent years building his dream home on the eastern side of the village, a two-story cement place that towered above the old adobe buildings nearby. Each year he would add a window or wall.

In the 1980s and 1990s, like Marcelo, most men who went to the United States still had families in the village, and almost all of them planned to go back. Even in the first decade of the 2000s, as border enforcement made it harder to move back and forth, both men and women continued to hope for return (as detailed in chapter 2). They sustained close connections, with 87 percent of U.S.-based respondents, for instance, making at least one call to the village per month. For them Retorno was not just a backup plan like among migrants in Los Angeles; it was a vision for the future.

Therefore, even though Retorno excluded migrants from politics, more than two-thirds of them participated in the PCPR. In 2011, for instance, 68 percent of those surveyed attended the HTA's annual fiesta for Retorno's patron saint, and 73 percent participated in committees involved in organizing that festival or other activities for the HTA. In the same year 30 percent contributed money to public projects back home—a rate that had likely been even higher in years past, before migrants began fighting among themselves (as described in chapter 5). In addition, like the OIP in Los Angeles, several different groups of migrants from Retorno applied to the Mexican government's 3x1 Program, to request resources that would help build up the village for their imagined return. In short, just as migrants in Los Angeles tried to separate from their hometown, those in North County San Diego reinforced their cross-border ties.

The FIOB and the Link to Mexican Politics

Migrants' mobilization in North County San Diego also helped them forge an alliance with the rising Mexican opposition party, the PRD. In 1988 Cuauhtémoc Cárdenas emerged as the first Mexican presidential candidate to oppose the rule of the PRI. During his campaign Cárdenas traveled to California to meet with several migrant groups, including the PCPR. While Mexican political parties had historically neglected emigrants, Cárdenas had heard of the Mixtecs' marches in California, and he saw that they could be a long-distance political force. Domingo García, who helped organize the visit, remembered the migrants' sense of awe. He recalled, "For us, [Cárdenas] was like the icon, the most important leader of the Left. . . . And his proposals convinced us. So at that time with Cuauhtémoc, we organized meetings so he could present in San Jose and San Diego, and those of us in San Diego [County] got together and we went. And that made this [U.S.-side advocacy] into a movement that was now politicized [via Mexico]." Not only did the PCPR (and later the FIOB) connect to the PRD, they also began to see the weight of their voices in Mexico.

Although Cárdenas lost the 1988 elections, he roused emigrant workers in the United States to decry Mexican government neglect, call for absentee ballots, and advocate for democracy in Mexico. In the early 1990s, as described in chapter 3, the PCPR joined together with other migrant hometown associations in California to form a coalition they called the Oaxacan Indigenous Binational Front (FIOB). Ultimately, the FIOB took the place of the PCPR, as migrants who had formed Retorno's HTA participated in the coalition as well as in a village-specific branch of the FIOB. Building on their history of leftist and labor activism, FIOB members embraced an anticolonial narrative and challenged the mistreatment of migrants in the United States. At the same time, they also advocated for greater party competition in Mexico, punishment for PRI corruption, and the redistribution of state resources, especially to indigenous pueblos. Through the FIOB migrants strengthened their alliances and their influence in Mexico.

Perhaps surprisingly, the FIOB's mobilization also gave migrants leverage with the PRI. The Cárdenas campaign revealed that to sustain PRI power—particularly in long-term strongholds like Oaxaca—the party needed migrants' support. Between 1988 and 2000, all three PRI governors of Oaxaca visited Oaxacan migrants in California. At each meeting with the PRI leaders, FIOB members staged protests. The first was Gov. Heladio Ramírez. When Ramírez booked his visit, Basilio joked, "Maybe he was ignoring the fact that we [in the FIOB] were a radical movement." The migrants reproached Ramírez, shouting at him and addressing him in the *tu* (informal "you") form to show disrespect. Surprisingly, the governor did not respond with the usual repression in migrants' hometowns. Instead, one FIOB leader remembered,

> He listened carefully, did not disrespect [the migrants], and was tolerant as he should be. He did not even return to Oaxaca to initiate a repression against his opponents. . . . [He] showed tolerance and listened carefully to all the complaints. Although in Oaxaca he governed with an iron hand against indigenous farmworker, popular, and union organizations, he never made up lies against migrant organizations, and particularly the FIOB.[27]

The competition between the PRD and the PRI showed migrants their power in relation to Mexican politics. In turn, these early experiences stimulated a wave of HTA activity and emigrant engagement by people from all over Mexico, including the FIOB.

In 1993, when the next PRI governor visited California, the FIOB made a list of demands. It called for the state of Oaxaca to (1) intervene in land disputes between Mixtec communities, (2) end police and customs extortion in border cities, (3) prevent the theft of money remitted from California to Oaxaca, (4) promote effective community-development projects in the Mixteca, (5) provide legal assistance to Mixtecs accused of crimes and unjustly imprisoned in the United States, and (6) intervene with the U.S. government to stop human-rights abuses, including killings of Mixtec migrants by the U.S. Border Patrol.[28] The governor responded by extending further support to migrants, creating new programs to advocate for their interests in the United States, and helping them channel dollars back home.

As a result, just as migrants began feeling ever more alienated from the United States, they gained a sense of efficacy toward Mexico. While U.S. politicians grew more hostile, ignoring migrants' protests, Mexican politicians responded to emigrant advocacy. These Mexican officials not only promised to help the migrants make change back home but also offered support with the problems they faced in the United States.

Though migrants from Retorno earned too little to contribute very much to their hometown, the FIOB brought media attention, funding, and thus economic influence in the village. After the visits from Cárdenas and the Oaxacan governors, U.S.-based foundations and immigrant-advocacy groups began supporting the FIOB. In the 1990s and early 2000s, the organization won grants from the Welfare Foundation, the MacArthur Foundation, the Ford Foundation, the Vanguard Foundation, the Rockefeller Foundation, the Inter-American Foundation, the National Endowment for Democracy, and the California Endowment, among others. These grants enabled the FIOB to launch new community-development programs in Oaxacan hometowns, including Retorno, promoting human, labor, and women's rights.

Mexican institutions reached out to the migrants as well. By 2000 Mexico's National Indigenous Institute, National Program of Solidarity with farmworkers, and the Office of the Governor of Oaxaca had forged formal ties with Oaxacan migrants in California. While migrants were once Retorno's excluded poor, and continued to be underpaid in the United States, their organizing gave them new access to resources and leverage over their hometown government. In 1995, as I discuss in chapter 5, migrants from Retorno used these ties to overthrow the local PRI elites, this time for good.

Migrants' influence in Mexico made their homeland seem dynamic. Although arbitrary policing eventually silenced migrants' protests in the United States, participating in Mexican politics reinvigorated their advocacy. As the FIOB garnered widespread public attention, its members felt inspired to push for Mexican democratization. Over time many of them withdrew from U.S. advocacy and concentrated on changing their homeland instead. Despite Retorno's history of exclusion, migrants' new alliances gave them hope that they might change Mexico from the United States. Rather than echoing U.S. ideas, their movement remitted resistance.

How Men Came to Champion Women's Inclusion

When the FIOB was founded, almost 90 percent of its members (and migrants from Retorno in general) were men. Women rarely came to meetings in North County San Diego, for fear of their husbands or of getting stopped by the police. In Retorno, as in Partida, women still had no voice or vote. In the late 1990s that changed. Migrants wanted to return, especially men, but they needed support in the village. Women were now the demographic majority in Retorno and key nodes in split families. Many had been migrants themselves, having returned from northern Mexico or the United States. Therefore, in the late 1990s the FIOB began urging women in Retorno to join their fight for rights and resources from the Mexican state.

Male migrants needed these women to wage their long-distance struggle on the ground. So people like Domingo and Basilio began reaching out to women, brokering ties between the housewives in the village and their husbands and brothers in North County San Diego. In particular, the FIOB members invited women in Retorno to attend protests and meetings and, for the first time ever, to vote. They even began providing training in women's rights. Why would such men—the very people who abandoned, threatened, or beat their wives—promote such a radical change in women's participation?[29] Domingo explained,

> We wanted women to come [to the village assembly] because it was necessary. Look, we had been struggling *[luchando]*. . . . So we started to incorporate the women. I remember that the first women leaders there in the pueblo were Alma, Adelina, Irma, and another woman, Chavela, [with] her husband in the United States. There are several, but—we thought that women were the other force, the other half of our power. Even more because they are the ones who are there. They are the ones who see [what's going on]. . . . So we started to incorporate them and work on questions of their training, human rights, women's rights, and productive projects.

Migrants like Domingo may have observed new gender practices in California. But gender equity was not simply a cultural idea they adopted in the United States and then shipped back home. Indeed, some of these very same men reinforced gender inequities while they lived in North County San Diego. Rather, activists like Domingo encouraged women's involvement primarily because they recognized that women could help strengthen the FIOB in Mexico. To make long-distance mobilization effective, men and women had to change gender relations and struggle together. The FIOB gave them new ground to do so.

Though women had their own motivations to mobilize (see chapter 5), men like Domingo encouraged them. Alma Sandoval, for one, had stayed out of politics her whole life. She feared that if she spoke up, her husband would beat her. Yet when Domingo organized Retorno's first road blockade, he invited Alma and several other women to bring coffee and tortillas to the people staging the protest. In Retorno it was common for women to contribute food to community affairs, so the favor didn't seem out of the ordinary. Once the women arrived, however, Domingo asked them to stay. A few months later Retorno held its tri-annual assembly to appoint new village leaders. To Alma's shock, the men invited her to the meeting. "How," she shot back, "if they don't accept us women?" But Domingo did not waver. He told her, "They are going to accept you. I already talked with the president."

The process was far from simple. As Alma and other women leaders began attending marches and knocking on doors, men in Retorno screamed in their faces and denounced them as streetwalkers and whores. Yet the more support Domingo mobilized—financial and moral—the more courage Alma gained. She explained, "Domingo got us [women] involved. He said the government was sending resources for women, and he brought people to train us, about the law, about the government, about human rights. We didn't even know that we could complain about our husbands' abuse. Rather, they [male migrant activists] would go and denounce our husbands for us." In later years men from the FIOB solicited "women's empowerment" programs from the Mexican government to train women in Retorno to defend their rights and mobilize politically. Such experiences helped women act on their own agendas for change.

Male migrants also pushed men in the village to let their wives participate. As with Alma, for instance, Domingo encouraged Adelina Juárez to attend political meetings. At four foot ten, and with experience in the strikes in Culiacán, Adelina was a firebrand. Domingo quickly began to see her as crucial to the FIOB's strength in Retorno. But when Adelina's husband realized what she was up to, he got mad. Domingo intervened, helping convince Adelina's husband to accept her new civic role. She described,

> He started to get jealous, my husband, saying that he didn't want me to go [to assemblies]. I told him, "Ay, well, if you don't want it, then I won't go anymore. I am not going to be fighting about this. If you don't want it, well, then I won't go." . . . But then [Domingo] said to him, "Who do you want to do it? They need—the people need [state] support, but there is no one to stand in front other than Adelina, and I see that she is sharp."

Once a fellow man encouraged Adelina's husband, highlighting their shared political cause, he agreed. Even though some men hesitated to let their wives participate, their class-based struggles and desires for state funding spurred them to change old gendered patterns. As I discuss in chapter 5, women's involvement in the FIOB made gender relationships more fluid in Retorno, inverting the assumption that migrant women's empowerment happens primarily in the United States.

The Breakdown of Transnational Ties

Though members of the PCPR and FIOB forged extraordinary cross-border alliances, they also faced hurdles and counterattacks. Even though the state-level PRI publicly honored the FIOB's demands, it furtively planted wedges between key FIOB leaders. In 2002, for instance, as I describe in chapter 5, the PRI governor of Oaxaca alleged that FIOB figureheads Domingo García and Luis Pérez, both from Retorno, had embezzled donations to the organization. A series of media stories erupted, marking the FIOB corrupt. In turn, Domingo and Luis split into separate factions, and their supporters were wracked by internal infighting. Uncertain what to make of the chaos, migrants also began to sour against the organization, dismissing its leaders as self-oriented liars. During my fieldwork in Vista, they often talked of the FIOB with cynicism and distrust, admitting that though they once sympathized, transnational organizing was hard. Some, like Marcelo, said that while they were still motivated to help their village, they felt they did not have the education or means to work at the state level. Others said that in the context of recession, they needed to dedicate their time to their jobs.[30]

Cross-border collaboration also grew harder when migrants stopped circulating. Though migrants still tried to support the village—through both the FIOB and a smattering of smaller-scale efforts—many complained that their counterparts in Retorno were disorganized and unresponsive to their efforts. During my fieldwork, for instance, a group of migrants sympathetic to the FIOB and PRD sent funds and technical staff to Retorno to design an irrigation project. Yet the village government was run by a newly revived PRI. These PRI leaders disregarded the migrants' engineers and hired their own team instead, duplicating the project so they could take credit for themselves.[31] When I met with the migrant group, they lamented the conflict. It had become too *pesado* (burdensome), they said, to mobilize people politically. While some, like Marcelo and Basilio, formed new groups to promote Mixtec culture in California, these organizations lost the binational, anticolonial mission that had first driven the FIOB. Though migrants remained alienated in the United States, their cross-border cohesion fizzled, leaving it unclear where dissent would land.

For Mexican migrants from Retorno and beyond, the period from the mid-1990s to the early 2000s had been a heyday of transnational advocacy. However, the PRD was repeatedly defeated between 1988 and 2012, disheartening many of its long-term sympathizers. Meanwhile, state and paramilitary repression stifled resistance movements like the Zapatistas on the ground, sapping some of the energy that had inspired the FIOB in the first place. At the same time, intensified U.S. enforcement made migrants nervous to be too visible. Over time their efforts on behalf of the PRD waned. While groups like the FIOB (and Zapatistas) persist as of this writing, they had fewer adherents and less public prominence.

POLITICIZING MIGRANTS' GLOBAL ENGAGEMENT

Migrants from Partida to Los Angeles and Retorno to North County San Diego illustrate the ways transnational practices are political. Migrants can send money and U.S. ideas to their hometowns, as scholars have shown. But they can also remit dissent. Divergent conditions in the United States—and the different legacies migrants bring from their hometowns— provoke distinct relationships to the homeland, some polarized and other solidary. Migrants' lived experiences of "illegality" influence which kind of transnationalism they adopt. Migrants pathways also shape whether or not they engage with political shifts occurring in their country of birth, such as the rise of the PRD.

The case of Los Angeles illustrates how a strategy of U.S. belonging can fuel transnational polarization. As migrants from Partida tried to earn U.S. inclusion, most abandoned their village. Others fought to dismantle Partida's communalism from afar. When migrants did support Partida, they took a charitable and even paternalistic approach, highlighting their own progress and framing their village as "behind." Partida's HTA also stayed out of Mexican politics, claiming to be politically neutral. Yet this "progress" narrative was not just an indicator that migrants felt they had found a better life. The "modernization" framework was also political, symbolically rein-forcing immigrants' efforts to earn inclusion in the United States.

In contrast, migrants in North County show how arbitrary control— and migrants' consequent strategy of withdrawal—can drive cross-border solidarity. Alienated from the United States and divided from their fami-lies, migrants from Retorno identified with those back home. They also hoped to return. Though they initially fought for rights in the United States *and* Mexico, they were more effective in mobilizing responses from the sending side. Even as migrants faced increasing repression in California, party competition made them darlings of the PRD—and later the PRI. Therefore, though most did not return in person, they shifted their attention back home to Mexico. As I explain in chapter 5, these cross-border connections helped them translate disillusionment with the United States into demands for resources and representation from Mexico.

This chapter also reveals how migrants' transnationalism intertwines with women's empowerment. In both cases migrants used new gender arrangements (particularly women's involvement in HTAs) to reinforce their political agendas. In Los Angeles women took on leadership roles in the OIP to display their newfound influence, insisting that their home-town remained stuck in a patriarchal past. Yet women's empowerment was not always situated in the United States. Indeed, migrants in North County San Diego reversed common assumptions about the mechanisms of women's liberation. First, defying expectations, men actively helped draw women into new political roles. Even though men in San Diego County often dominated women at home, the goal of hometown change inspired them to help organize women from afar. Second, women took new roles not in the United States but in their once-patriarchal village. Because families were divided, women became critical players on the sending side. As women like Alma and Adelina got involved in political advocacy, they converted Retorno into a more dynamic site of gender change than North County San Diego.

Migrants' transnationalism also reflected the interplay between the legacies they brought with them and the modes of control they faced in the United States. The histories and ongoing structures of their hometowns, including their (in)equity, their patterns of family separation, and migrants' reasons to leave, informed their feelings toward Mexico. For instance, Partida's collective, autonomous history kept its migrants skeptical of political parties. Meanwhile, Retorno's migrants' prior activism and ongoing war against the PRI helped connect them to broader networks like the FIOB and PRD. But their paths also shifted, thanks to conditions in the United States.

Ironically, each community's transnational actions may have helped diffuse their dissent against U.S. exclusion. In both Los Angeles and North County San Diego, migrants critical of the United States tended to return to Mexico (or plan to return). In Los Angeles, migrants' idea that California represented "modernization" reinforced their investment in the United States. To the extent that migrants abandoned their hometown, they gave up the option to return. Thus, they increased the stakes of earning inclusion in California. Meanwhile, in North County San Diego, migrants' investment in Mexico may have further encouraged them to hold out for a promised return. Migration has long been thought of as a safety valve for the sending country, allowing dissident factions to vote with their feet. But on the receiving end, migrants may also let off steam through transnational ties.

At the same time, viewing politics binationally is promising. As the case of the FIOB shows, migrants who seem withdrawn in the United States may in fact be waging fights across borders. They may also leverage their ties in Mexico to put pressure on an unresponsive United States. Still, a full understanding of transnational politics requires looking beyond the actions of migrants. As I show in chapter 5, returnees and nonmigrants respond to migration as well, shaping their stances toward Mexico and transforming the very places migration began.

5 Pathways to Hometown Change

In 2004 the citizens in Partida held a meeting. Gathering all day at the village hall, they lamented the apathy and "egotism" of their counterparts in Los Angeles. Many argued that emigrants were abandoning the commune, while those at home were "killing themselves" to sustain the pueblo. They questioned migrants' "Americanized" notions of dismantling community-service requirements or giving women the right to vote. They decided it was time to formalize their stance. Over the next few years, they codified their communal structure and made demands of those who had left. In the resulting statute, they proclaimed,

> The community of Partida agrees to continue enjoying its lands and natural resources in a communal manner, that being the closest to our way of life and form of community organization . . . [including] the participation of all community members [as well as migrants] to maintain the core institutions of the community, including tequio [communal labor], the cargo system [civic posts], *cooperaciones* [monetary contributions], the fiestas, the assembly, the way of life, and the heritage of the community.

The hometown highlighted that emigrants were *comuneros* (members). If migrants did not contribute their time and money, villagers would reclaim the land and houses they still had in the village, dump their belongings just outside of town, and throw the migrants in jail should they try to return.

Partida's statute was not just an internecine quarrel between migrants and those "left behind." It was also a shield against state attacks on communal landholding and political participation. Starting in the 1990s the Mexican federal and Oaxacan state government started pressing indigenous villages to dismantle Usos y Costumbres, open up to political parties (which were banned under the indigenous system), and turn over common resources to individual property and corporate control. State agents also argued that indigenous self-government should be dismantled, to give women equal rights. In Partida, however, many people dismissed women's participation in politics as an external intervention. They used their community statute to defy these outside demands, legally and symbolically. By codifying their collective, male-run structure, villagers positioned themselves against the individualistic ideas of "modernization" promoted by both migrants and the homeland government.

Residents of Retorno also faced radical changes driven by both migrants and the Mexican state, but they responded differently. Instead of rejecting political parties, they aligned themselves with the left-wing PRD. They also collaborated with their long-distance counterparts, particularly through the Frente Indígena Oaxaqueño Binacional (FIOB; Oaxacan Indigenous Binational Front). With the help of these allies, villagers challenged the longtime corruption of the local- and state-level PRI. They demanded resources, insisting that Oaxaca's government deliver roads, irrigation, health services, and productive projects. They also took advantage of the emerging mandate for "women's empowerment" to garner more state support. In the process women in Retorno began to vote and take on political posts for the first time in history. Thus, they staked their claim to resources and representation.

Why did people in Partida shore up their communal structure and reject state intervention, while those in Retorno demanded inclusion in local and state democracy? This chapter traces how each hometown's experiences of emigration shaped its approach to Mexican politics. Rather than focus on migrants' long-distance impacts, as many scholars have done, I look at how those on the sending side reacted to their own or others' histories of migration.

HOW HOMETOWNS FACE MIGRANT GLOBALIZATION

For those in Mexico, emigration was a political spark plug: a catalyst for change. In the 1990s and the first decade of the 2000s, people of Partida and Retorno faced both "illegality" in the United States and vast political shifts on the Mexican side. For one, Mexico began to democratize. Though the PRI had ruled the country for seventy years, opposition parties including the Partido de la Revolución Democrática (PRD; Party of the Democratic Revolution) and the Partido Acción Nacional (PAN; National Action Party) began to challenge its clientelistic control. Along with advocacy organizations of various stripes, these parties put pressure on the PRI and exposed its corruption. During this period, Mexico also privatized state resources and rolled back welfare support. The federal government then reformed the constitution to enable the sale of communal lands. Finally, Mexico decentralized, shifting responsibility for "development" to the municipal level.

Though indigenous villages were historically isolated from Mexican politics, democratization and decentralization made them battlegrounds for political control. In 1995 Oaxaca's PRI legalized the long-standing indigenous system of Usos y Costumbres, granting 418 of the state's 570 municipalities the right to self-govern.[1] Nevertheless, the state also began pressuring indigenous people to dismantle their traditions of public service and independent self-government. In the late 1990s, for instance, the state began paying stipends for cargos, undermining the tradition of unpaid public service. At the same time, the PRI also created new funds for sanitation, reforestation, agriculture, education, household infrastructure, and training in entrepreneurship, in hopes of holding the rural vote.[2] To get such funds villagers needed the signature of the municipal president. Thus, village authorities came to control both new salaries and state development funds. If migrants and their allies took over a village, they would gain access to these funds and put wind in the sails of the PRD opposition. Despite the ostensible political independence of indigenous pueblos, many faced clashes over local control. Municipal governments were now a strategic arena in which to challenge the PRI.

In the 1980s Mexico also started integrating women into state-led development.[3] By the 1990s women's empowerment was a central axis in rural state programs. In particular, the Oportunidades program, started in 1998 under the name Progresa, granted cash transfers to women across Mexico, on the condition that they participate in health workshops and send their children to school.[4] Since indigenous villages often excluded women, "women's rights" also gave the state an excuse to dismantle indigenous control. Together these changes laid the terrain on which hometowns remade their Mexican citizenship, in dialogue with the criminalization of their counterparts in the United States.

But how did migration play into these shifts? Traditionally, scholars argued that migration was a political "safety valve," allowing people who might otherwise protest to leave the homeland instead. Emigration thus freed the sending state from accountability to migrant-sending villages, consigning them to political irrelevance.[5] Indeed, some scholars show that migrant-sending villages tend to see less political participation than non-migrant towns.[6] Others argue that as people leave and get exposed to individualism and class stratification, cohesive communities disintegrate.[7] In such formulations communal governance figures as an inadequate and antiquated form of resistance, eroded by capitalist globalization.[8]

Increasingly, social scientists have grown interested in how migrants' remittances and "voice after exit" might have the opposite effect, fueling hometown growth or democratization.[9] These scholars argue that migrants send back not only remittances and cultural habits ("social remittances") but also "political remittances": attitudes and alliances that can either help democratize their hometowns or exacerbate instability.[10] Yet it remains unclear why migrant involvement encourages democracy, development, and gender equity in some hometowns, while making others less secure.[11] Many scholars conclude that emigration helps sending communities if migrants (1) make money in the United States, (2) are exposed to "egalitarian" U.S. norms, and (3) remit the "right" productive investments, democratic ideals, and social practices (like gender equity).[12] Such frameworks imply that economic development, democratic participation, and women's empowerment "trickle down" from Global North to Global South. They also make such prospects appear to rely on migrants' economic and cultural integration, depoliticizing the interplay between sending and receiving sides. In turn, more recent studies have highlighted the mediating effect of homeland contexts, revealing that successful cooperation between migrants and hometowns also hinges on sending state programs, homeland democracy, and interstate relationships.[13] Still, studies of migration and development remain largely divorced from the realities of U.S. exclusion.

This chapter shows how people in the homeland adapt their political strategies in relation to their perceptions of migration, including negative images of the United States. As Mexico evolved, it suggests, Partida and Retorno each forged new forms of citizenship on the sending side. Yet they did so quite differently. Each community's political pathway—including its historical power dynamics, the mode of control its migrants faced in California, and the character of its migrants' transnationalism—provoked distinct reactions in Mexico.

For people in Partida both migration and state interventions threatened communal autonomy. Those in the hometown responded with what I refer to as *antiglobalization backlash*.[14] Most people remaining in the village had never been to the United States. They denounced emigrants for being selfish and abandoning the common good. They dug in their heels to protect collective governance and insist that migrants help out. They also rejected efforts at modernization by the Mexican state. Instead, they remade indigenous "tradition" as a political tool. Framing land privatization, corporate intervention, and party politics as threats to equity, they shored up their long-standing autonomy. Collectively, they blocked state "development" programs and refused to convert traditional cargos into paid public posts.

For people in Retorno, however, outreach by migrants and Mexican political parties presented an opportunity to transcend the village's long history of exclusion, fueling a fight for *alternative globalization*. Due to family separation and historical patterns of circulation, many people in Retorno had been migrants themselves or had family members in California. They shared migrants' disillusionment with the United States. Under the mantle of the FIOB, therefore, they sought a greater voice in Retorno and the state of Oaxaca. Locally, they continued their ongoing fight against the village and state-level PRI. They dismantled traditions that had forced indigenous people to do unpaid labor and blocked them from local leadership. They won migrants and women political rights. Inspired by migrants, they also joined other hometowns and the PRD to pressure the state for support. Thus, they used their indigenous identity to build solidarity with other villages. By exercising political voice, they claimed new rights to belong on the Mexican side.

Women's empowerment weighed critically on both pueblos' politics, representing the peril or promise of outside ties. In Partida antiglobalization backlash was also patriarchal: men spurned women's rights as a form of outside meddling. They argued that Western notions of gender equality clashed with indigenous traditions of complementarity (in which women and men played reciprocal, mutually supportive roles).[15] Ultimately, however, Partida relied on migrant women's support, so it had to make accommodations. In Retorno, meanwhile, women became important leaders in the battle for democratization. Due to family separation, women were the majority in the village, so organizers realized they needed women to stage successful marches—as well as to garner resources targeted at women's empowerment. Thus, the people of Retorno embraced what I call *gendered jujitsu* (a martial art where a small adversary uses an opponent's force to set the opponent off balance), using state funds to expand their own movement.

The contrast reveals that just as transnationalism is political, hometown politics are transnational. Not only do migrants impact their villages from afar, but the people in migrant hometowns also react to migration, reconstructing the meanings of indigeneity, gender, and Mexican citizenship. Ethnicity is central to this process, but it plays out in different ways. Usos y Costumbres, for instance, is not a stable indigenous tradition but instead a dynamic political tool that changes depending on hometowns' goals. For Partida, indigeneity represented autonomy; for Retorno, ethnic connection. In Retorno, democracy also required abandoning the old, corrupted version of Usos y Costumbres altogether. Thus, politics were processual, altering long-standing structures as villagers navigated both U.S. exclusion and evolving homeland dynamics.

RESISTING GLOBALIZATION IN PARTIDA

The first time I visited Partida, landslides tore at the mountains of Oaxaca's Sierra Norte, spilling over the road and stripping the skin off the dense forest slopes. By the time I tumbled out in front of Partida's bright-blue town hall, public loudspeakers were calling the *comuneros* out to slosh mud and rocks off the street (see figure 5). Men emerged one by one from their homes to do tequio, a duty they still traded for membership in the village and access to its communal land. When I met with the village leaders, they were also suspicious of me. Though migrants from Partida had been going to California for decades, they stiffened when I mentioned the United States. They asked whether, like those who had left, I would push them to change their values. Migration had incited Partida to defend its communal ways. Villagers used their long-standing participatory structure to restrict the meddling of migrants, political parties, corporations, and even wayward graduate students from the United States.

Figure 5. Villagers doing communal labor on the main street of Partida. Photo by the author.

Defending the Commune

Leonel Vega and his wife, Nadia Parra, illustrated the local penchant for self-protection. One long, cold evening I sat with the couple, eating yellow mole over their flowered, plastic tablecloth. Leonel had worked in Los Angeles before coming back to Partida to marry Nadia in 2001. These days, however, he was breaking his back to manage Partida's water infrastructure *and* its system of public labor—one of the pueblo's more rigorous civic jobs. Migrants did not appreciate this hard work, he complained. Across from Leonel's small cement home, his brother-in-law Bernardo Cruz, who lived in Los Angeles, had built a gleaming, three-story house. Migrants like Bernardo—those with papers anyway—would come back to Partida to relax or even rent out their homes for pay. Looking across at the empty dwelling, Leonel was angry:

> I'm working so that they can have running water, so that the roads are well maintained, and they're profiting from that. . . . [In the communal system] we have obligations, and we have rights. . . . When you do tequios, you see all the work that needs to be done. Being the person who manages the tequios, for instance, is a huge amount of work, because you're responsible for the water system, and if that breaks you have to go in the middle of the night and fix it . . . or right now that we have to [do tequios to] plant all these trees . . . and when you're there [in the United States], you don't even know what's going on.

As more people left, cargos from road maintenance to village secretary fell heavily on those who remained. People who stayed in Partida, Leonel felt, had been saddled with unfair burdens.

Just the day before Leonel and several dozen men had marched out to the home of a migrant who failed to pay his "tax." In the late 1980s, as described in chapter 4, villagers decided that if emigrants wanted land or rights in Partida, they would have to contribute a hundred dollars per year and participate in the community's HTA in Los Angeles. Though this man kept his (usufruct) land in Partida, he never remitted the requisite hundred dollars. The pueblo decided it was time. Machetes in hand, they fenced off his property for return to the collective holding. Other times, the *comuneros* cut off electricity, water, or sewage to the homes of "reluctant" migrants (those who failed to contribute to the village), even if family members still lived in the house. If migrants tried to visit without having paid, they locked them in cells below the town hall. They explained to the wayward, "Only the people who have worked and contributed have rights, but you don't contribute. You don't help, and you [migrants] just come to help yourselves to what's already here." If migrants did not support the community, the village revoked their membership.

Residents like Leonel endorsed such sanctions because they resented their migrant counterparts. Only 35 percent of men and 3 percent of women in Partida had ever been to the United States. I heard of just one married couple separated across borders. So instead of feeling tied to migrants, most people felt betrayed—including returnees like Leonel. Parents would sob into the phone, begging their children not to leave or accusing them, "Why did you abandon me?" Some even cursed their migrant sons and daughters, refusing to hear their names. The resentment was palpable in families like Ernesto Galindo's. Ernesto grew up on a three-thousand-square-foot plot, where he now lived with his wife and seven children in a one-room adobe hut, with two large beds and an open fire. Just feet away his brother who lived in Los Angeles had built a three-story home, sealed with a padlock. Every time Ernesto looked at the lock, his eyes filled with rage. Though some migrants sent money to Partida through their HTA, those at home felt they never quite did enough.

Tomás Ríos, one of Partida's senior statesmen, explained why they felt so mad. Once a teacher, Tomás had worked in Los Angeles in the mid-1990s, but he returned disillusioned with the individualism and isolation of U.S. life. Now in his midfifties, Tomás lived with his wife and their teenage children and ran an embroidery shop at the top of Partida's hill. In his spare time Tomás played guitar at local parties and tried to document and bring back the Zapotec language. He was skeptical of me when I first arrived, wondering why on earth I was asking so many questions. He would look at me pensively from under his thick eyebrows, as his foot click-clacked on a sewing machine. Gazing through his window over the clouds, he told me, "Those of us who are always here have the idea that the more we help one another the more we can advance. But when someone comes back from the city they think differently. . . . People sometimes get very apathetic when they migrate. They forget. They leave and they don't send money; they don't participate. . . . It pains us that they don't want to contribute." Not only had migrants shirked their responsibilities, Tomás felt, but when they did turn back it had been to "fix" Partida. The people at home, he added, were fighting for a counterweight to these impositions. They valued the feeling of community that came from serving the common good. Doing public service gave them strength, he added, teaching them to care about the village as a whole.

Such resentment was both material and moral. While one might expect migrants' economic success to appeal to other villagers, emigrants threatened Partida's values of service and equity. Tomás's views were widely shared. Almost daily, while I hung out at the taco stand in Partida's town square, I heard villagers lament the "egotism" of migrants. As Naila Marcos, a fiery young health promoter in her midthirties, complained,

> [Migrants] get used to those comforts, and they don't want to come back here anymore. They start to think they come from Los Angeles, and they come to show off and to say how pretty Los Angeles is. . . . Instead of thinking about the common good, about our children, people start to think about why that guy has money and not me. Then they lose the ideology and the habit of mutual aid. . . . Those people start thinking they can have everything easy, and they come back with very hard hearts.

Like Naila, many villagers disliked migrants' individualism. In particular, returned men like Tomás were often especially adamant, having given up the United States and come back to the village in search of a collective alternative.

Partida's rules had key implications for those who returned. If a migrant was deported or chose to come back for good, he had to petition the pueblo to start at the bottom of the local public-service ladder. For instance, Mario Vargas lived in Los Angeles for almost twenty years. In 2009 he was deported for drug use. He had nowhere to go but Partida. When he returned, he described, "I had to start from the bottom. To go to the village leaders and say, 'This is what happened.' I had to promise to stop drinking and using drugs. And I had to do lots of cargos. I have already been a guard at the town hall, and now I have to be a guard at the church— lots of cargos." For Mario the obligations actually fostered self-esteem. Staffing his new hot-dog stand in Partida, he told me, "Take a picture of me! I want my boys [in Los Angeles] to see that I'm working. I'm not like I was there."

The village also used community service to reindoctrinate returned migrants to communal life. Abel Espinoza, a former village president, described one memorable incident. In 1999 and 2000 a set of deportees returned to Partida and began drinking, beating people up, and vandalizing village property, "throwing stones at an old man or any person who might be passing by." In a neighboring town the village leaders put these *cholos* (gangsters) in jail, throwing them out on the earliest bus in the morning. In Partida, Abel boasted, the assembly assigned community service *and* jail:

> There was a time when there were a lot of drunk young men [back from the United States], and the pueblo had to put them in jail. We said, "If you don't have work to do we have some for you here," and we gave them a few days of tequio as punishment. And fines too. From tequio to jail, then back to tequio. Tequio is a way to straighten the young people out *[enderezarlos]* when they are loitering around.

Later, these returnees complained to the state government that Partida was abusing their human rights. In answer, the village leaders told the police, "Here, we don't live by your laws. We are a village of Usos y Costumbres, and here we make our own laws." By asserting collective practices, the people of Partida disciplined wayward returnees. They also asserted their independence.

Autonomy from the State

Insisting that migrants support the commune gave Partida tools to reinforce its autonomy from Mexican government and political party interference. Initially, Partida developed its community statute to manage emigrants. But the law also helped the village, for instance, to protect its communal land. Partida's communal land included resources—such as wood—that were attractive to corporations. In the 1970s and 1980s several nearby villages lost their communal land because paper companies, and in particular a corporation named Maderas de Oaxaca (Oaxacan Wood), bought out individual landholders, promising to "help" the sellers earn money.[16]

Mexico's federal and state governments greased the wheels of such corporate takeovers by pressing villages to privatize land. Starting in 1992 Mexican president Carlos Salinas de Gortari revised article 27 of the Constitution to create loopholes that enabled communal land like Partida's to be converted to private holdings.[17] Salinas also created a program called the Program to Certify Communal Lands, which sent bureaucrats to rural villages several times a month to induce people to convert their land into smallholdings. While villagers were not legally required to privatize, representatives from the *procuraduría agraria* (attorney general of agriculture) visited villagers and invited them to meetings. These agents also mapped and measured villagers' parcels, offered them "certificates of rights," talked about smallholdings, and provided fencing to mark off individual territory.[18] They also offered incentives and spoke as if land were already private. Often, such agents told villagers that the state's *free* program to measure and certify land was about to end. If the pueblo changed their minds later, the visitors threatened, they would no longer get money for reforestation, and they might have to pay for titles to land. Ignacio Baca, a lawyer for an indigenous-advocacy organization based in Oaxaca City, became involved with people in Partida as they confronted their issues with migrants. As he did, he also helped them fight back against such actions by the state. He reflected, "It's a daily pressure, every week, every two weeks, there is the bureaucrat telling them to join the [privatization program]."

By putting their communal status in writing, the people of Partida resisted this pressure. The village statute reinforced their traditional values: not only would everyone, including migrants, participate, but resources would also continue to be held collectively. After passing the statute, villagers defied privatization by actively demarcating *communal* land. Ignacio told me, "Now even the young people are really, really enthused. They have gone around the village on foot, marking off all the old land demarcation points, interviewing the elders . . . and they made their own map of all the [communal] lands." Once again, migrant returnees who had grown disillusioned with U.S. unfairness, such as Juan Serrano and Alejandro Campos, were especially enthusiastic. Such efforts helped protect Partida's valuable forests. Pablo Velasco, a village councilman, noted,

> There is wood [in Partida]. They [corporations] have not exploited the wood, and we have worked hard to conserve it. . . . No company has touched it. They have wanted to, but the pueblo is very bullheaded and they say no. Now, on the contrary, the young people want to reforest more. There are places where their grandparents planted corn in the mountains, and they want to put more trees there.

In the first decade of the 2000s Partida also banned felling trees and began to require members to help reforest whenever the government cut them down. So when the state cut trees to widen the road, the village leaders called for teqiuo (communal work) to plant new ones. Residents took pride that they had some of Oaxaca's only virgin forests, untouched by corporations.

Linking outside meddling to the degradation of communal life, people in Partida also rejected political parties and the state's "productive projects." Though political parties were technically illegal in Usos y Costumbres communities, they often became involved in local elections, especially as the PRI and the PRD vied for control. This competition fractured many rural communities, leading the state to cut off their funding until conflicts had been resolved. To avoid such a fate, Partida's assembly blocked political parties. When a state senate candidate for the PAN came to the village in 2010, for instance, residents heckled her and threw stones, yelling, "Who is this woman to come and tell us what to do in our pueblo?" When I asked why, Juan explained, "Because political parties come in— you're red [PRI], I'm yellow [PRD], and it's divide and conquer." Tomás extended his criticism of migrants to parties as well, telling me, "Political parties . . . are purely destructive criticism, not constructive. We should have politics but constructive, to unify people not to separate them. But we came to the conclusion [that parties] divide." In Tomás's reckoning indigenous pueblos' hopes lay in their own, grassroots control. Thus, people in Partida rejected affiliations like Retorno's alliances with the FIOB and the PRD.

Partida's protectionism also extended to the traditional system of cargos. Migrants had long insisted that instead of requiring people to serve, cargos ought to be paid. Then the state of Oaxaca also started offering such salaries. People in Partida, however, feared that if cargos were paid (instead of unpaid, as they had been), they would lose the moral value of reinforcing people's mutual obligations to the community. Refusing migrants' and the state's vision of modernization, hometown citizens voted to pool the money intended for stipends and use it for public works. To insist that public posts served the people, they also held civil servants accountable for every peso that came in from the state. One village president carped that in Partida, "They check your accounts; they check everything, and if something comes up they put the evidence before the group and charge you a fine, and if they're angry, then to jail."

Because people in Partida were so wary of outside influence, they rarely solicited resources beyond the standard municipal funds. While Retorno had dozens of state programs during my fieldwork, Partida had only one in 2010, for chicken coops, and none in 2011. Though microfinance institutions and small NGOs were ubiquitous in rural Oaxaca, respondents had never heard of such an organization entering Partida. Terrified of cultural degradation, the few funds they accepted tended to reinforce indigenous culture, such as a community museum, a village radio station, and a program to revive the Zapotec language. When funds were tied to outside impositions, the village refused.

Patriarchal Backlash

Men in Partida also rejected women's rights as part of the outside attack on communal traditions. Historically, indigenous men and women had practiced gender complementarity, playing reciprocal roles. Men took responsibility for public service, voting on behalf of their wives and daughters, while women attended to the family and home. Men argued that protecting women from the burden of village governance was a form of respect. Everardo Segura, a former village president, explained, "If us men don't want to participate [in civic posts], the women want to less. It's a burden. We can't name women to posts because they're our mothers. I would go [serve] on behalf of my daughters but not to take their rights from them."

Perhaps surprisingly to a Western eye, most women in Partida accepted this distribution of work. In surveys 55 percent said they preferred not to attend village assemblies. These all-day meetings were onerous: tiresome, boring, and a "lot of work," the women explained, on top of the chores they already had to do in the female domain. Tomás's wife, Victoria Maldonado, explained, "I don't go [to the assembly], because my husband goes [for our family]. No, we [women] don't go. That's the custom: the woman doesn't go. If she doesn't go, it's because it's our way that men go, not women. Us women participate only in women's things." Those who did attend assemblies were largely single mothers, who were required to join and would be fined if they failed to appear. As mentioned in prior chapters, women otherwise viewed cargos as an insult. Even when Partida nominated a woman as town president in 2012, as I describe later, the nominee started to cry, recognizing how much she would have to give up in order to run the village.[19]

When Partida was writing its community statute in 2004, Ignacio, the nonprofit lawyer, encouraged villagers to formally include women in their assembly, where all local voting took place. Yet women themselves refused. Ignacio recalled,

> There was a debate that lasted all day about whether or not women would participate in the assembly. Because if we were going to define cargos, the women should be there to define their cargos. So people talked and talked, and at the end [men] said, "Okay, let women join." . . . But the women said it was not the moment, that there was too much to do, and they couldn't have the whole family in the assembly. . . . Having gone through the whole morning, after lunch the women said, "No, we'd rather not return. We don't want this to be an obligation *or* a right to come to the assemblies, because coming the whole day—no, we'd prefer not to. Let it be optional."

The men eventually reasoned, "We have to respect women too; we have to give them their space." Thus, the pueblo decided that women would be exempt from public service. While men in Partida told me they allowed women to join assemblies, I never saw a woman attend. Given that many women (and men) left the village to escape male abuse in the household, migration may also have helped to sort people born in Partida, leading the most rebellious women to leave.

Whether or not women wanted to engage in local politics, their absence left them with little leverage to stop gendered violence. From the day I arrived in Partida, doctors, teachers, and other urban workers described the village as rife with domestic abuse. In the first few hours I spent in town, a teacher from the city professed in hushed tones that the gender situation there was "brutal" *(canijo)* and that men of Partida were some of the most abusive in the state. Despite her resentment of migrants, Naila, too, angrily shook the ruffled sleeves of her black shirt as she explained, "Maybe there's not as much abuse as before, but, still, if a man hits a woman, people will say it's the woman's fault. Or women themselves denounce her. . . . [Even] women say that if I have husband, I can't go out. . . . They say that if I'm walking around in the street I'm just a *cualqui-era* [slut]. *Está canijo aquí* [It's rough here]." Others told gruesome stories, such as one woman's tale of her sister beaten to death by *sillazos* (chair hits) or another's description of a sixteen-year-old girl "enslaved to her in-laws." Men, meanwhile, were known to gather at a local cantina called Nacho's Bar to swap stories of hitting their wives with the end of a hose. They joked, as one confessed to me privately, "You're not from La Partida unless you go to Nacho's Bar, and you beat your wife."

When women did push for greater political influence, men threatened, teased, or silenced them. Claudia Vega, the fierce mother who sent her seven daughters away from Partida to school, had been demanding a say in assemblies since the 1960s. She attended the meetings, often as the only woman present. Puttering in her courtyard one day, she railed, "Here they [women] are used to the idea that women don't have the right to go [to assemblies]. 'No!' I tell them. 'You have to see that the women go to the meeting, to participate, to know. Not from other people's mouths, who don't even talk or know anything.'" Yet when women like Claudia did go to meetings, men mocked and muffled them. Several women were afraid of the village assembly. It was embarrassing, they said. Noemí Torres, for instance, told me, "If we go to meetings, men are the ones who speak, and women are still afraid to speak. If a woman speaks up, they make fun of her." Lorena Padilla, a single mother, added, "I went to the assembly once, but they don't let you speak; they say what we say is worthless. We don't talk—because what's the point of talking?" In short, as Claudia put it, "We [women] have neither voice nor vote."

Women's influence in the Los Angeles HTA threatened men in Partida. Women questioned the pueblo's traditions of gender complementarity, and they denounced its widespread domestic abuse. As they raised money for the village, migrant women also worked to remit some of their own "liberation," demonstrating their power to men back home. Those men resisted. They called migrant women "streetwalkers" *(mujeres de la calle)*, "bitches" *(perras)*, or "loose" *(andalonas)* and said that when women migrated, they lost their honor and respect. Others added, "Over there [in the United States] men are no longer men." Otilio Santos—a former president of Partida—suggested that the women's takeover of the HTA left men in the pueblo especially vexed: "The men are afraid of women, afraid that at some point one of the women is going to take charge here [in the village]. . . . The men of Partida are really defeated, because they got a woman [as HTA president]. They say, 'How can it be that this damn old lady is telling us what to do?' They're waiting for her to make mistakes so they can take her down."

At the same time, the Oaxacan state had started using women's rights to subvert indigenous self-governance. Even though women won suffrage in Mexico in 1947, many indigenous villages, including Partida, continued to exclude them from voting and village posts. Generally, this practice was accepted as part of indigenous peoples' right to set their own electoral rules. In the late 1990s, however, the federal government and the state of Oaxaca began insisting on women's rights to political participation, property, and law enforcement. The state also used women's individual rights to question the legality of collective self-governance.[20] In 2007, when a Zapotec village near Partida blocked a woman named Eufrosina Cruz from running for community president, she appealed to the PRI and later to the president of Mexico, leading Mexico to impose a constitutional restraint on indigenous communities' rights to self-govern. In 2009 the Oaxacan electoral institute then mandated that indigenous women be allowed to vote in local elections and considered for municipal councils.[21] But men like Everardo, who had been president of Partida in 2008, argued that these outsiders were trying to square indigenous practices "with urban eyes." When the mandate for women's participation arrived in Partida, the village assembly ignored it.

State-led women's empowerment programs also proved sticking points between outside advocates and men in Partida. One of Oaxaca's key state services in the first decade of the 2000s (indeed, its third-largest source of income) was the conditional-cash-transfer program Oportunidades. Even though the program offered villagers cash, Partida refused it for years, due to its focus on women. The local doctor—a young woman from Oaxaca City sent to Partida for her internship—was especially incensed. One evening I sat with her in the clinic after close, chatting about how stubborn the men had been. She explained, "I have asked for permission to come speak to men in the assembly, to talk to them about domestic violence here, but they won't give it to me. The problem is they're very *machistas;* they're afraid of a woman who speaks up." The more the doctor encouraged women to resist domestic violence, she added, the more the men refused to listen or help her—even to help themselves. When the doctor went out of her way to get supplies for the village, such as dozens of much-needed wheelchairs, the men retaliated as well, refusing to approve her proposals and costing them critical support. To men in Partida, gender equality was a symbol of outside values, incongruent with collective life.

Coda: The Contradictions of Defying the "Outside"

Sometimes villagers' bullheadedness deprived them of important resources. Partida relied on migrants and the state for money. At certain moments, its leaders were so focused on refusing outside impositions that they put this support in jeopardy.

In particular, if the hometown was too stubborn, it risked alienating its migrants. Partida's HTA in Los Angeles played a key role in funneling money to the pueblo, by monitoring migrants' participation and collecting the "migrant tax." During my fieldwork in Los Angeles, I often saw HTA members knocking on doors and checking whether migrants had purchased their allotted tickets to upcoming fund-raisers. OIP leaders like Blanca held thirty years' worth of event tickets, meeting invitations, and other proof of contributions to the organization. If a wayward migrant returned to Partida, the local authorities phoned these HTA leaders to verify whether the person had lent them a hand. Guillermo Reyna, who lived in Los Angeles, argued that by punishing "reluctant" migrants and appropriating their property, "they [the hometown leaders] are exposing themselves. . . . They need things from us, the people who are outside." Santiago Morales added that while the villagers had effectively manipulated the meaning of *comunero* to demand migrants' participation, migrants also had tools of their own, including access to government grants like the 3x1 Program. In his mind, migrants were "the most important [economic] motor of Partida." The more money migrants sent, the more they had leverage to change things back home. Villagers faced a catch-22: while they wanted to "recommunalize" migrants, they also depended on those in Los Angeles.

To keep migrants happy, the people of Partida had to adapt. Thus, the pueblo acquiesced to migrants' demands to reform the system of cargos. In the first decade of the 2000s, they reduced the total number of cargos by half and the number of years someone worked in each cargo from three to one. They also monetized these positions, eventually agreeing to use state funds to pay civic stipends. While villagers initially insisted that migrants return to serve, they later accepted the HTA's proposal to pay substitutes instead. Ultimately, they began allowing community members to hire other people to do the cargos and tequios they had been assigned, at the rate of about US$3,000 to $5,000 per year for civil-service positions and US$15 per day for communal labor.

Monetizing Usos y Costumbres transformed Partida's communal government. While the pueblo had historically assigned leadership positions to the most prosperous villagers to equalize income disparities, these posts now fell on people who could not afford to hire substitutes or who needed the money they'd earn from serving on others' behalf. As a result, cargos no longer rotated among citizens. Instead, they became stratified toward the poor. The shift to a paid system also put migrants in the position of literally funding the functioning of the hometown government. It was unclear how long such an arrangement could last.

In what Nazanin Shahrokni and I (2014) call "patriarchal accommodations," Partida adapted its gender order as well. Since the 1990s women migrants had been some of the most active participants and fundraisers in Partida's HTA. Therefore, even as village leaders kept women out of assemblies at home, they encouraged women *migrants* to stand up to men in Los Angeles, to convince them to contribute. When Blanca Martínez was president of the HTA in the early 1990s, for instance, she reached out to the hometown government to complain about migrant men. She told the village president,

> It's hard for us women that the men rebel against us and protest. Us women are contributing more than the men. It's as if it's harder for [migrant] men

to submit to us women. . . . They say that we have no authority to make them contribute, and it's hard to fight with people who are like that and don't want to help. I don't know what's in their heads. They think they're going to stay here their whole lives, and they won't need any help from the pueblo. What can we do with them? If you want support, then help us make them do their part.

Perhaps surprisingly, the leaders replied, "You women should rule, because you wear the pants more than us men. Just take a hard rod and make them do it." Because the village needed support, men there not only accepted women in the HTA; they also encouraged them to take a heavy hand with male migrants who failed to help out.

In 2010–11 Carmen, Concha, and Renata's leadership also inspired some of the men in Partida to push for women's inclusion. Esteban Báez, who was hometown treasurer during my fieldwork, was one. He reflected,

> What really gets my attention is that when there were men [leading the HTA], they never took advantage of the program [3x1], and now that three women head the group, they're doing it. . . . [Men in Partida] think that women are still not capable of being town leaders, and I tell them that's not true. The clearest example is what Renata and her *compañeras* [female companions] did [in Los Angeles], that women can do it as well as us—or better.

Esteban was so inspired that when Partida nominated him to serve as town president the following year, he said he would do it only if they appointed women to serve alongside him. While the pueblo declined, such efforts eventually built momentum to give village women the vote.

In 2012, led by men like Esteban, along with returnees like Alejandro Campos and Juan Serrano, Partida agreed to shift from voting publicly in assemblies to voting by secret ballot. They also began requiring women to vote, just like men. Then, after centuries of all-male politics, the pueblo elected a woman as president. In a rather literary twist, Isabel Vega—the president-elect—was the seventh daughter of long-time, outspoken feminist Claudia Vega. The last time I visited Claudia, she bounded around her small cement patio, clutching her gingham apron and telling me, "It's high time that women ruled! How we have fought for this!" Leonel reflected more stolidly, "We have made history here in Partida, Abigail." Ultimately the shift echoed decade-old changes at work in nearby Retorno. The contexts, however, were dramatically different.

ALTERNATIVE GLOBALIZATION IN RETORNO

The day I arrived in Retorno, its roads buzzed with women hawking homemade tamales and tattooed men in baggy black jeans (see figure 6 for an image of Retorno's main road). Unlike in Partida, people talked often of California. The following week, on a bright July morning, the village held its secondary-school graduation. Mothers filled folding chairs first, bedecked in traditional Mixtec *rebozos* (scarves). Then came a second group: young men with shaved heads and jeans, who looked like they had just landed from California. The contrast between the two groups was striking. Yet all of their faces shared signs of strength and strain. Both stayed quiet, arms crossed over their chests. As the ceremony concluded, the principal gave a speech. He implored the eighth-grade graduates to

> continue with your studies. Get college degrees, because in this country of Mexico we need more professionals. We need anthropologists, psychologists, biologists, lawyers, and teachers. We have had enough with migrating to serve as cheap labor in the north [the United States]. *Ya basta* [enough already]. Let us stop being slaves to the *gringos!*[22] We need graduates and no more *braceros* [manual workers]![23]

As he spoke, three girls glanced at me, stifling giggles. The speech hinted at how Retorno's migration pathway had compelled the pueblo to fight for a future in Mexico. Goaded by cross-border ties, villagers joined migrants, the FIOB, the PRD, and other indigenous communities to demand representation and resources from the shifting Mexican state.

Throwing Out the Caciques

For Retorno's poorer villagers, aligning with migrants, the Mexican opposition, and other indigenous villages offered new leverage at home. Once migrants organized in California, they inspired their allies to help expel the PRI caciques in the pueblo.

Figure 6. Women walking down the main street of Retorno. Photo by the author.

For one, migrants' long-distance advocacy helped link them to a small, educated, and politically mobilized group of teachers in Retorno who bolstered their fight. In the late 1970s teachers in Oaxaca had begun to rebel against the national teachers' union, which was associated with the ruling PRI.[24] They waged marches and sit-ins to democratize union leadership and educational practices and to seek change in Mexico as a whole. Many of the rebel teachers came from rural areas, including Retorno. In the

1980s they aligned with the Mexican Socialist Party, the same group that migrants met in the fields of Sinaloa. Like the party, they emphasized social struggle and solidarity with the vulnerable. Blockading roads and occupying Oaxaca City, the teachers became the core of popular mobilization in Oaxaca in the 1980s and continue to lead its biggest social movements today.[25] In the mid-1990s teachers also started to grow increasingly involved in rural communities. Their class consciousness linked them to workers and peasants, echoing migrants' own goals.[26]

Other villagers were sympathetic to migrants as well. In Retorno 88 percent of men and 57 percent of women had once worked as migrants—63 percent and 20 percent, respectively, in the United States. In addition, two-thirds of couples had separated across borders, and a third of young people had at least one parent living elsewhere. Returnees' and family members' stories had a ripple effect, convincing villagers that instead of going north, they should focus on making Retorno a place to feel "free." Even those who had never been to the United States would say things like, "Why would I go to the United States? Only to suffer." Their experiences as internal migrants made them receptive to negative accounts of life in North County San Diego.

In the mid-1990s, such villagers began to rally with migrants to democratize Retorno. Luis Pérez, a short, eloquent teacher with heavily gelled hair, became a leader of the opposition—and later of Oaxaca's branch of the FIOB. Luis was the youngest child of a family of five. All of his siblings migrated, and he hoped to avoid the same fate. To make that possible, however, he had to advocate for government programs and public support. So he joined the teachers' movement—and the village rebellion. He explained,

> My goal was, above all, the possibility of having a pueblo that was different— a developed pueblo, a pueblo that could count on educational institutions that would raise the level of development, a pueblo that might have access to public programs from the state government. But we couldn't imagine Retorno getting access to these things if we didn't organize ourselves [to demand support]. Therefore, the fundamental step—in order to influence things and have a different town—was in the organizing.

Together, migrants and teachers recruited much of the village to challenge Retorno's inequity. By the late 1990s nearly 90 percent of adults in Retorno aligned themselves with the FIOB branch in the village and, with it, the PRD.

In 1995 local FIOB sympathizers revived the fight to overthrow the local PRI and democratize village control. They physically ousted the sitting PRI president and installed a teacher named Martín Alvarado in his place, putting FIOB allies into all the village leadership posts. Martín's government dismantled the "customs" the caciques had used to exploit the poor. First, they ended the requirement that villagers do unpaid labor, insisting that all government jobs be paid. Second, they reduced the number of cargos in Retorno to ten per year, welcoming state stipends for those who served. Third, they abandoned public voting in favor of secret ballots. With the new system, it was harder for elites to suppress indigenous voices or deliver votes on the poor's behalf.

The FIOB-affiliated leaders also enabled migrants, indigenous people, women, and the poor to vote and hold civic posts. They eliminated all but one of Retorno's twelve religious festivals, so villagers would not have to give so much money to the church. They also ended the requirement that civic leaders sponsor a village fiesta, which tacitly tied positions of power to wealth. For the remaining yearly festival, they replaced onerous sponsorship requirements *(cofradías)* with a small annual contribution from everyone in the village. Basilio Ramos, who prodded these shifts from afar, reflected,

> One of the great satisfactions—something that FIOB has given us and that was in our plans from the beginning, one of the great dreams—was to end the *cofradías* in the pueblo. Many people thought that the *cofradías* were a detriment to the community, but there was also a lot of resistance to change. . . . Still, after six or seven years [without them], people were really happy, because now families don't sacrifice themselves [economically]. Many families from Retorno had to leave, and many couldn't return because they were so in debt.

Dismantling tradition alleviated the kinds of debts that had driven migrants to leave. Ironically, it was only by doing away with Usos y Costumbres—the very customs that protected participation and redistribution in Partida—that the new government made Retorno more democratic.

Martín Alvarado and his colleagues also held a series of consultations with migrants in North County San Diego and Baja California, in which migrants participated in hometown politics and made suggestions to restructure the village. The caciques had once barred former migrants from holding political office. By 2010, however, returnees held ten of eleven village leadership posts. In that year's municipal election, ten of twenty-two proposed representatives had worked in the United States in the past three years and another ten at some point in their lives. As I discuss later, the new leaders also decided to require women to attend assemblies and serve on public committees alongside the men.

Finally, the FIOB-allied government redistributed resources. Not only did the FIOB obtain new funding from foundations, nongovernmental organizations, and the state of Oaxaca, but its allies also spread those resources more evenly among the people of Retorno. Javier Ortíz, a long-time FIOB advocate and twice president of the organization's branch in the village, explained, "Around that time [the late 1990s] a lot of money was coming in from the government, from SAGARPA [Secretaría de Agricultura, Ganadería, Desarrollo Rural, Pesca, y Alimentación; Ministry of Agriculture, Livestock, Rural Development, Fisheries, and Food], and so on. But Martín also distributed a lot of resources, or at least they started to be distributed more evenly." Rather than siphoning state funds into their cronies' pockets, Martín's government used the money for infrastructure, paved roads, and projects that benefited the village as a whole.

Nunca Más un México sin Nosotros (Never again a Mexico without Us)

In 1994 the FIOB opened an office in the Mixteca and established branches in many migrant hometowns, to fight for greater inclusion of indigenous pueblos in Mexico. Galvanized by strikes in North County San Diego, the fledgling organization unified migrants who came from across the region, and it hoped to animate similar dissent among those on the sending side. In individual villages, including Retorno, the organization also backed allies' bids for control. When they were successful, FIOB allies gained new leverage over municipal funds. By the late 1990s the organization had also begun promoting the PRD agenda.

In addition to pursuing municipal seats, the FIOB mobilized pueblos across the region to fight for more state support. Indigenous political autonomy, they insisted, did *not* mean the government could abdicate its responsibility for community development. In a 1996 communiqué to the state and federal governments, for instance, the FIOB demanded immediate assistance in Retorno to install potable and irrigation water and to pave roads. To promote similar demands across the Mixteca, the organization mobilized marches, road blockades, and sit-ins in Oaxaca City.[27] In August that same year, it announced an "indefinite takeover" of the main highway near Retorno: the protest that brought Alma Sandoval into politics. It demanded that the government of Oaxaca provide piped water, roads, services, solutions to communal-land disputes, productive and cultural projects for indigenous communities, and a halt to the militarization of the Mixteca and the harassment of FIOB members. By the early 2000s, the FIOB and its allies in Oaxaca had secured funds from more than ten different state offices as well as direct grants to FIOB leaders and the municipalities they represented.[28]

These funds supported irrigation, paved roads, bridges, roofs, cement floors, agricultural projects, and credit and loan groups. They also provided training in human rights and women's empowerment. In addition, the FIOB secured collective taxi licenses (the main mode of public transportation in the area), enabling villagers to earn almost three times as much driving taxis as they did in day labor. By 2000 the FIOB had more than twenty thousand members in seventy Oaxacan towns, and its assemblies in Mexico drew more participants than its meetings in the United States.[29] By positioning itself as a new interlocutor with the state, the FIOB gave indigenous people access to resources they had never had before. These resources also helped the FIOB mobilize votes for the PRD.

Where people in Partida avoided political parties, those in Retorno got *more* involved. Not only did the FIOB help solicit funding for migrants' hometowns; it also promoted the leftist ideals of the PRD. Its movement in Oaxaca built on demands made by the Zapatistas, in nearby Chiapas, for inclusion and fair treatment of indigenous people and an end to neoliberal globalization. Emphasizing inclusion, the FIOB took up the Zapatistas' slogan, *Nunca más un México sin nosotros* (Never again a Mexico without us). FIOB leaders, particularly those from Retorno, denounced Mexico's disregard for its indigenous people. In a communiqué to state and federal authorities, for instance, they wrote, "We are interested in expressing our opinions in the National Consultation about indigenous rights and participation, hoping that this is not one more consultation that turns to smoke and leaves our communities forgotten. . . . We do not permit nor will we permit more discrimination based on the fact of having deep indigenous roots."[30] They added that they would not allow the PRI to divide them. Thus, even as Retorno dismantled some of the customs associated with Usos y Costumbres, it reconstituted indigeneity as a tool to unify neighboring villages and oppose state neglect.

The FIOB also backed PRD efforts to challenge the federal- and state-level PRI. When the FIOB emerged in Oaxaca, the PRI had held power at both levels for almost seventy years. The FIOB and the PRD rallied Retorno and other nearby hometowns to contest its control. In 1998 they launched Luis Pérez, the teacher from Retorno, as a left-wing PRD candidate for Oaxaca's state senate. Throughout the region FIOB members knocked on doors, helping the PRD wage a massive campaign to support him. In 1999 Luis was elected as the first-ever indigenous representative to Oaxaca's state congress. The campaign tied the FIOB so closely to the PRD that the FIOB started describing itself as the FIOB-PRD. A decade later villagers still had trouble distinguishing between them. Drawing on the alliances and critical politics that migrants developed in northern Mexico and the United States, the FIOB helped indigenous people claim greater voice back at home.

Cross-border connections also helped the FIOB-PRD weather counterattacks by the PRI. As I describe at the end of this chapter, in 2002 the state-level PRI retaliated against the FIOB, slandering Luis Pérez and throwing him in jail. The FIOB fought back by launching a binational campaign to defend him. In Europe, Canada, South America, Mexico, and the United States, human-rights organizations supported their cause. Thanks to their efforts, Luis was released after seven days. As the PRI assaulted the FIOB, its members in the United States also mobilized to protect their allies in Mexico, waging hunger strikes and demonstrations at Mexican consulates in California. Given the PRI's long-standing dominance in Retorno, villagers could not avoid political party competition. But their cross-border ties gave them strength to push for the parties that spoke to them best.

Gendered Jujitsu

In what I call *gendered jujitsu*, the FIOB also used women's rights programs to broaden its movement. Before the FIOB entered Oaxaca in 1995, women could hardly approach Retorno's town hall, let alone vote in village assemblies. By 2010 they were 62 percent of Retorno's voters and ran most of its school committees, health councils, and government social programs. The FIOB promoted this shift, and women, in turn, gave the movement momentum.

Before the FIOB took off, women had already begun to do civic work in Retorno when men were absent. From the 1980s on, women had been the majority in Retorno, the nexus of divided families, and some of the first returnees. From 1970 to 1990, as more men left for California, the proportion of local men who were working age fell from 60 to 38 percent.[31] Several women did public service in their husbands' stead. Dora López, the first to serve on a town committee in the mid-1980s, explained, "Women had to be on the committees because all the husbands went to the United States, and there were just women alone, so the only ones who went to the meetings were mothers." When the FIOB began to organize in Retorno, therefore, it realized it needed women to serve as its eyes and ears on the ground.

In the coming years, as the FIOB organized in Retorno, Alma, Adelina, and a few other female leaders did the bulk of the mobilization, walking from house to house and inviting other women to meet and march. If a PRI representative came to the village, the women would grab him and demand that the government bring them programs. Whether or not they longed for influence *as women,* most described their early political work as a burden. Often, villagers shamed them as sluts and streetwalkers. Yet the women soldiered on, determined to avoid the abuses they'd faced as migrants in Mexico and the United States. As Alma put it, "We women made that [FIOB] government."

Women got involved in this movement because they cared about the "right not to migrate." In 1996 Martín Alvarado's government announced, "[Women] have a right to participate in the elections too, to have a voice and vote." Alma Sandoval, Adelina Juárez, and four other women answered the call. All had been migrants themselves. When Alma arrived at that first assembly, she recalled, she felt "such a shame! We [women] would have preferred to cover our heads and faces with our shawls, and we didn't say anything." At the time, FIOB sympathizers had identified a program that would replace their thatched roofs with tiles, but it required a woman to be at the helm.[32] They named Alma president of the program. Alma could hardly speak out of shame, and she never said if she would accept. Nevertheless, she took the post for the good of the village, thinking, "I care about my pueblo . . . because I want to live here." Without the participation of women like her, Alma worried, Retorno would lose the resources the FIOB had promised—and with them, her chance to stay home. From that moment on, Alma added, "We [women] were in."

Other women mobilized to avoid displacement as well. As a young woman, for instance, Adelina had worked for nearly a decade in Culiacán, going on strike at age sixteen and watching her firstborn baby die in the fields. Like Alma, Adelina avoided assemblies at first. Yet she eventually realized, "It's for a just and noble cause that we [women] are going, because it's not acceptable for just a few people to control us and put whomever they want in as president." Likewise, Dolores Muñoz recalled that when she left the fields of northern Mexico to come back to Retorno in the 1990s, she was inspired to change the village. She described,

> I used to tell the women, "You [women] have to go [participate]! How are we going to help Retorno advance if we don't say anything, if we don't speak, if there are meetings, and we don't go? No. We have to go. We can!" . . . I told the women they didn't have to let anyone take advantage of them. "Stop being abused. You have to fight for what is yours. If you see that something is not working well in Retorno, you have the right, you know? You have to go to the government, form a group, and ask about the corruption. You have the right to have the village be different. . . . Don't let yourselves be cheated by the people who are high up in [PRI] politics, because the only thing they do is just come to the village to trick people. And then in the end, the ones who benefit are those people, and our village remains the same."

In some ways, Dolores's language sounded like Western feminism. Yet her reason for urging women to participate was not *gender* abuse but the risk of village stagnation at the hands of manipulative politicians. Clientelism, she felt, deprived villagers of the only resources that might enable them to avoid migrating to northern Mexico or the United States.

New programs for women in development also made their inclusion crucial to garnering state support. Javier Ortíz, who was president of the FIOB branch in Retorno in the late 1990s, explained, "Foundations [in the United States and Mexico] also started to see that women's participation was critical, so they started to give projects for women." They offered chicken rearing, palm crafts, mushrooms, Lorena stoves, and microbanks. As they did, Javier added, they made women's participation "fundamental." To get such funding, the FIOB insisted that women like Alma be involved. They also used women's rights workshops as organizing tools, training women to advocate for resources and to contribute to FIOB mobilization.

As women participated in such trainings, they began to pay increasing attention to their rights as women. Adelina, for instance, attended FIOB-run workshops on human and women's rights. She went to talks on how women should participate in assemblies. She reflected, "[The FIOB] taught us about the rights every citizen has, that every person has. That we [women] have our own names and that we have the right to travel—they taught us that, as well as our responsibilities." A decade later during my fieldwork, Adelina led a group of women into the village square for Retorno's election. Crowded together, they demanded fair distribution of state resources and reprimanded men in the pueblo for poor financial management. Planted at the center, Adelina grumbled when the emcee did not call on her. To all assembled, she insisted, "It's because I'm a woman; he's ignoring me because I'm a woman." Adelina's effort to avoid dislocation and exclusion had driven her into new, gendered struggles. Now she claimed voice *as a woman*, even around issues like fiscal transparency, which fell outside the "feminine" domain.

Meanwhile, men in Retorno began to realize that by involving women, they, too, might get access to resources from the state. Slowly, they began urging their wives and daughters to serve on municipal committees and engage in civic affairs. At first, for instance, Adelina's husband resisted her involvement in politics. Then, he realized she could access state funds on their shared behalf. He started to tell her, "Go [to the assembly], woman! Go, because they're going to get support for the pueblo. Support is going to come for village, and for women! Come on." Similarly, Tamara Huerta, one of the early women activists, explained that when she, Alma, and Adelina began organizing,

> There were many houses where the men threw us out with sticks. Yes! Many, many. But today, everyone participates because ever since the Oportunidades program came in 1999, support started to come here. That year men set their wives free to join. Because before that, no; we were only a few that would go out. We were maybe forty, fifty women who went out. But then when the Oportunidades support came, that's when everyone in the pueblo joined.

State funds swayed the men to "set their wives free."[33]

The more women gained voice in Retorno, the more they saw their hometown as a dynamic alternative to emigration. Instead of associating Retorno with patriarchy, for instance, Dolores Muñoz found "liberation" in the village. Not only could she escape her husband's beatings by staying in Retorno when he went on to the United States, but she could also avoid the "slavery" of farmwork in northern Mexico and factories in North County San Diego. As Dolores mobilized, she also gained confidence. She explained,

> I was on the school committee, so when the school needed something I had to go ask for it. For instance, a delegate would come from Oaxaca, and we would have to go. . . . So I started developing more as a person at that point. Like I learned how to fight for things for Retorno. The people who were managing things badly—well, I would go and say to them, "No. This is not okay. You have to do it like this." So a lot of people told me—a lot of people started to respect me. . . . So when I was back in Retorno, I was another person; I was no longer the same submissive Dolores that bowed her head when they punished her, that just cried and cried and never said anything. No. At that moment I changed.

Despite the burdens of community service, many women who participated in politics felt a stronger capacity as women. Activists like Alma and Tamara described an "awakening," saying that they could now "see themselves," that life in the village "felt great," and that they would no longer tolerate abuse by politicians, employers, or men.[34]

As women took on new political roles, they also began to confront domestic violence, the lack of divorce, and men's control over property and children. María Robles, a divorced single mom in her forties who ran a mini-mart near the town square, remembered that her father had refused to let her go to school. She quipped, "In the old days almost all the men used to beat women. But now, no; now it's the reverse. Women control the men! [Laughs.]" While women in most Oaxacan villages still lacked recourse to report domestic violence, with the help of the FIOB, those in Retorno regularly went to the district court to denounce abuse.[35]

Yet household relationships were not their only point of comparison. Rather, women of Retorno measured their quality of life against their experiences in the United States. They felt "strong," as they put it, not just because they gained influence toward their husbands but also because they avoided exploitation, abuse, and discrimination in North County San Diego. In Retorno they built lives they had reason to value. Of course, they faced ongoing economic pressure. Many also made great sacrifices to support public programs. Nevertheless, most echoed Alma: in Retorno, they said, they felt "free." As in other countries, these women became feminist activists in and through their other kinds of struggles.[36] Fighting against the degradations of migration gave meaning to their efforts as women. By incorporating these women into politics—along with migrants and the poor—the FIOB transformed the pattern of authority in Retorno.

Coda: The Fragmentation of Solidarity

Still, the FIOB's gains were fragile. For one, the PRI retaliated. As described in chapter 1, several of Retorno's wealthier, PRI-affiliated families migrated to Mexico City in the 1970s and 1980s. When these families heard of the FIOB takeover, their blood boiled. In particular, a sixty-seven-year-old woman named Esmeralda Ruiz, who had worked for the PRI in Mexico City for years, decided to return and reclaim her pueblo. Esmeralda owned a grimy, paid bathroom in the nearby town square, charging two pesos (about twenty U.S. cents) per person to enter. The first time we met, she reclined in the entryway to this business, in a billowing pink poncho and gold earrings. She explained that she had come back to the pueblo because by 2001, "The PRI was dead in Retorno; [the FIOB] had blocked the PRI." Esmeralda took it upon herself to revive Retorno's ruling party. Drawing on a wide, wealthy, and long-standing PRI network of patronage and her ties in Mexico City, she got funds for reforestation, beauty courses, and even cash handouts. She also twisted women's empowerment to her own ends. In workshops targeted primarily at older women, she denigrated the "licentious" behavior of FIOB leaders like Alma and Adelina. She told the *señoras* that these girls, the wives of their hardworking sons away in the United States, were getting drunk and prostituting themselves to activist men. She also trained the elder women to defend Retorno's "old stability" by supporting the PRI.

The PRI in Oaxaca City struck back as well. In 2001 Oaxaca's PRI governor José Murat, who was known for manipulating social movements and their leaders, attempted to pay both Domingo García and Luis Pérez to abandon the PRD and shift the FIOB's allegiance to the PRI. Domingo and Luis refused. In answer, the governor spread word across the press that the men had failed to account for US$120,000 worth of donated funds, most of them for women's committees. In April that year the Oaxacan newspaper *El Universal* reported that the state branch of the Ministry of Social Development (Secretaría de Desarollo Social) had found corruption in the FIOB, led by Domingo and Luis. The governor arrested them both. Many people believed these rumors, and they may have been true. Regardless, Domingo argued, the PRI—profoundly corrupt itself—brought the case to light to break the FIOB. Had the PRD won in Mexico, the outcome might have been different.

Instead, the PRI accusations dramatically weakened the FIOB. One-time participants felt angry, insulted, and swindled. As Javier, who was once again in charge of its node in Retorno, put it, "All the confusion and chaos means that many people prefer not to participate in any organization; they'd rather stay out of it." Even Alma reflected that with the FIOB, "You break off quickly [*se zafa uno rápido*], because you don't get anything from them." Though almost everyone in Retorno had participated in the FIOB's actions from 1996 to 2001, by 2007 only 31 percent identified with the organization and by 2011, only 6 percent. While the remaining FIOB members continued their grassroots movement, the organization had far more trouble securing support. Mexican state agencies and U.S. foundations halted their funding to the group.

U.S. enforcement also weighed on the village. For one, most migrants stopped circulating, with men either returning or bringing their families to the United States. By 2011 only 15 percent of couples were divided, compared to 67 percent two decades before. A growing number of young men were also deported to Retorno. While their predecessors had returned voluntarily, these deportees tended to feel more hostile toward their hometown. Most had gone to the United States as children, and they fit awkwardly in Retorno. Julio Molina's parents, for instance, brought him to the United States in 1995, at age five. In 2009 the Vista, California, police caught Julio in a stolen car and deported him. During my fieldwork he was twenty-one. We chatted often, as he hung around Retorno's streets with little hope of a job. He constantly complained about being bored. Gesturing at his father's house at the bottom of the hill, he grumbled (in English), "This shit is dirt. . . . In the States when are you going to have a house like this?" Every so often I heard that Julio had brutally beaten another young man. One weekend he landed a fourteen-year-old in a coma. Rumor had it that he was also at the helm of a string of robberies of elderly women's homes. When I asked Julio why he and his companions fought, he replied, "What I see? The main reason is alcohol. That's basically it. Because they [we] got no life. They have nothing to do. So you drink, you drink, you get happy, and you don't feel so bad. Know what I mean? Like when you're drunk, you drink, everything seems fine. . . . It makes you feel good for a certain amount of time." As we talked, Julio pointed to a cartridge from a .22-caliber pistol, lying on the ground in his driveway. "Know what this is?" he asked. Julio promised me he wouldn't cause trouble. But his history hinted otherwise. He had been in a gang in the United States. He was used to a life where, as he put it, "If you don't get shamed, you get shot."

Whereas Partida's collective structure helped discipline its deportees, those in Retorno were far less controlled. As people like Julio brought drug use and petty crime to the pueblo, they also sapped residents' sympathy for migrants in the United States. Young women began to describe their male counterparts—both deportees and nonmigrant men—as "slackers," "scrubs," or "slimeballs." Carmelita Caballero, a twenty-nine-year-old single mother, cut hair in the village salon. She'd been married for a bit but not for long, she explained, as she spun me in front of her mirror. She reflected, "Men are assholes, so I think some women are just meant to be alone." In reference to the rise in robberies, others told me that things had gotten bad. As Ximena Ortíz, a longtime migrant and mother of eight, put it, "This town is disintegrating fast."

PRI attacks and U.S. enforcement eroded the ties that had fueled Retorno's resistance. They diluted the hometown's links to both migrants and the PRD. They also splintered the village itself, crippling its political capacity. After 2001 the results of every single election in Retorno were contested, requiring appeals to the state government. Such postelectoral conflicts were common throughout the Mixteca and sometimes lasted for months.[37] As they went on, the government froze all municipal resources, leaving the villages starved for money. Sometimes the state even let the conflicts fester, to avoid distributing funds. Ironically, the entry of competing parties into Retorno—which began with the goal of getting *more* state support—sparked conflicts that ended up inhibiting its access to cash. Without strong allies and transnational ties, the FIOB was more vulnerable, Retorno grew less stable, and the PRI reclaimed authority.[38] Nevertheless, women, indigenous people, and the poor maintained their voice and vote. Retorno's *caciquismo* was gone for good.

THE ROLE OF MIGRATION IN MEXICAN DEVELOPMENT

Students of emigration sometimes assume that hometowns get "left behind." Others focus on migrants' remittances of ideas or money as motors of so-called development. This chapter complicates both models, illustrating how each community's migration pathway shapes its relationship to political change. It shows how, even as migrants weigh in from afar, nonmigrants and returnees also develop their own attitudes about emigration and, more broadly, globalization. These understandings then influence how hometowns navigate broader political shifts, such as Mexican democratization.

In a place like Partida, where migration creates tensions between tradition and Western individualism, it can spark antiglobalization backlash. As migrants from Partida embraced Los Angeles, their counterparts in Mexico reinforced their communal participation and landholding. For the latter, indigenous self-governance was not just an antiquated, passive form of resistance.[39] It also offered a tool to stand up to pressure to "modernize," from both migrants and the state. By reviving communal values and political autonomy, the pueblo could make demands of migrants, manage deportees, and avoid some of the fragmentation associated with land privatization and Mexican political parties. That said, the insistence on tradition also tended to *re*-create characteristics supposedly endemic to indigenous villages, including being closed, insular, and patriarchal.[40]

In a place like Retorno, meanwhile, villagers' sympathy with migrants can fuel demands for alternative globalization. Due to Retorno's history of circulation and family separation, women, teachers, and other residents often felt close with migrants. Like migrants, they realized that to avoid the United States and live in Retorno, they had to end the pueblo's old hierarchies. Through the FIOB and the PRD, they joined migrants to take down the PRI caciques and claim a new voice in local politics. The rebels scrapped the rules elites had once used to pinch their money and time. They gave migrants and poor people access to leadership roles. They also sought state funds and representation in Mexico as a whole.

As gender relations shifted in the process of migration, they also got caught up in hometown battles. In Partida men associated women's rights with outside imposition, sparking patriarchal backlash. For many years they rejected state funding tied to women's participation. Nevertheless, the village relied on migrants for money, and some villagers admired women's actions in Los Angeles. Ultimately, therefore, the pueblo agreed to let women vote. By contrast, people in Retorno used women's empowerment programs strategically, drawing women into politics to fuel their movement for change. Not only were women the majority in Retorno, but state programs also encouraged the FIOB to include them in funding requests. Both men and women embraced such gender shifts as a means to meet their broader goals. As a result, women began to vote, run village committees, and attend meetings as never before. In short, migration drew women into politics not just through "social remittances" from the United States but also through the pueblo's own mobilization.

As time went by, both hometowns were vulnerable to shifting policies in the United States and political warfare in Mexico. Though people in Partida wanted autonomy, they also relied on their counterparts in the United States. To the extent the pueblo alienated migrants, it risked losing not only its collective traditions but also its very ability to survive. As migrants from Partida settled into Los Angeles and grew ever more distant, the village had to moderate its stubborn commitment to patriarchy and communalism. Retorno's democratization also relied on outside supporters—particularly the PRD and the FIOB—who were vulnerable to fragmentation. Its migrants' alienation from the United States was not enough for a transnational movement. Rather, the community needed cross-border connections and political allies to back its demands on the sending side. U.S. border enforcement and Mexican party contention threatened these ties. As my research came to a close, drug violence also wracked Mexico, destabilizing rural life. While Oaxaca remained relatively insulated as of this writing, other hometowns disintegrated. As broader politics evolved, hometowns' struggles remained precarious.

Still, both of these cases highlight how sending sites can be a staging ground to challenge globalization and question migrants' experiences of "illegality" in places like the United States. Some observers argue that Mexico should stem the flow of migrants by building better economic development. This chapter demonstrates that it is not so simple. Rather, rural villages' engagement with party contention and state-run development *reflects* their ties to migration. Hometowns *use* state programs to struggle against the broader process of globalization and the conditions of U.S. exclusion. As migrant communities seek to maximize democratic control, access to resources, and environmental stewardship, their approaches are molded by the political institutions already at their disposal as well as the prospects and threats they face in their destinations.

Conclusion

A decade after my research began, eleven million undocumented immigrants continued to live in the United States with few political rights.[1] They slogged at the nation's most toilsome jobs. Most complied meticulously with the law. Almost 40 percent had children born in the United States. Still, the U.S. government branded them "illegal" and hunted them down for deportation. State force kept migrants terrified, pushing them into segregated neighborhoods and leaving them vulnerable to police and labor abuse.[2]

Voiceless and faced with violence, migrant communities fought tirelessly for space to be "free." They worked for change across state borders, as well as in their everyday lives. Yet they did so in surprisingly different ways. Some, like Carmen Rojas, strove to belong in the United States. Through hard work and humility, they sought to prove themselves worthy. They joined marches for legalization. In the 1990s and the first decade of the 2000s, this advocacy fueled vibrant social movements, exposing the torment of unauthorized families. Where immigrants' voices were loudest, they won protection from labor abuse, domestic violence, and even federal enforcement. At the same time, other migrants, like Alma Sandoval, adopted a strategy of withdrawal. While decrying unjust U.S. treatment, they channeled their protests to Mexico. In the meantime, they endured abuses at work and at home—along with the fear of deportation.

These struggles echoed in Mexico too, as hometowns responded to migrants' paths. Once again community strategies varied. Some villages, like Partida, resisted globalization, insulating themselves from pressure to change. They protected communal traditions. Yet they also left themselves severed from state and migrant support. Others, like Retorno, joined Mexican fights for democracy. In the 1990s and the first decade of the 2000s their movements helped bring down the long-standing rule of the PRI and draw funding to rural villages. As they claimed a new voice in Mexico, these pueblos revealed that the United States was not always the source of "freedom." On the contrary, many people longed for a "right to stay home."

Finally, migrants' advocacy upended the roles of women. As Carmen Rojas, Alma Sandoval, and their counterparts struggled for freedom, they also took major, new political roles. Blocked from politics a decade before, they began to tie their advancement as women to their struggles to earn inclusion. In the process they defied hometown patriarchy. Yet, once again, they did so in contextually contingent ways. Those like Carmen, who had access to state protection in Los Angeles, linked gender liberation to life in the United States. Those like Alma, who feared North County police, found "awakening" in Mexico, with help from programs for women's rights. As they did, they inverted gendered geographies that located women's empowerment exclusively in the United States.

This conclusion explores how the political-pathways approach presented in this book can transform existing thinking about gender and agency in undocumented migrant communities. I reconsider theories of politics, globalization, gender, and social change. Then I extend these insights to other people, places, and moments. I also look at how migrants' pathways may change over time. I close by considering what U.S. cities, Mexican leaders, and migrant men and women might do to expand their political voice.

PLACE, GENDER, AND THE PROCESS OF POLITICS

Undocumented people face great hurdles to political inclusion. They must, of necessity, work outside traditional civic bounds. Nevertheless, scholars have celebrated the possibility that such grassroots mobilization can challenge global inequity.[3] Understanding when, where, and how such groups fight back requires examining their pathways, meaning the places they leave, the places they go, and their courses of action between. As Partida and Retorno make clear, migrants' politics are not homogeneous. People find freedom in different places. They may or may not leave their hometowns behind. Therefore, a coherent account of undocumented struggles must explore local practice, historical process, and gender. Local control shapes hometowns' and migrants' political projects. At the same time, advocacy is a process; that is, migrant communities strategize in relation to their own specific histories, local U.S. contexts, and ongoing homeland shifts. Finally, gender is part of politics. Places affect men and women distinctly. And communities may fight exclusion partly by changing their old gender roles.

The political-pathways approach reframes existing theories of state power, globalization, and gender in migrant communities. First, my focus on place helps rethink the role of the state. Scholars have drawn crucial attention to how state laws *make* immigrants "illegal" (especially in the United States) and mark them as less than human.[4] Researchers also denounce the use of force to control undocumented families. They show that surveillance fuels racial stigma, while deportation keeps migrants terrified, exploited, and politically silent.[5] In the realm of local policy and state actions, however, a battle rages. In some places advocates defend the undocumented from the trauma of state abuse. In others police and bureaucrats target migrants as "criminals." Thus, "illegality" is not just a legal status but a patchwork of place-based practices.

These local modes of control condition migrants' feelings about race, gender, the state, and belonging. Local-level outreach, public services, and limits on policing, as in Los Angeles, can give migrants a sense of hope, expanding civic engagement and mitigating racial exclusion. Yet good/ bad divisions can also pit people against one another, pushing them to perform as "good." By contrast, arbitrary enforcement provokes more acute fear, as in North County San Diego. Unpredictable policing makes migrants cynical. As angry as these migrants may be, however, they tend to feel powerless, subduing dissent. These local modes of enforcement also shape workplace control. Even within the same industry, city- and county-level protections can curb labor violations, while anti-immigrant policing may enable abuse. In short, police and bureaucrats can open or close space for political mobilization, both in civil society and at work.[6]

Sending states are not unitary actors either. They, too, vary with local practice. Histories of egalitarian governance and resource control, as in Partida, can give migrants access to more desirable urban jobs in the first place. By contrast, hierarchical hometowns like Retorno may leave their members more vulnerable to farmwork and hostile destinations. Such legacies shape migrants' options and give them distinct understandings of their prospects at home.

These variations also make it clear that even in a context of state violence and disenfranchisement, there are spaces for agency. Both at home and away, the state is not just a juggernaut; it is also a terrain of possibility. Local practices mediate exclusionary laws and fuel different collective identities. For instance, Los Angeles's (relative) support for immigrants inspired some migrants to march for rights. Yet when combined with deportation, it also divided them. In North County, meanwhile, repression kept migrants silent. At the same time, they forged a shared oppositional identity, seeking allies and resources elsewhere. Social scientists might extend this insight by exploring how other local laws and practices can make room for political say.

My second core point is that hometown globalization and development are a process, linked to U.S. exclusion. As other scholars insist, migration is not a linear act; rather, migrants, returnees, and hometown residents often exist with "feet in both worlds."[7] For one, migrants bring hometown legacies with them when they arrive in the United States.[8] Those who leave for opportunities or gendered escape may feel more kindly toward their U.S. destinations. Those who carry histories of oppression or radical protest, meanwhile, may extend their critical lens to life in the United States. Grassroots advocacy relies on such long-term histories for building political will.

Immigrants' reactions to local U.S. policing also shape their transnationalism. As this book underscores, cross-border relationships vary. When immigrants see benefits to presenting themselves as "modern," as in Los Angeles, they may distance themselves from their hometowns. This polarization is not just fallout of assimilation but also a strategy by which immigrants show they belong. By contrast, when migrants feel alienated from the United States, as in North County San Diego, they may look to their homelands for substantive change. In such cases transnational solidarity is a tool to escape exclusion. This focus on the homeland displaces contention from the source of discontent—the United States—to the places the state seems to hear.

Hometowns, meanwhile, are not just objects of change. Homeland contexts are dynamic as well, shaping the impacts of migrant engagement.[9] As sending communities cope with the threats and benefits of migration, they may sanction migrants—as did Partida—or call on them to engage. In Retorno, for instance, party competition drew migrants into a fight to democratize Oaxaca. Hometowns can also offer symbolic alternatives to life in the United States. As returnees and nonmigrants react to emigration, they alter indigenous traditions, engage with national politics, and seek routes to democracy at home. Indeed, vibrant movements against the degradations of migrant globalization—whether led by migrants, as in Retorno, or by those who resent them, as in Partida—occur on the sending side. Emigration shapes homeland development not just by providing remittances but also by provoking new forms of citizenship.[10]

My third main point is that the relationship between gender and migration is complex and contingent. Understanding how gender relations change during migration requires a contextual, dynamic lens. As scholars have long known, migration sparks major shifts in the roles of women and men. Traditionally, analysts attributed these changes to women's wages and egalitarian ideas located on the receiving end. By framing U.S. (or European) culture as liberating, however, they obscured practical constraints on women who were undocumented, poor, and racially marginal. More recent research shows that gender relations vary with legal status, class, race, and place.[11] I add to these accounts by illustrating how women's political mobilization is shaped by local institutional contexts and by migrants' own cross-border struggles.

Gender varies with local modes of control. This relationship begins in the homeland. Where sending villages create urban opportunities, as in Partida, they can enable women to leave for escape. Where debt drives families to migrate together, as in Retorno, patriarchy travels with them. Similar contrasts appear in the United States. In areas like Los Angeles, police and employers may offer unauthorized women particular perks or protection. These gendered policies can mitigate the burdens of U.S. exclusion for women. In such contexts women are more likely to embrace the United States and feel they belong, even when they lack legal status. Men may be more ambivalent. In contrast, arbitrary policing can intensify "illegality," keep women trapped at home, exacerbate their dependence on men, and block them from access to services. Thus, local practices create *different* intersections of gender and legal status. Cities can open options to women like Carmen and Alma, or they can shut them down.

Gender is also processual, and migrants' struggles against exclusion can help give women greater political voice. In some cases women pursue inclusion in the United States (as scholars usually assume). In places where women believe that they can belong and fight to do so, as in Los Angeles, they may also feel empowered as women. They may even extend their new influence to the sending side. Yet women do not always feel free as migrants. In other cases, like Retorno, women's efforts to *avoid* U.S. suffering push them into new roles back home. These movements can change men as well. When men see benefits to women's participation in immigration-related struggles, they may be more flexible and encourage gender inclusion. In this regard, migration resembles war: both situations force men and women to contend with trauma, mobilize, and change their approaches to politics.[12] By creating ruptures, they open new roles to women.[13]

THE RANGE AND EVOLUTION OF UNDOCUMENTED STRUGGLES

Partida and Retorno are just two of many possible pathways. As I insisted in the introduction, their stories cannot account for the actions of all undocumented migrants, even in California or Mexico. Neither is a model that repeats itself elsewhere. On the contrary, the contrasts between them underscore precisely why aggregate analysis or singular narratives are inadequate to explain migrants' struggles. While Partida and Retorno may be unusual, my goal was not to obtain a representative sample. Instead, I used qualitative insights to flesh out mechanisms by which migrants' pathways can shape their politics.[14]

Even these cases themselves continued to change. As this book went to press, people from Partida and Retorno faced new democratic closures and forms of racial exclusion on both sides of the border. In Mexico, drug cartels took lives nationwide, wracking the country with violence. The PRI reclaimed power as well. In the late 2010s xenophobic nationalism also swept the United States and Europe, fueling hostility toward immigrants. Such attacks threatened to enervate both the U.S. immigrants' rights movement and migrants' transnational advocacy. Last I heard from Carmen, she had forsaken marching and remained stoically waiting for papers. Alma, meanwhile, abandoned the cross-border movement she herself helped to build. Fed up with transnational politics, she grew resigned to stick to her own affairs. As Retorno endured the defeat of the PRD and got cut off from members in California, its rebellions faltered as well.

Carmen's and Alma's stories raise questions. How durable were their pathways and their efforts at mobilization? What are the scope conditions for similar struggles? And where else could gender relations change? One might also ask how these findings extend to other groups. Who else fits into pathways, and who else can or will organize? What variations exist on migrants' strategies of inclusion or gender change? What might happen, for instance, without the democratic competition that enabled resistance in Mexico, without the government support for women's rights on either end, or without the groundswell of protest that swept Los Angeles into marches for immigrants' rights? When can migrants' struggles really dismantle exclusion? And under what conditions is the Global South a viable site of alternatives? Finally, if struggles are local and built historically, how might migrants come together to mobilize and learn from one another's experiences? I do not have all the answers.

Still, these two communities offer clues about to what to look for in other marginal groups, especially in an age of migration, exclusion, and policing. Despite their specificities, the people of Partida and Retorno exemplify a class of disenfranchised actors who lack power against states that exclude them. To understand such migrants' identities and advocacy, scholars must look to their hometown legacies, the modes of control they confront in their destinations, and the relationship between politics and gender. There are signs that similar processes of control resistance, and gender transformation resonate elsewhere.

On the sending side, Partida and Retorno symbolize a range of power dynamics, from redistributive to hierarchical. Indigenous Oaxacans have uniquely high rates of communal landholding and democratic participation. Indeed, in Mexico as a whole, only 16 percent of municipalities have a democratic assembly, 27 percent have a citizen council or board, and just over 33 percent have some kind of citizen committee. Partida, in particular, was unusually egalitarian. Retorno's unequal dynamics resemble more sending communities in Mexico and around the world.[15] Future research might ask whether homelands can also *build* more favorable options for migrants, such as by expanding redistribution and democratic representation.

On the receiving end, the contrast between Los Angeles and San Diego speaks to the importance of street-level discretion in creating a range of local modes of control. Admittedly, California has large concentrations of Latinos, plays host to some of the most active immigrant advocacy in the United States, and is now among the most immigrant-friendly states in the nation. Migrants in other locales have fewer institutional resources to encourage a sense of belonging. Nevertheless, local actors across the country have also taken immigration into their own hands. The variation between institutions and practices in Los Angeles and North County hints at this spectrum of modes of control.

On one end are spaces of conditional treatment, where immigrants may feel more hope and belonging. In the United States today, this category includes major cities and Democratic areas, all of which now have coalitions for immigrants' rights. As of 2017 twelve states and Washington, DC, offered limited-function driver's licenses to the undocumented. Los Angeles's conditional approach might be especially common in places where migrant-friendly publics are stymied by coercion. It might also expand under U.S. presidents who walk the line between enforcement and inclusion, as did Barack Obama. Research shows that institutional support fuels similar feelings of belonging—as well as mobilization—in other locations too. Even within hostile receiving sites, supportive institutions like schools or health practitioners can bolster migrants' sense of inclusion.[16] At the same time, good/bad contrasts can push immigrants to self-regulate both in Los Angeles and in other places as well.[17] Even outside California such practices may encourage an ambiguous combination of "good behavior" and immigrant mobilization.

On the other end of the spectrum are times and places of arbitrary hostility, which may leave migrants more cynical and alienated. Such treatment is likely in agricultural and Republican areas, as well as under right-wing federal leaders like Donald Trump. As of 2016 more than 150 U.S. cities had laws targeting immigrants.[18] Many more policed them arbitrarily by race. Evidence suggests that across the United States, these policies leave migrants afraid and alienated, as, for example, in rural Texas.[19] Autocratic rules and intensive policing isolate migrants in other countries as well, creating barriers to advocacy. For instance, the United Arab Emirates and Israel make it difficult for migrants to move about in public, let alone organize collectively.[20] Even in more moderate nations such as Belgium or the Netherlands, immigrants are more alienated in places where policing is rigid.[21] Future research should explore whether and how hostile local laws provoke mobilization, force immigrants to "pass" as American, or leave immigrants stoic and hopeless, as I argue here.[22]

Contrasting local practices produce similar gender patterns in other places as well. In areas that promote opportunities for female migrants, like police protection and U visas, women tend to feel more faith in the host community. Such local support may help women and men open up to new kinds of gender roles. But there can also be unintended consequences, such as pitting women against men. In a nonmigrant parallel, police in African American neighborhoods have framed women as deserving and set them against their male counterparts.[23] Still, hostile control is far worse. Arbitrary assaults on immigrants make women more vulnerable and enable domestic abuse. Such approaches often coincide with the disavowal of existing protections for women.[24] Thus, women are best off under tolerant policies, especially those that support their particular needs.

There are variations on these trends as well, including more extreme cases and hybrids in between. Many cities mix arbitrary and supportive treatment. In other areas, jurisdictions within the same region take opposing approaches to migrants. And migrants' experiences can vary by class, gender, and racial appearance. Local practices also change over time. Broader power relations shape the constraints on state agents, the positions of migrants, and the possibilities for mobilization. In moments of nationalism, radical populism, and police crackdown, as under President Trump, even friendly cities become subject to federal intervention, making migrants more isolated and angry.[25] Under such conditions, immigrants may relocate to supportive sites within the United States (if they can), or they may hunker down and dream of a future elsewhere. On the other extreme one might hope for a time when immigrants enjoy a path to citizenship and are no more policed than those who are native born.

Social mobilization (and demographics) also shape the treatment of migrants. California offers a telling example. In the mid-1990s California was openly hostile to immigrants, threatening to bar them from public services. As California's Latino population grew in size and influence, however, the state became more supportive. Receiving communities began to recognize the benefits of welcoming immigrants and the drawbacks of collaborating with ICE. Migrants also fought hard for greater rights. In the late 2010s California shifted course, passing statewide bills that prevented police from assisting ICE, extending driver's licenses and in-state tuition to undocumented immigrants, and making California the nation's first sanctuary state. Such welcoming policies curbed the restrictionism of cities like Escondido and Vista, even at a time of greater federal crackdown. Perhaps the combination of immigrant mobilization and demographic change will convince other areas to alter their treatment of migrants as well.

As for transnational mobilization, one might argue that indigenous communities sustain closer social networks, more connections to Mexico, or more democratic vibrancy than their counterparts elsewhere.[26] Indigenous people were at the helm of some of the strongest social movements of the 1990s and early 2000s, giving them a framework to challenge U.S. exclusion. Indigenous hometowns have also been more assertive than others in demanding participation from emigrants abroad.[27] In other instances migrants from the same hometown may not follow cohesive pathways at all. Indeed, one study found that only 9 percent of migrants engage in cross-border politics.[28] Migrants who come from cities or scatter to various destinations might have weaker ties with one another and their homelands. In cases where migrants flee gangs or war-torn countries, meanwhile, they have little recourse to return at all. Likewise, other forms of exclusion—including homeland patriarchy—give certain groups of migrants little choice but to seek inclusion on the receiving end. Still, pathways vary, and detachment from the homeland can be a path of its own.

Even on cohesive pathways members may grow disconnected. Rigid border enforcement, for instance, blocks migrants from circulating. As of 2017 back-and-forth trips to Mexico had all but ceased among undocumented immigrants, hindering flows of ideas, money, and solidarity. While many migrants in the United States felt afraid, angry, and alienated from mainstream society, they had fewer outlets for their dissent. In the 2010s northward migration also reversed. The United States deported roughly 400,000 people per year. At the same time, the rate of voluntary return rose to almost 450,000 a year. Net migration from Mexico fell below zero for the first time in half a century.[29] It will be important to understand how these changes transform migrants' cross-border actions.

Despite such variations, the concept of pathways can be helpful in understanding the trajectories of many migrant communities, from small groups to countries as a whole. Almost all migrants follow social networks to their destinations. Three-quarters of migrants actively connect to their hometowns, such as by calling or visiting.[30] While not all migrants come from villages as cohesive as Partida and Retorno, they can also *build* unity, such as through labor unions, civic associations, or family ties. Even migrants who are fragmented from one another can find ways to seek rights and dignity. For instance, sociologist Amrita Pande (2012) found that in the highly restrictive context of Israel, live-in maids talked across balconies to build camaraderie with one another. Migration streams that appear "dead" can also evolve in response to political contexts. Take the example of migration between Central America and the United States. In the 1980s several Central American countries sent refugees fleeing civil wars to the United States. Then migration diminished. Thirty years later, however, deportation and gang violence produced a new refugee crisis, leading women and children to leave Central America and seek U.S. asylum.[31] The direction of each migration pathway is hard to predict in advance.

These cases also highlight how certain conditions can enable or hinder homeland battles for alternative globalization. They suggest that cross-border organizing is most likely when (1) migrants are willing to engage, (2) allies help them do so, and (3) the sending state is "open for business." Elsewhere, one might expect greater transnational engagement when migrants feel rejected on the receiving end but have institutional allies and democratic openings (or ongoing struggles) on the sending side.

Institutional support helps migrants mobilize across borders, as they did in the FIOB. For instance, sociologists Patricia Landolt and Luin Goldring (2010) show that Chileans in Toronto were able to advocate against Augusto Pinochet's dictatorship thanks, in part, to supportive Canadian activists. Likewise, in the Netherlands, local solidarity groups helped Filipino emigrants continue their struggle against dictator Ferdinand Marcos.[32] Future research might dig deeper into how migrants can build alliances that further their transnational causes.

Emigrant engagement is also more extensive when encouraged by sending countries. In Mexico in the 1990s and early 2000s, party contestation elicited increased political participation among both migrants and their hometown counterparts.[33] Similar political battles in other countries may also incite migrant advocacy, as among Hindu nationalists in the United States or Kurdish activists who left Turkey after the 1980 revolution and fought for rights from afar.[34] Yet other sending states refuse or lack the capacity to recognize their emigrants abroad. Indeed, after a heyday of migrant outreach in the 1990s and early 2000s, Mexico itself was hamstrung by violence and drug trafficking. In turn, migrants grew afraid to return. In some hometowns, residents' hands were tied by threats from cartels. Likewise, Somali refugees face the effective collapse of their home state, so when they send remittances, it is only at a subnational level.[35] Scholars of other migrant groups have found that such unstable conditions deter migrant engagement and suppress democracy at home.[36]

Transnational openings for women rely on sending nations as well. State support for women—such as Mexico offered in the first decade of the 2000s—can help link gender equity to other kinds of political inclusion (such as of migrants and the indigenous). "Women in development" programs also encourage some men to be open to change. One might expect particularly strong women's advocacy on the sending side when gender oppression in the destination coincides with such opportunities at home. By contrast, homelands threatened by gender shifts in the United States, such as Iran, might reinforce patriarchal norms and deter women from return. Further research should consider the range of conditions that can help women struggle for resources and political rights.

Finally, one might ask how second-generation immigrants alter their parents' paths. Given the constraints of multisited research, this book focuses on the first generation. Still, 1.5- and second-generation immigrants are critical to undocumented communities. As of 2017 almost six million U.S. citizen children lived with an undocumented adult (usually a parent).[37] Many such young people stay connected to their ancestral homelands.[38] My observations suggest that this second-generation engagement varies by pathway. First, the family structure of migration matters. When young people migrate for opportunities, as in Partida, they are likely to have children after migrating. Their children are born in the United States, with prospects to overcome the constraints of "illegality." But these children may also be less attuned to their parents' hometowns. By contrast, where parents leave children behind, as in Retorno, those children also cross the border undocumented. Faced with a hostile receiving environment, they too grow critical of racism, exclusion, and injustice. In Retorno's case, however, they could not circulate as their parents had or sustain the same cross-border connections. U.S. border enforcement made it too hard. Meanwhile, other young people remained stuck in Mexico, with few economic resources and unable to cross. For both sets of children, long-term prospects hinge on the conditions in Mexico and the criminalization of Latinos in the United States.[39] Later research should examine how long and to whom pathways extend under different political conditions.

TOWARD INCLUSION AND EQUITY

Many countries, including the United States, are founded on the promise that even the vulnerable can have political voice. Contemporary immigration enforcement defiles this democratic vision, shattering families and leaving immigrants voiceless. In the face of exclusion, how can U.S. cities, Mexican locales, and migrants expand gender equity and political rights? This book suggests that resistance must be both place-based and open to transnational process. It must also attend to gender.

First, advocates must look for openings locally. As this book has shown, on-the-ground practices mediate federal control. Federal immigration reform is crucial. At the same time, law alone does not determine migrants' fates. Rather, the actions of U.S. cities, bureaucrats, and police affect migrants' emotional well-being and day-to-day lives. The state can fracture migrant families only if there are police officers to take young mothers to jail. Police and other state agents can also help build living examples of how *else* things could be done. Policy advocacy must therefore go hand in hand with local-level support. In this regard, sanctuary cities like Los Angeles serve as both examples and warnings. On one hand, sanctuary cities have been emblems of social inclusion. As discussed throughout this book, they insulate immigrants from violence and fear. Studies also show that sanctuary policies encourage better outcomes for immigrants, improve the local economy, and decrease rates of crime.[40] On the other hand, immigrant advocates make a deal with the devil by separating "good" from "bad." Such contrasts pit migrants against one another and even legitimate continued exclusion. Those who care about equity might avoid such moral distinctions, both between citizens and immigrants and among migrants themselves.

Second, migrants' supporters must look for agency in unexpected places and offer their support. As this book reveals, migrants are *already* advocating against U.S. exclusion. Unable to engage in formal electoral campaigns, migrants use "everyday politics" to find places they can belong. Their struggles offer insights into what they want and a vision of what might be possible. At the same time, financial support, connections with other migrants, and institutional allies can help communities scale up their efforts. For instance, in Retorno's case, migrants' ties with one another, the FIOB, foundations, and the PRD helped amplify their demands and institutionalize their fight for democracy. Similarly, when migrants from Partida joined LA-based organizations to march for immigrants' rights, they shifted the conversation around migrant exclusion, especially in California. By sharing stories and resources, migrants might also expand their sense of the options available. They cannot fight exclusion alone.

Mexico can help as well. Rather than seeking to become more like the United States, Mexico might listen carefully to its people's demands for economic support, self-determination, and political rights. Indigenous communities, in particular, offer an example of participatory governance and of the possibilities for transforming women's participation. Mexico might further its own democratic trajectory by honoring such pueblos' demands for inclusion. As Mexico copes with the outfall of U.S. hostility, it might also continue to advocate for its emigrants in the United States (as it started to do in the early 2000s and has promised in answer to President Trump).

Finally, local governments in both Mexico and the United States could go beyond putting resources toward gender equity (a good start!) by supporting women and men in their broader fights for inclusion. Instead of assuming that U.S. culture drives gender change, scholars and advocates might promote both institutional openings and migrants' mobilization. If they did, they would see that concrete benefits like U visas and funding can offer women leverage, inspiring both women and men to shift their traditional ways. But they would also see how women like Carmen and Alma are struggling to escape "illegality" and economic desperation. Indeed, women's empowerment programs have little effect when patriarchy is compounded by poverty or state persecution. Meanwhile, movements that appear to bear little relation to gender may be among the greatest sources of women's emancipation.

Migrant communities' prospects hinge on this work to secure rights and resources. Their political attitudes and everyday actions influence social justice, along lines of gender, race, legal status, and class. In addition, their advocacy has critical implications for social stability in their host countries and homelands. Therefore, the public must pay attention to migrants' struggles. Yet they must also go beyond migrants themselves and hold local-level actors accountable for human suffering. In this, U.S. citizens and allies have a key role to play.

Political inclusion—and alternative globalization, as I have put it in this book—requires breaking down divisions between citizens and unauthorized migrants, "good" immigrants and "bad" immigrants, women and men, migration and development, and Mexico and the United States. In their struggles against exclusion, communities like Partida and Retorno are already doing this work. Their actions cross the borders of nation, legal status, gender, and scholarly categories. Following this lead may help migrants and those around them rethink our approaches to change. As we listen to migrants, we might reimagine inclusion, equality, and even our visions of "freedom."

Methodological Appendix

LISTENING TO DIFFERENCE

This appendix is about how being a young, white, U.S.-born woman shaped my relationships with indigenous Mexican villagers and undocumented migrants in the United States. As I built rapport across social divides, tensions molded the questions I asked, the methods I used, and the sites I considered important. Instead of erasing inequities, I tried to stay open to what I might learn from migrants' responses to me.[1]

In October 2009 I set out to begin my dissertation in sociology. I had lived in Latin America for several years, spoke fluent Spanish, and had run a volunteer program in thirty Oaxacan villages in 2004–5. I returned to Mexico thinking I would study the complexities of rural women's empowerment. The first thing I did was reach out to NGOs and tag along as they visited indigenous villages. Often I was the only white person who had been to the pueblos in months. At five feet five I also stood a head above most indigenous people.[2] And of course I had U.S. citizenship. I worried that being a foreigner could complicate my relationships with Oaxacans. But I also thought of our differences as obstacles I must overcome. Eventually, I realized that I would learn more by *listening* to difference. When I got to the villages, people did not want to talk about women's empowerment. They wanted to focus on me and where I had come from: the United States. That redirection fundamentally shaped the research: to get what was going on in the pueblos, it became clear, I had to look at migration.

Thus, I scoured local libraries and pored over statistics from the Mexican census, choosing Retorno, Partida, and a dozen or so other villages as possible examples of Oaxaca's emigrant history. On a dry November afternoon, I made my first trip to Retorno. I hopped on a van from the city, arcing over the mountain pass. In what was left of the local cornfields, farmers drove wizened donkeys, kicking up dust on the sunburned grass. My experience in Oaxaca had taught me that the right way to do anything in an indigenous pueblo was to request permission from the local authorities. So when the van lurched to a stop, I approached the village town hall. Outside a few men sprawled on thin wooden benches, waiting to talk to the village heads and turning straw hats in their hands. Circumspect but curious, one asked where I came from, and why *tan lejos* (so far)? They perked up when I mentioned California. They "knew" California too, they told me: the strawberry fields just north of the city of San Diego. Perching beside them to wipe off the dust, I asked when they had gone north. "Who knows how many times?" one replied. No one could quite remember the first year he crossed or even the last, nor did they know if they were now back for good. Until the jobs picked up, they had some space to be "free."

When my turn came to enter the *municipio* (town hall), I fidgeted nervously with a folder of papers, worrying that the village would reject my request to do research or, worse, refuse me permission to stay the night. But the four civil servants had other things on their minds. Almost immediately, they interrupted my speech. They were far more concerned about California than about my presence in—or potential threats to—their town. One after another, they offered tales of Escondido, Vista, and Oceanside. I flipped my pen in my hands, eyes glued to the faded clock and the growing queue of people outside, eager for these men's attention. Nearly four decades after Retorno's first migrants crossed the border to California, almost everyone in the village had ties to the United States. Sure, I had permission, they nodded, stashing my papers in a spare desk drawer.

Nostalgic stories aside, as I started to roam the village, people's words resounded with fury. Women spilled out of doorways, poking their heads from their houses to yell, *Cómo le hacen sufrir a nuestra gente!* (How they [you?] make our people suffer!). Elvira González, a fifty-eight-year-old shopkeeper, offered a frigid Coke. Though she'd never visited California, she had several sons there. "They [you?] pay us terribly," she lamented. "They don't even realize how we suffer to cross [the border], or how much we bear. . . . They kick us out; they send us home even though we're there to work. *No es justo* [It's not fair]." Spanish left the grammar ambiguous as to who ("they" or "you") was inflicting this pain. Likewise, the preschool teacher talked of her childhood in the fields, of how her mother had scrounged for food when her father was gone. I was a trigger, I realized, for places that tormented the town. This anger felt like failure. But it also gave me an early clue to what I would later understand as their rejection of "illegality" in the United States.

On paper Partida seemed just like Retorno. It was remote and rugged as well, set off from the city by a winding drive through the mile-high mountains. Both were poor and indigenous; both were municipal seats; both once survived on corn; and both were about the same size. Migrants left in the same waves too, and by the time I arrived, about half of the people born in each pueblo lived in the United States. Yet, unlike in Retorno, I knew, those from Partida had gone to Los Angeles.

Three months later I went to Partida. In a pause between downpours, my truck wove around boulders and heaps of red earth to reveal the village before me. It was a town that clouds covered in the blink of an eye, closing out the world—or perhaps closing *this* world in. It was also eerily quiet. By this point I was looking for impacts of U.S. migration. Yet no women yelled from their houses. When I stepped out of my taxi near a group of ten elder ladies, in gingham aprons and braids, they scattered like sparrows at the sound of a gun. Despite decades of migration to Los Angeles—and with the exception of a few cement homes—the pueblo seemed not to have moved an inch. Instead, I saw practices I had stereotyped as remains of the past: collective politics, communal labor, and a gender oppression that scholars wrote off as a relic of bygone days.

When I learned that Partida's government opened only from seven to nine at night, I bucked up and started poking my head into doors. Stories of abuse seemed to stalk me from house to house. One housewife whispered that her forty-five-year-old sister had been beaten to death last year, hit on the head with a chair. Another woman, visiting from Los Angeles, tried desperately to convince her sixteen-year-old niece to leave an abusive marriage. The new urban doctor had been pushing them to tell her when they were hit. And the men didn't like it. If women's empowerment was an afterthought in Retorno, here it seemed absent. Gender changes, I saw, were not just an echo of U.S. equity, shipped back from California.

When my turn came to meet with Partida's leaders, it had been dark for hours. In the foggy streetlight some thirty men clustered together, their hands in their pockets for warmth. When one gestured for me to go in, I clutched my papers to my chest and climbed the stairs to the second-floor office. There sat a gauntlet of men, lined in their high-backed chairs. I shuffled forward, hoping that I would be ready. When I mentioned the United States, however, the men seemed to stiffen. In a regal desk, the president asked about my agenda. Was I religious? Was I from the government? What did I plan to take from them, and what would I give? Then he dismissed me with a wave of the hand: "Yes, there's permission. But you have to find your own place to stay." What I later learned was that here I stood in for migrants' abandonment and their efforts to import U.S. ideas. Partida was not as detached as it seemed. Its fierce communal commitments—and its patriarchy— reflected a politics of its own. While Oaxacans' relationships to the United States were critical, the character of those interactions varied from place to place. To understand these interplays I would have to talk to migrants in the United States.

Though I set out to study Mexico, my U.S. citizenship (and graduate fellowships) made it possible to follow the forces that shaped Oaxacan lives, in ways that members themselves could not. I gained insights by "going home" to where I had come from: California. As I moved between Mexico and California, I began to connect the stances I heard in each hometown to the experiences of their counterparts in Los Angeles and North County San Diego. As I moved, I traced the far-flung effects of the U.S. (mis)treatment of migrants, and I built the idea of "pathways to politics."

Fieldwork in California presented a new host of tensions. Though I had already lived in migrants' hometowns for several months, in the United States I was a white stranger, and most respondents lacked legal authorization. Many were deeply suspicious. For instance, Santiago Morales, who became a close friend and informant in Los Angeles, admitted that when he first met me, "To me it seemed, I can tell you, half, even half-stupid, that a little girl from—I don't know where the devil you come from—has to go to the south of Mexico because she wants to do a study." Others, like Lupita Suárez, at first would not open their doors.

If my thinking in Oaxaca was guided by how people responded *to* me, in California I also learned from the contrasts between us. I spent my first several months in Vista, where being with migrants made me acutely attuned to privileges I took for granted—and to the everyday impacts of migrants' fear. Respondents often lived eight or ten to a one-bedroom home. So as not to bother them, I rented a room in a nearby complex. Most other renters were white military veterans, who openly argued that migrants were criminals and should "go back where they came from." I felt desperate and isolated. I could only begin to imagine how migrants themselves must feel. I got hints in our interactions. As I describe in chapter 2, most migrants had lived in Vista two decades without ever once going into a restaurant. If I took them to Starbucks, they would hide while drinking their coffee, waiting for police cars to pass. Scared of the simplest actions, they were like captives in their everyday lives.

If Vista showed me how much I took for granted, Los Angeles challenged my assumptions about how undocumented people "ought to" respond to an exclusionary state. Coming to Los Angeles from the cynicism and fear of Vista, I was shocked when people like Carmen Rojas told me they "loved" the United States. While Carmen may have inflated such language because I was a U.S. citizen, migrants from Retorno had not shared similar feelings. In Los Angeles, even when I argued that U.S. laws were unfair, many respondents insisted my country had treated them well. Just as visiting Retorno primed me to be surprised by Partida, living among cynical migrants in Vista made these pro-U.S. attitudes seem strange. In this case my challenge was to be serious about migrants' appreciation, even if I disapproved of U.S. immigration control. Each time I moved between places, I saw new ways the two groups were different—and new connections between them.

While my identity certainly shaped my discussions, over time I got to know people, as all ethnographers do. Despite our social differences and the tensions of early visits, I used humor to build intimacy. I talked often of my personal life. The more people knew about me, I found, the more they were willing to share. In the United States my car made me a resource: without licenses of their own, people often prevailed on me to shuffle them to parties, the grocery store, or children's schools. Several migrants also adopted me as a courier to Mexico, piling me with gifts and photos (and boosting my popularity in the hometowns!). I was also able to help some people access critical information. I translated everything that came home in English, from bills to student report cards. As I talked migrants through the results of biopsies or the methods to access legal aid, I often landed at the center of intimate family affairs. Being an outsider also allowed me to be an "independent" confidante—and occasionally got me caught in internal battles— as women complained about men, or migrants about those back at home. The more I stuck around, the more people could tell that I cared.

My (then) status as a single woman also helped me build friendships, especially with women. When I arrived in Oaxaca, respondents almost always remarked on the fact that I was alone. Often they offered to take me in. While villagers rebuked me for walking alone at night as a woman, no one batted an eye when I shuffled into household kitchens and wedged my way into closed-door gossip. I talked constantly with women about relationships. I had been through a recent breakup, so *mejor sola que mal acompañada* (better alone than in bad company) became a favorite refrain. The women reciprocated, offering advice and stories, including of household abuse. My interactions with men were mostly more formal, though I ultimately grew close with some of the men as well.

While I had been concerned about imposing on respondents, they were not inert in our interactions. They made demands on me as well, especially in the United States. Cell phones and the Internet were not yet available in the villages, but they were omnipresent in Southern California. There respondents would regularly call me to check up on where I was and what I was doing. Compared to their hometown counterparts, U.S. migrants were also more willing (or able) to take charge of the story. They would joke, for instance, that I was obligated to attend the HTA's fiesta, explaining, "Abigail, the community sociologist has to be at the fiesta. If you're going to learn, you need to know this stuff." More seriously, they would dictate decisively what I could or could not write down.

Many ethnographers have been reflexive about the dynamics between researchers and the people they study. Though I at first wished to act as much like an insider as I could, it turned out that my gender, race, and U.S. citizenship guided— and enabled me to do—the project I did. Though power-laden relationships were challenging and sometimes created barriers, they also offered sources of insight. Just as I interviewed respondents, their questions and comments pushed me to places I could not have predicted when the research began. Over time I grew intimately involved in the lives of several transnational families. These relationships persistently posed new question of power. They also challenged me to interrogate my role in the institutions that kept migrants' lives constrained.

Rocío León, whom I call Paula throughout this book and to whom the work is dedicated, brought these tensions home to me perhaps more than anyone else. Rocío lived in East Los Angeles and had three children: two teenage girls she had raised on her own and a five-year-old son with her new boyfriend. Born in Partida, she had worked in garment factories on Alameda Street for more than fifteen years. I met Rocío through her younger sister, Irene, who subsisted by selling *tlayudas* (a Oaxacan specialty) on the main road back home. A single mother and a survivor of household violence, Irene lived in a two-story brick structure Rocío had sent money to build. I spent hours chatting with Irene, and when I mentioned my plans to visit Los Angeles, she gave me Rocío's number. I was immediately drawn to Rocío as well. She was sweet and soft-spoken, incredibly earnest in her commitment to building a life for her children. Though she acted reserved at first, she eventually invited me over to her one-bedroom apartment. On weekends she would insist on cooking for me or giving me clothes she had sewn at work. When I traveled to and from Oaxaca, I also brought videos of Rocío to Irene and vice versa. Every time, the videos made them cry.

On one visit Rocío mentioned that she had gotten a biopsy a month earlier but had not received the results. I was worried. Since Rocío spoke limited English, I offered to call the doctor on her behalf. It quickly became clear that there was a problem. At my urging, Rocío accepted a ride to the hospital. We waited for almost five hours. I was livid. I suspected that Rocío would not have been seen at all had I not complained to the staff. Finally, a frosty doctor informed us that Rocío had a rare form of sinus cancer. I blamed the dense dust and lack of ventilation in the garment factories. She was thirty-six years old. The doctor ordered an MRI, but staff said flatly that they had no appointments for eight months. The tumor had already begun to distort Rocío's face. I screamed for another time. Eight months later, I suspected, Rocío could be dead.

Rocío died in 2012, just as my research came to a close. When she found out about the cancer, she asked me to help tell her children and boyfriend: a sobering moment in which I spelled out the gravity of the disease. She let me drive her to appointments at the hospital and just be there to talk of the pain, so searing she could barely hold back her tears. On my own I also asked Partida's hometown association to gather money for Rocío's children. Rocío had not always been a consistent participant, and some of the members hesitated. I convinced them that it was precisely for these situations that they built their HTA. It was inspiring to see how much money and support the members raised for Rocío, though almost all worked twelve-hour days at barely the minimum wage, and most were undocumented themselves. In Rocío's final weeks she returned to Partida, so her children would not have to see her die.

Looking back at those interactions, I could have recused myself. Perhaps my analysis of Rocío's fate might have been more "real" if I had watched the constraints she faced from a distance instead of getting involved. Yet I couldn't help but use my privilege, both in the institutions that ignored her directly (like the hospital) and in the immigrants' rights protests and sanctuary city battles that continued after her death. While I had initially agonized about my own impositions, neutrality felt less important to me than doing something about the injustices my country imposed on people like Rocío, as they quietly suffered and worked.

Rocío's death also exposed the limits of my capacity to help. I was there the moment she learned of her illness, and I visited often in the months she was sick. Nevertheless, I could not fix the conditions that gave her cancer, obtain her legal authorization, or, ultimately, prevent her death. During my fieldwork I hoped my commitment to respondents would endure. I became *madrina* (godmother) to a girl in Retorno. I brought my family to spend Christmas in Partida. And as Facebook came to the villages in the years that followed, I shared more about my life with people from all four field sites, even as it grew harder to visit in person. When I learned in 2013 that I had been offered a job in San Diego, I was thrilled at the prospect of living closer to respondents and just twenty minutes away from the Mexican border. But as I grew closer in some ways, I grew further away in others. I was pinned down—ironically—by the demands of crafting their story. Though I asked the migrants for feedback, they rarely replied. I wondered how many would ever read the book I had made of their lives.

Notes

1. I use pseudonyms for everyone surveyed or interviewed, and I occasionally scramble details to avoid identifying respondents. I also use pseudonyms for both hometowns and hometown associations. In the community I refer to as "Retorno," I draw on research by other scholars that identifies the village, so I take particular care to mask the identities of interviewees. I make two exceptions. First, I use the real name of the Frente Indígena Oaxaqueño Binacional, because it is a widely recognized, public organization. Second, I use migrants' real names when quoting their words from other texts where they are identified. All translations are my own.

2. *Pueblo* means both "town" and "people." Many Oaxacans use this word to refer to their hometowns.

3. Ironically, rigid border enforcement increased the number of undocumented Mexican migrants living in the United States. From 1995 to 2007 the undocumented population grew from about 5.7 million to a peak of 12.2 million (Passel and Cohn 2011). While enforcement did little to stop Mexicans from coming to the United States without authorization, it raised the costs and risks of crossing. As a result, fewer migrants went back and forth. Migrants who had once left their families behind also began bringing spouses and children across the border. Even those eligible for family visas sometimes brought family

members undocumented, because visas could take as long as eighteen to twenty years (Massey, Durand, and Pren 2016).

4. Krogstad, Passel, and Cohn (2017).

5. Taylor et al. (2011).

6. In 1986 the U.S. Immigration Reform and Control Act closed off legal entry to most new Mexican migrants, blocking them from obtaining legal authorization except through employer visas or immediate family.

7. By comparison, in 1997 the United States deported about ninety thousand people. The Obama administration deported more people than all past presidents put together (U.S. Department of Homeland Security 2012). In 2012 the United States spent almost $18 billion on immigration control, more than the budget for all other federal law enforcement combined, and over fifteen times what it had spent (adjusted) in 1986 (Massey 2012; Meissner et al. 2013; Waters and Pineau 2015).

8. When deportees *were* convicted of crimes, their offenses consisted primarily of illegal entry (25 percent), traffic violations (23 percent), and drug charges (21 percent), mostly marijuana (Golash-Boza 2015; U.S. Department of Homeland Security 2012).

9. In the 1990s and the first decade of the 2000s, U.S. laws, including the 1996 U.S. Illegal Immigration Reform and Immigrant Responsibility Act and Anti-Terrorism and Effective Death Penalty Act, expanded the grounds for deportation to include "crimes" ranging from traffic violations to entering the United States without authorization. Under such policies almost two-thirds of *legal* immigrants also became deportable, because they had previously crossed the border unauthorized (Massey and Malone 2003; Provine et al. 2016).

10. Peter Evans defines alternative globalization as a "globally organized project of transformation aimed at replacing the dominant (hegemonic) global regime with one that maximizes democratic political control and makes the equitable development of human capabilities and environmental stewardship its priorities" (2008, 271).

11. Following the Mexican census, I define villages as "indigenous" based on self-identification and state-level rights to political autonomy.

12. Political theorist Partha Chatterjee (2004) argues that security technologies have enabled governments to manage groups like unauthorized immigrants without providing space for democratic participation. Giorgio Agamben (1998) extends this point to argue that people deprived of rights are reduced to what he calls "bare life" and lose the ability to use their voices or represent themselves.

13. McAdam (1999); Meyer (2004); Meyer and Staggenborg (1996); Tarrow (1993); Tilly (1995).

14. L. Martínez (2005, 2008); Voss and Bloemraad (2011).

15. Michelson (2016); Ryo (2013, 2015).

16. Calavita (1998); Hagan, Eschbach, and Rodriguez (2008); Holmes (2007); Piore (1979); Walter, Bourgois, and Loinaz (2004).

17. Burawoy (1976); de Genova (2002); Golash-Boza (2015).

18. See Berry (2017) for a review of research on patriarchal backlash to women's political gains. See also Kibria (1990).

19. Rodriguez and Rouse (2012); Schussman and Soule (2005); Verba, Schlozman, and Brady (1995); Waldinger (2008).

20. Barreto et al. (2009); Ebert and Okamoto (2013); Jiménez (2010); Okamoto and Ebert (2010); Sanchez and Masuoka (2010); Zepeda-Millán (2017).

21. Gutiérrez and Hondagneu-Sotelo (2008); Hondagneu-Sotelo and Salas (2008); Voss and Bloemraad (2011).

22. De Genova (2010); Vargas (2011). In particular, youth known as the "DREAMers" were at the vanguard of undocumented activism. Young immigrants took this moniker thanks to the DREAM (Development, Relief, and Education for Alien Minors) Act, proposed in 2001 and reintroduced in 2009, which would have offered a path to citizenship for young undocumented migrants brought to the United States as children if they attended college or served in the military. The act repeatedly failed in Congress. But in 2012 President Barack Obama created the Deferred Action for Childhood Arrivals program, which granted this group protection from deportation. DREAMers developed slogans such as "here to stay" and "undocumented and unafraid" (Abrego and Gonzales 2010; Milkman and Terriquez 2012; Nicholls 2013; Patler 2018; Terriquez 2015).

23. Milkman (2006); Varsanyi (2005).

24. Bada et al. (2010).

25. Waldinger (2008).

26. Benedict Anderson (1998) calls this form of activism "long-distance nationalism." See also Gosse (1996); Hamilton and Chinchilla (2001); Pedraza (2007); and R. Smith (2003).

27. Luis Guarnizo, Alejandro Portes, and William Haller (2003) find that one-sixth of migrants are core transnational activists and another one-sixth are occasional activists. Meanwhile, Roger Waldinger (2007) finds that 9 percent of migrants are involved in hometown associations.

28. Délano (2011); FitzGerald (2008); Iskander (2010).

29. Fox and Rivera-Salgado (2004); Kearney (1996); Kearney and Besserer (2004).

30. The Zapatista movement was formed by indigenous peasants in Chiapas, Mexico, beginning in 1994, to fight the harms of neoliberal globalization. The movement became an inspiration to the global Left in the 1990s, especially after the fall of the Berlin Wall.

31. Partha Chatterjee (2004) suggests that in India "political society" (namely, the struggles of those excluded from formal citizenship) is where political modernity is being formed. Similarly, Asef Bayat (1997, 2013) shows that in the Arab

Spring protesters set up their own existence beyond the state. Such theorists build on long-standing arguments by scholars like James Scott (1985), who shows that dominated groups resist by using "weapons of the weak" such as non-cooperation, and Giorgio Agamben (1998), who contends that those deprived of basic freedoms use their bodies to protest inhumane prison conditions. Such theorists built on postcolonial scholars such as Frantz Fanon (1963), who argued that because the colonized had no formal voice, they had to resist through violence.

32. Evans (2008); Tarrow (2005).

33. Brown (1992); J. W. Scott (1988).

34. During and after the 2016 presidential campaign, Donald Trump used this phrase to describe undocumented immigrants and justify expanded immigration control. See also Golash-Boza and Hondagneu-Sotelo (2013).

35. Levien and Paret (2012).

36. Sometimes scholars worry that such geographic and temporal "extensions" may sacrifice depth for breadth, diluting the focus that historically characterized participant observation (Marcus 2009).

37. Levitt (2001); R. Smith (2006).

38. Cohen (2004); Kandel and Massey (2002); Massey et al. (1993); Wilkerson (2010).

39. Most comparative studies of migration, such as Pedraza (1985) and Portes and Borocz (1989), look at entire nations, such as Mexico and Cuba, with a few exceptions, like Goldring (1992).

40. For instance, one might look at how people from the same hometown fared under different U.S. practices of control.

41. Relational comparison is similar to "linked ethnography," which Nazanin Shahrokni and I describe in Andrews and Shahrokni (2014). It is *not* the same as "relational ethnography," proposed by Desmond (2014) and others. Desmond focuses on the relationships between players in a case rather than the relationships between cases and of cases to the context as a whole. See Burawoy (2017) for a cogent critique of Desmond's approach.

42. Cohen (2004).

43. Zapotecs and Mixtecs are the two largest indigenous groups in Oaxaca, with Zapotecs making up 32 percent of the state's indigenous population and Mixtecs 21 percent (INEGI 2010).

44. Barrera-Bassols (2006); Velásquez (2004).

45. As of 2011 Oaxaca was one of only two Mexican states that had not adopted a 2007 federal law prohibiting violence against women in its state constitution or penal code (Gibson 2005).

46. See Paul (2011).

47. Novo (2004).

48. In the 2010 U.S. census, 685,000 people self-identified as indigenous Latinos, and it is estimated that at least that number would not self-report (Stephen 2007; U.S. Census Bureau 2012).

49. Kay (2004); Massey et al. (1987).

50. By 2014, 59 percent of Mexican migrants still concentrated in these states, along with New York, New Jersey, and Florida (Passel and Cohn 2016; Riosmena and Massey 2012).

51. Passel and Cohn (2016); U.S. Census Bureau (2017).

52. The causes of this divergence are beyond the scope of this book. Common knowledge associates anti-immigrant practices with factors such as high unemployment, high crime, city size, and rapid influxes of Latinos (Hopkins 2010; Walker and Leitner 2011). But nationwide surveys of police conducted by Provine and her coauthors (2016) show that these factors are relatively unimportant for local policing. Rather, partisanship is the most important predictor of local immigration control. Left-wing areas tend to push pro-immigrant practices, while right-wing areas tend to encourage restrictionist policing. For more analysis of the factors that drive local immigration policy, see Chand and Schreckhise (2015); de Graauw and Vermeulen (2016); Ebert and Okamoto (2015); Gleeson (2010); Gulasekaram and Ramakrishnan (2013); Lewis et al. (2012); Ramakrishnan and Wong (2010); and Walker (2014).

53. Walker and Leitner (2011).

54. Tramonte (2011). Under the Trump administration, these cities risked federal sanction for failing to cooperate in immigration enforcement.

55. Coleman (2012); Coutin (2000); Donato and Armenta (2011).

56. In 1996 the U.S. Illegal Immigration Reform and Immigrant Responsibility Act created an optional provision called 287(g), empowering police to turn migrants over to ICE. In 2008 the federal government phased this program out and replaced it with Secure Communities, which mandated that police take individuals' fingerprints upon booking. From 2004 to 2011 Congress increased funding for these programs from $23 million to nearly $700 million. The programs became notorious for racial profiling, often turning immigrants over to ICE for things like "appearing undocumented" (Armenta 2015). Obama later introduced the Priority Enforcement Program, which he promised would focus on convicted criminals. As of 2017 Trump planned to return to the Secure Communities model.

57. For accounts of agent discretion, see Armenta (2015); Coleman (2012); Jones-Correa (1998); and Marrow (2011).

58. By substantively responding to migrants' needs, they promoted what Helen Marrow (2009) calls "bureaucratic incorporation."

59. De Graauw (2014); Fujiwara (2005); Gleeson and Gonzales (2012); Hallett and Jones-Correa (2012); Lewis and Ramakrishnan (2007); Yoo (2008).

60. I focused on hometowns that were municipal seats and had at least a thousand inhabitants, to obtain better information about municipal policies and have enough respondents to conduct the study.

61. CONAPO (2005).

62. Earlier waves of migrants moved straight to the United States from western Mexico, often setting roots through the U.S Bracero Program, which recruited temporary Mexican farmworkers during and after World War II (Fox and Rivera-Salgado 2004). Even though Partida and Retorno sent a few people to this program, their U.S. migration remained at a trickle until the late 1980s (Velasco Ortiz 2005a, 2005b).

63. Even though each community had also sent migrants to internal destinations, and Retorno sent a few people to other parts of the United States, I focus on their primary U.S. destinations. The wider dispersion of migrants from Retorno may reflect the repression they faced in North County and their efforts to find better opportunities. To confirm my observations I visited migrants from Retorno in Brentwood, California, and from Partida in Oaxaca City.

64. U.S. Census Bureau (2017).

65. Later Oaxacan migrants were more dispersed across the United States.

66. Aquino (2009); Aquino Moreschi (2010); Besserer (2002); Ibarra Templos (2003); Kearney (1998); Krissman (1995); López and Runsten (2004); K. Martínez (2005); Nagengast and Kearney (1990); Rivera-Salgado (1999); Stephen (2007).

67. For counterexamples, see Cohen (2004); Mines, Nichols, and Runsten (2010); and R. Smith (2006).

68. Campaigns included an early effort by the United Auto Workers to stop plant closures, the SEIU campaign "Justice for Janitors," the Domestic Workers Movement, and organizing by Local 11 and the Bus Riders' Union, among others. Through repeated collaboration these campaigns built trust, mobilized resources, and translated grievances into action (Keil 1998; Milkman 2006; Nicholls 2003, 2008; Pulido 1996).

69. Milkman (2006).

70. Chavez (1998).

71. I discuss these local dynamics in more detail in chapter 2.

72. I had worked in rural Oaxaca from 2004 to 2005, giving me both on-the-ground connections and a sense of how to interact with indigenous communities.

73. Since there is no list of undocumented migrants, scholars often recruit them through institutions. Such methods can overrepresent civically active migrants, neglecting the 75–95 percent who are not involved in such groups.

74. I decided not to live with families in California because most migrants lived several people to a room, and I did not want to add extra strain. Though the neighborhood of Echo Park was undergoing rapid gentrification, some of Partida's earliest migrants still lived there.

75. Abrego (2011).

76. I did not interview 1.5- or second-generation immigrants. Since most respondents arrived in the 1990s, second-generation immigrants were largely still under the age of eighteen. In the conclusion I address how my analysis may apply to later generations.

77. When I mention the percentage of respondents who share a particular viewpoint, I do so only to give a picture of the distribution of attitudes or demographics across each community.

78. Spanish was the lingua franca among respondents, even though some interviewees also spoke Zapotec or Mixtec.

79. While snowball samples may produce skewed groups of respondents, they offer one of the only means to survey undocumented migrants, who are not "listed" systematically (Cornelius 1982). When I pooled the samples, I weighted the cases by the inverse of the sampling fraction at each site. For a detailed description of the UCSD survey methodology, see FitzGerald, Hernández-Díaz, and Keyes (2013).

80. Interestingly, my ethnographic experiences helped me see biases in the surveys, revealing how respondents interpreted categories differently than researchers. For instance, the UCSD survey asked women in Retorno whether they were employed. I observed that nearly all women in Retorno did wage labor, ranging from running small businesses to paid farmwork. Nevertheless, most female respondents selected "housewife" as their job and did not mention this other work. While scholars often see surveys as "harder" data than qualitative accounts, these variations in respondents' reports led me to take survey results with a grain of salt. In turn, our surveys also revealed significant gaps in government data, particularly the Mexican census. Mexico's Consejo Nacional de Población (National Population Council; CONAPO 2005) tracks several municipal-level indicators of migration. Compared to our surveys, CONAPO dramatically underreported rates of migration and remittances. For instance, CONAPO reported that, in 2005, 14.9 percent of households in Partida and 9.7 percent of those in Retorno had migrants in the United States, while our surveys show numbers closer to 60–70 percent in both cases. Likewise, CONAPO estimated that 3–5 percent of households in each site received U.S. remittances, while we showed numbers between 35 and 37 percent. Such observations underscored the importance of triangulating surveys with qualitative reports.

81. In Retorno in-depth studies by Curiel (2011) and Velasco Ortiz (2002, 2005a, 2005b) were invaluable, along with the two major surveys conducted by the UCSD Mexican Migration Field Research Program in 2007 (Cornelius et al. 2009) and 2011 (FitzGerald, Hernández-Díaz, and Keyes 2013). I also drew on research in neighboring towns by Besserer (2002); Caballero and Ríos Morales (2004); and Krissman (1995). In Partida studies of neighboring villages proved informative, particularly those by Aquino (2009); Aquino Moreschi (2010);

Hirabayashi (1993); Nader (1991); and Worthen (2012). On the U.S. side I built on studies of Mixtec migrants by Chavez (1998); Holmes (2013); K. Martínez (2005); Rivera-Salgado (1999); and Zabin (1992), among others. I also relied on extensive prior research on Zapotec and Mixtec communities by Kearney (1996, 1998) and Stephen (2005, 2007) as well as the studies compiled by Fox and Rivera-Salgado (2004) in their volume *Indigenous Mexican Migrants in the United States*.

82. Mahoney (2000, 2010).

83. Chavez (2008); de Genova (2002, 2005); Ngai (2004).

84. Following Bourdieu (1989), scholars refer to the legitimation of migrants' subordinate status as "symbolic violence" (Golash-Boza and Hondagneu-Sotelo 2013; Holmes 2013; Menjívar and Abrego 2012). They also show that policing and deportation terrify migrants into submission (de Genova 2002; Golash-Boza 2015; Menjívar and Abrego 2012).

85. Portes and Rumbaut (2006); Portes and Zhou (1993); Stepick and Stepick (2010).

86. Castles (2010); Delgado-Wise and Cypher (2007); Hirschman (1970).

87. Peggy Levitt (2001) refers to ideas sent home as "social remittances." See also Duquette-Rury (2016); FitzGerald (2008); Goldring (1992, 2003); Kapur (2010); Pérez-Armendáriz (2014); Pérez-Armendáriz and Crow (2010); Rivera-Salgado (1999); and Soyer (1997).

88. Grasmuck and Pessar (1991); Hirsch (2003); Hondagneu-Sotelo (1994); Mahler and Pessar (2006); Parrado and Flippen (2005).

89. Abrego (2014); Crenshaw (1991); Dreby (2010, 2015); Dreby and Schmalzbauer (2013); Kibria (1990); Menjívar (2000); Parrado and Flippen (2005); Schmalzbauer (2009).

90. Evans (2008); Keck and Sikkink (1998); Smith, Chatfield, and Pagnucco (1997); Tarrow (2005); Vertovec (2009).

91. Brubaker (2010); Castles and Davidson (2000); Yuval-Davis (2006).

92. Regarding place, see Hart (2002); Martin and Miller (2003); Miller (2000); Nicholls (2008); and Wolford (2003). Regarding local organizing, see Armstrong and Bernstein (2008); Buechler (2000); Friedman and McAdam (1992); Polletta (1999); Polletta and Jasper (2001); Snow and Soule (2010); and Voss and Williams (2012). Such scholars show that when people identify with a group, they are more likely to engage in collective action (Hunt and Benford 2004; Klandermans 2003).

1. LEGACIES OF (IN)EQUITY

1. INEGI (1940).

2. In the 1940s labor recruiters from Veracruz had also come to Oaxaca, drawing a few workers from Retorno and Partida into sugarcane contracts. But

agroindustrial recruitment became far more extensive in the 1960s (Garduño 1991; Stephen 2007).

3. Cornelius et al. (2009).

4. Hulshof (1991); Mines, Nichols, and Runsten (2010); Stephen (2007).

5. López and Runsten (2004); Stephen (2007).

6. Portes and Bach (1985); Sassen (1990).

7. FitzGerald (2008); Massey et al. (1987); Paul (2011).

8. Durand and Massey (1992); Massey et al. (1987).

9. Aguilera and Massey (2003); Massey and Espinosa (1997); Massey, Goldring, and Durand (1994).

10. Massey, Goldring, and Durand (1994).

11. López and Runsten (2004); Massey et al. (1987).

12. Wolf (1957, 1969).

13. Sociologists show that when migrants work within their home countries, they build skills and networks that link them to similar sectors abroad (Hagan, Hernández-León, and Demonsant 2015; Paul 2011).

14. López and Runsten (2004); Stephen (2007).

15. Hondagneu-Sotelo (1994); Massey, Fischer, and Capoferro (2006).

16. Cerrutti and Gaudio (2010); Cerrutti and Massey (2001).

17. By contrast, as I show in other work, men remained more tied to the village by their obligations under Usos y Costumbres (Andrews and Shahrokni 2014).

18. Selee (2011).

19. These technologies would later spread around the world. While the innovations enabled poor countries to grow food at much larger scales, they also introduced toxic pesticides, undermined small farmers, and diminished the nutritional value of food (Wright 2005).

20. Krissman (1995); Thompson and Martin (1989).

21. Kearney (2004).

22. Wright (2005).

23. Alba (1982).

24. Hirabayashi (1993).

25. Dillingham (2012).

26. Arizpe (1981).

27. Fox (1992); Light (2006); Singer and Massey (1998); Stephen (2007).

28. Babb (2001); White, Salas, and Gammage (2003).

29. In 1992 Mexican president Carlos Salinas de Gortari reformed article 27 of the Mexican Constitution, which had granted rural villages in Mexico communal land rights (Barkin 2002).

30. Taylor et al. (2005).

31. Stephen (2007).

32. Rivera-Salgado (1999).

33. From 1980 to 2002 migration from rural Mexican villages to other parts of Mexico increased by 352 percent and to the United States by 452 percent (Taylor et al. 2005).

34. Parreñas (2001); Tyner (2004); Yinger (2006).

35. Krissman (1995); Velasco Ortiz (2002).

36. Rubin (1996); Selee (2011).

37. Joseph and Nugent (1994); Kearney (1998); Nagengast and Kearney (1990); B. Smith (2009). Because villages in Oaxaca were so remote and their land of relatively low value, colonial intervention and early Mexican state presence were more limited there than elsewhere in Mexico and relied on indirect rule (Chance 1989; Rivera-Salgado 1999). The villages' isolation made them models of what Wolf (1957, 1969) calls "closed corporate communities."

38. Hernández-Díaz (2007); Kearney (1998); Stephen (2007).

39. A village of 1,500 might appoint 50 to 100 people to cargos per year, including a mayor, sheriff, four councilmen, four alternates, a judge, four elders, eight police commanders, and numerous others, including several committees of 4–5 each that oversaw water, communal landholdings, education, health, and so on (Stephen 2005, 2007).

40. Oaxaca's isolation and rugged terrain helped it avoid the dispossession that swept Mexico in the nineteenth and twentieth centuries, leaving most rural families landless (Massey et al. 1987). The extent of communal landholding in Oaxaca is unique within Mexico, a country that itself saw more land reform than other parts of Latin America.

41. Communes *(comunidades agrarias),* which predominate in Oaxaca, are governed by similar laws as *ejidos* but their communal status dates to the colonial era, giving them more protection from privatization (Esteva 2007; Kearney and Besserer 2004). Under both forms, families can pass on usufruct rights but are not allowed to sell land on the market (Nagengast and Kearney 1990).

42. Hernández-Díaz (2007); Kay (2004); Massey et al. (1987); Stephen (2007).

43. Scholars find that Usos y Costumbres could provide as much as 30 percent of a villager's annual food budget through redistribution (Dow 1977; Greenberg 1981).

44. Aquino (2009); Esteva (2007); Kearney (1998); Nagengast and Kearney (1990).

45. Eisenstadt (2011).

46. Guardino (2005).

47. Chance (1989).

48. Chance (1989); Guardino (2005); Mallon (1995).

49. Aquino (2009).

50. B. Smith (2005, 2007).

51. A parcel is around two acres. By "having" land, Samuel meant they had usufruct rights.

52. Across the Sierra Norte region, there was no individual landholding more than 250 acres (Aquino 2009).

53. Amita Baviskar (1995) notes that communal labor can check inequality. Since all farmers require others' labor, they cannot acquire too much wealth at others' expense without losing goodwill.

54. In the 1970s anthropologist Lane Hirabayashi (1993) found that in one nearby village, 70 percent of families lived on communal labor, while 10 percent hired workers and 20 percent worked for wages.

55. See Stern (1983).

56. Hirabayashi (1993); Stephen (2007).

57. In the 1950s and 1960s a few men from Partida went to the United States to do farmwork through the Bracero Program (Stephen 2007). Their reaction was the same.

58. These urban migrants also gained literacy. Though both Retorno and Partida had around 20 percent literacy in 1940, by 1970 literacy was 80 percent in Partida and still only 45 percent in Retorno, despite the introduction of primary schools in both pueblos (INEGI 1940, 1970). Literacy may have helped migrants from Partida to read everything from employer want ads to urban transit signs.

59. CONAPO (2005).

60. In Mexico there were some live-in public schools called *internados*, targeted at children who did not have secondary schools in their hometowns.

61. Some men also left for gendered reasons, to escape their father's violence.

62. Anthropologists such as Klaver (1997); Stephen (2005); and Young (1978) demonstrate that women emigrated alone from many villages in the region.

63. Worthen (2012).

64. Hulshof (1991); Stephen (2007); Worthen (2012).

65. Similar patterns reverberated across the Mixteca, the region where Retorno is located.

66. Respondents' accounts and local archives are unclear about where the new landlords came *from*, stating that they came from a nearby community, which was presumably a waystation from farther afield.

67. Chance (1989); B. Smith (2009); Spores (1967).

68. Velasco Ortiz (2005a).

69. Bartolomé (1997).

70. B. Smith (2005).

71. Chance (1989); Monaghan, Joyce, and Spores (2003); Pastor (1986); Velasco Ortiz (2005a).

72. Aquino (2009); López Bárcenas and Espinoza Sauceda (2003); B. Smith (2009).

73. "Reporte Municipal," 1960, Registro Agrario Nacional, Archivo Municipal de San Miguel Tlacotepec, Oaxaca City, Mexico.

74. Curiel (2011); Rivera-Salgado (1999).

75. INEGI (1950).

76. Kearney (1996); Stuart and Kearney (1981); Wright (2005).

77. Wright (2005).

78. See chapter 4 for a discussion of how farmworkers from Retorno joined mass strikes in Sinaloa, coordinated by students sympathetic to the Communist Party.

79. For a similar account, see Stephen (2007).

80. U.S. growers often used independent farm-labor contractors to avoid potential penalties for recruiting undocumented workers.

81. Krissman (1995, 2002).

82. Zabin (1992). A few migrants from Retorno went on to California's Central Valley (particularly to the area around Brentwood, California), a site I also visited as part of my fieldwork.

83. Cornelius et al. (2009).

84. Brenner (1976).

85. Despite the egalitarian aims of communal landholding, in most Mexican *ejidos* and communes, state pressure coincided with local power struggles to encourage *caciquismo* (political bossism) and the de facto privatization of communal land (B. Smith 2009).

86. Whether Zapotec or Mixtec, Oaxacan pueblos were more likely to lose their communal structures if elites operated as privileged agents of the colonial powers, the PRI, and the state (Chance 1989; B. Smith 2009). Villages that had stronger political bosses and more local dispossession were more likely to send members into debt and farmwork, even if they were Zapotec. The more land equity in a village, meanwhile, the less susceptible it was to farm migration (Van-Wey, Tucker, and Diaz McConnell 2005). Those that were more egalitarian had greater access to urban options, including ethnically Mixtec communities such as those in the nearby state of Puebla (Chance 2003; R. Smith 2006). The consistency of these patterns across ethnic lines suggests that the differences cannot be attributed to cultural or ethnic variation alone. While some Zapotec migrants have been found to be more fluent in Spanish and less attached to their indigenous identity than Mixtecs (López and Runsten 2004), I argue that these differences represent an effect of the Zapotecs' mostly urban migration patterns rather than a cause. See also Cohen (2004) and Mines, Nichols, and Runsten (2010).

87. Levitt and Lamba-Nieves (2011); Waldinger and Duquette-Rury (2016); Waldinger and FitzGerald (2004).

88. Cornelius et al. (2009); Schlosser (1995).

89. Zabin (1992).

90. Holmes (2007); Mines, Nichols, and Runsten (2010); Stephen (2007). As of the early 1990s, 72 percent of California's indigenous farmworkers were paid piece rate, and nearly 100 percent earned below the federal poverty level (Kresge 2007; Zabin 1997).

91. Balderrama and Molina (2009). In general, farmwork is associated with relatively hostile receiving areas, circularity, male migration, and family separation.

92. Hart (2002); Kearney (1996).

2. "ILLEGALITY" UNDER TWO LOCAL MODES OF CONTROL

1. Sterngold (2006).

2. Walter Nicholls (2008) points out that while analysts attribute Los Angeles's immigrant mobilization to Spanish-speaking DJs, similar radio coverage elsewhere did not produce large turnout.

3. Burawoy (1985); Hart (1991); Lee (1995).

4. For critiques of this good/bad immigrant logic and how it affects advocacy, see Bosniak (2012); Fujiwara (2005); Yoo (2008); and Yukich (2013).

5. Maricopa County, Arizona was one of the first and most notorious to do such racial targeting, but examples abound. See Coleman (2012); Holmes (2013); and Schmalzbauer (2014).

6. Capps et al. (2011).

7. Milkman (2006); Nicholls (2008).

8. For instance, Huntington Park city manager Gregory Korduner said, "I can tell you, these [unauthorized migrants] are good people. They pay their bills. They are respectful. They want to make this a better city. Who doesn't want that?" (Sterngold 2006).

9. Maya (2002); Tramonte (2011).

10. Elsewhere, police were asking for legal status at the time of booking (Capps et al. 2011).

11. This policy ended in 2015, after I concluded my fieldwork.

12. Alarcón, Escala, and Odgers (2016); Tramonte (2011).

13. Garment factories employed between sixty thousand and eighty thousand workers, making up 14 percent of manufacturing in Los Angeles County (Archer et al. 2010; Cummings 2009; Light 2006).

14. California was the only state to enforce labor laws for the undocumented (Milkman 2006, 2007).

15. Archer et al. (2010); Light (2006); Milkman (2006, 2007).

16. Narro (2005).

17. Burawoy (1985); Gleeson (2016).

18. Gleeson (2010).

19. Among U.S. Latinos in 2008, 73 percent disapproved of the arrest and deportation of immigrants, 76 percent disapproved of workplace raids, and 70 percent opposed the criminal prosecution of employers who hired undocumented migrants (Lopez and Minushkin 2008).

20. Regarding the comparatively welcoming context, see Alarcón, Escala, and Odgers (2016) and Pastor et al. (2016). In addition, the large presence of gangs in neighborhoods such as South Los Angeles and Huntington Park may have encouraged migrants like Gloria Chávez to appreciate the police (see García, forthcoming).

21. Waldinger (2007).

22. Cecilia Menjívar (2000) notes that women often had more economic opportunities in urban areas than men.

23. Quereshi (2010); Orloff et al. (2003); Shaw (2009).

24. It is worth noting, as Olivia Salcido and Cecilia Menjívar (2012) point out, that though the Violence against Women Act of 1994 and associated U visas were intended to support women survivors of domestic violence, undocumented women often face administrative hurdles to proving abuse.

25. Other scholars show that structural barriers like undocumented status may also be more salient for migrant men than women (Menjívar 2000).

26. In reference to British colonialists in India, Gayatri Spivak referred to a similar approach as "saving brown women from brown men" (1988, 297).

27. In the early 1990s the United States began targeted efforts to intercept undocumented migrants at the busiest crossing points in El Paso, Texas (Operation Blockade); Tucson, Arizona (Operation Safeguard); and San Diego (Operation Gatekeeper), making the U.S.-Mexico border one of the most militarized in the world (Nevins 2002).

28. The Minuteman Project was a group of anti-immigrant vigilantes founded in 2004.

29. Hall (2012).

30. The measure banning residents from renting property to unauthorized immigrants was later held up in legal disputes.

31. Maya (2002).

32. Marosi (2011).

33. Guidi (2011).

34. Between 2004 and 2011 the city of Escondido earned more than $500,000 a year from five tow companies. Each company paid the city for the right to charge an impound fee, a tow-hitch fee, and a thirty-day impound storage fee, totaling about $2,000 per car (Frey 2012).

35. Sifuentes (2011).

36. García and Keyes (2012, 12).

37. Chavez (1998).

38. Arnold (2007); Coleman (2012); Johnson (2003); Lacayo (2010).

39. García and Keyes (2012). California significantly restricted the use of E-Verify in 2016.

40. Danielson (2010).

41. Holmes (2013); Kearney (1998).

42. García and Keyes (2012, 16).

43. García and Keyes (2012, 13).

44. Velasco Ortiz (2005a).

45. Douglas Massey, Jorge Durand, and Karen Pren (2016) show this was a widespread response.

46. As of 2012 many who had applied for legalization in the 1990s were still waiting for papers.

47. Dreby and Schmalzbauer (2013); Kibria (1990); Parrado and Flippen (2005); Schmalzbauer (2009).

48. The distinctions may have been unintentional, as efforts to protect immigrants came up against ongoing criminalization.

3. STOICISM AND STRIVING IN THE FACE OF EXCLUSION

1. Ebert and Okamoto (2013); L. Martínez (2005, 2008); Okamoto and Ebert (2010); Piore (1979); Ryo (2013, 2015); Zepeda-Millán (2017). In her forthcoming book, *Legal Passing: Navigating Undocumented Life and Local Immigration Law*, Angela García takes a somewhat different view, arguing that migrants in more tolerant areas may have greater room to express their ethnic identity, while those in more hostile regions may be forced to perform assimilation to "pass" (as legal immigrants).

2. See Voss and Williams (2012) for a review.

3. Holmes (2013); Menjívar and Abrego (2012). Some scholars refer to such behavior as "neoliberal citizenship," in which migrants perform belonging in the face of political exclusion by working hard and refusing to depend on the state (Baker-Cristales 2009; Gleeson 2015; Gomberg-Muñoz 2010).

4. Some radical immigrant activists suggest that territory in the U.S. Southwest should be returned to or "reconquered" by Mexico.

5. Pedraza, Segura, and Bowler (2011). On immigrant optimism, see Branton (2007).

6. The use of Mexican flags also implies a critique of the U.S. government's failure to pass immigration reform. The flags recall the Chicano movement of the 1970s, where they were prominent symbols of ethnic pride. For some activists the Mexican flag also represents the demand to decolonize U.S. control over Latino immigrant populations and the territory that Mexico ceded to the United States in the Treaty of Guadalupe Hidalgo of 1848.

7. Bada, Fox, and Selee (2006).

8. This attitude was unusual. In general, 91 percent of Latino noncitizens, 86 percent of all Latinos, and 72 percent of U.S. citizens favor a path to legalization

for unauthorized immigrants as long as they pay fines, have jobs, and pass background checks (Taylor et al. 2011).

9. Ryo (2015).

10. Hallett (2012); Ribas (2015).

11. Ruth Milkman (2006, 2007) shows that 6.2 percent of Mexican-born workers and 12.6 percent of U.S.-born Mexican American workers unionized. From 1994 to 2004 Mexicans went from 1.8 percent of all U.S. union members to 2.3 percent, many of those in Los Angeles. In the United States in general, roughly 11.3 percent of workers were unionized as of 2013.

12. Milkman (2006, 2007).

13. Susan Berger (2009); Sally Engle Merry (2003); Roberta Villalón (2010); and others call such stipulations a form of "neoliberal citizenship."

14. As Leslie Salzinger (2003) demonstrates, factories often treat *both* men and women according to the trope of "third world women," as if they are cheap, docile, and malleable.

15. See Okamoto and Ebert (2010) and Ebert and Okamoto (2013) on how threat may unify migrants.

16. The march galvanized media attention, including from the *Los Angeles Times,* and drew public awareness to immigrants' rights (Zabin 1992).

17. Kearney (1998).

18. Students, who had been radicalized after the Tlatelolco Massacre and protests in Mexico City in 1968, quickly set their sights on the working conditions in Mexico's agricultural fields. Rejecting the official, PRI-run farmworkers union, the Confederación de Trabajadores de México (Confederation of Mexican Workers), into which the state and growers attempted to recruit migrants, they helped organize new, independent farmworker federations in Sinaloa and Baja California: the Central Independiente de Obreros Agrícolas y Campesinos (Independent Central of Agricultural Workers and Peasants) and the Federación Independiente de Obreros Agricolas y Campesinos (Independent Federation of Agricultural Workers and Peasants). These federations carried out additional strikes for several years. Supported by Cesar Chavez and the U.S. United Farm Workers, they won several wage increases. Nevertheless, their wages were outpaced by inflation and had a minimal lasting effect on the farm-labor market (Zabin 1992).

19. Domínguez Santos (2004).

20. The letter was published in Mexico's largest newspaper, *La Jornada,* as well as in San Diego.

21. Kearney (1998).

22. Two years later the Zapatista movement would arise in southern Mexico, fighting to protect the indigenous from globalization.

23. Fox and Rivera-Salgado (2004, 15).

24. Hernández-Díaz and Hernández Hernández (2013, 64).

25. Piore (1979).

26. While about 650,000 people marched in Los Angeles on May 1, 2006, only about 2,000 marched in Vista.

27. Ryo (2013, 2015).

4. CROSS-BORDER FIGHTS, RIFTS, AND TIES

1. David FitzGerald (2008) describes this process as "dissimilation," the counterpart to assimilation, in which migrants become *different* from those they leave behind.

2. Iskander (2010).

3. Délano (2011).

4. Carlos Salinas de Gortari, president of Mexico from 1988 to 1994, developed programs such as the Foreign Ministry's Program for Mexican Communities Abroad (Iskander 2010).

5. As of 2008 the 3x1 Program provided about US$38 million to 2,500 projects, up to US$60,000 per project. While these quantities appear large, the total collective remittances through this program still amounted to less than 1 percent of all family remittances from the United States to Mexico (Duquette-Rury 2016; Iskander 2010).

6. Duquette-Rury (2014, 2016); Goldring (2004); Waldinger (2015).

7. Iskander (2010). Arguably, the 1990s and the first decade of the 2000s were a high point for HTAs; in the 2010s growing violence in Mexico made engagement more difficult for migrants.

8. Goldring (1998).

9. Fox (2005); Rivera-Salgado and Escala Rabadán (2004); R. Smith (2003).

10. See Basch, Glick Schiller, and Szanton Blanc (1994); Levitt (2001); R. Smith (2006); and Stephen (2007). Early research in this area demonstrated that transnational engagement was not detrimental to integration; the two could also be complementary (Portes, Escobar, and Radford 2007).

11. FitzGerald (2008); R. Smith (2006).

12. Glick Schiller and Fouron (1999); Itzigsohn and Saucedo (2002); Portes (1999).

13. Duquette-Rury (2016); Waldinger (2015).

14. In the face of emigration, many indigenous communities extended their communal structures across borders, demanding that migrants serve or give money from afar. In the most extreme version, hometowns insisted that migrants return from the United States to serve in village cargos (Kearney and Besserer 2004; Stephen 2007; Ventura Luna 2010).

15. Goldring (2003); Hondagneu-Sotelo (1994); Jones-Correa (1998).

16. Levitt (2001).

17. The organization had antecedents in prior HTAs from Partida that were formed in Mexico City and Oaxaca City in the late 1950s, as migrants moved there and volunteered to help pay for festivals in the pueblo.

18. As other scholars note, communal traditions can give migrants a resource to facilitate organizing in the United States (Levitt and Lamba-Nieves 2011; Milkman 2006).

19. Among 300 to 400 migrant families from Partida in Los Angeles, somewhere between 35 and 120 participated in the HTA, depending on who one asked and how strictly that person defined "participation."

20. The irony is that indigenous villages are often better environmental stewards than "protection" planned from above.

21. This philanthropic stance is how many other HTAs have been portrayed as well, particularly those from western Mexico.

22. Their reasoning helps shed light on research by Guarnizo, Portes, and Haller (2003), showing that HTA participants tend to be more well-off and integrated into the United States than those who do not engage.

23. At the time the organization was formed, several of its key organizers were living briefly in Mexico City, working on the construction of the city's new metro system. Despite this short foray into urban migration—and the important outcome of establishing the PCPR—none stayed long enough to build strong urban ties.

24. Jonathan Fox and Gaspar Rivera-Salgado (2004) point out that in Mexico from the 1960s to 1980s the word *popular* suggested a broad class identity bridging workers, peasants, and Mixtec ethnicity.

25. Velasco Ortiz (2005a, 2005b).

26. See Cornelius et al. (2009) for details.

27. Domínguez Santos (2004).

28. Kearney (2000, 186–87).

29. Past research suggests that when male migrants return to Mexico, they revert to patriarchal practices (Guarnizo 1997).

30. Andrews et al. (2013).

31. See Hall et al. (2013).

5. PATHWAYS TO HOMETOWN CHANGE

1. Benton (2012).

2. Grindle (2007); Iskander (2010).

3. First, women entered "feminine" programs like sewing workshops, family planning, or handicrafts. Later, government agencies like the Ministry of Health and the National Indigenous Institute began to offer women-specific programs. The state of Oaxaca placed special emphasis on women's cooperatives, encouraging lending to women to develop productive agricultural, industrial, or artisan

activity (Dalton 1990). As elsewhere around the world, these gender programs framed women as ideal, "responsible" subjects of state development (Roy 2010).

4. Conditional cash transfers, which have become increasingly common in global poverty relief, aim to reduce poverty by offering welfare, contingent upon recipients' actions. By 2005 Oportunidades reached nearly a quarter of Mexico's population (Molyneux 2006).

5. Castles (2010); Delgado-Wise and Cypher (2007); Hirschman (1970).

6. Goodman and Hiskey (2008).

7. Kapur (2005); McKenzie (2005). Permanent migration, in particular, tends to drive depopulation and decreased remittances (Portes and Zhou 2012).

8. Kearney (1998).

9. Bravo (2009); Córdova and Hiskey (2015); Duquette-Rury (2016); Fox and Bada (2008); Pérez-Armendáriz and Crow (2010).

10. Bada (2014); Burgess (2016); Goldring (1998); Itzigsohn et al. (1999); Meseguer and Burgess (2014); Portes, Guarnizo, and Landolt (1999); R. Smith (2003); Williams (2012).

11. Iskander (2010); Kapur (2010).

12. Fox and Bada (2008); Hirsch (2003); Levitt (2001); Portes, Escobar, and Walton (2007); Portes, Guarnizo, and Landolt (1999).

13. Careja and Emmenegger (2012); Danielson (2017); Duquette-Rury (2016); Eccarius-Kelly (2002); Landolt (2008); Pérez-Armendáriz and Crow (2010); Pfutze (2012); Rother (2009).

14. The concept of *antiglobalization backlash* is inspired in part by Arturo Escobar's (1995) critique of Western-led development.

15. Marcos (2005).

16. Bray (1991).

17. While communes like Partida and Retorno were more protected than *ejidos*, the Program for the Certification of Ejido Rights made it legal to change a commune into an *ejido*, as well as to privatize land in *ejidos*.

18. Lynn Stephen (2005) describes a similar process in a nearby community.

19. Holly Worthen (2015) finds a similar reaction in a pueblo nearby. When the state mandated that women participate in local politics, women in that village refused, explaining that the government did not understand their indigenous political system.

20. See Danielson and Eisenstadt (2009); Hernández Castillo (2001); Newdick (2005); and Worthen (2015) for analyses of the contradictions between women's rights and indigenous autonomy.

21. Worthen (2015).

22. In Mexico *gringo* is a derogatory label for people from the United States.

23. The word *bracero*, derived from the word *brazo*, or "arm," refers to manual laborers. This term was used during the Bracero Program run by the U.S. government from the 1940s to 1960s.

24. Mexico's Sindicato Nacional de Trabajadores de la Educación (National Educational Workers Union) is the one of the largest and most powerful trade unions in Latin America.

25. In 2006, for instance, Oaxaca's teachers led a six-month uprising that unified leftist organizations and shut down the city (Stephen 2013).

26. Cook (1996).

27. Such contention was common in Oaxaca; indeed, protesting and blockading roads were among the only means by which grassroots groups could force the state to hand over money. This pattern ended, however, with the governorship of Ulises Ruiz, beginning in 2004 (Hernández-Díaz 2007).

28. State funds came from Oportunidades; the Ministry of Social Development; the National Commission for Supporting Housing; the National Institute of Social Development; the Commission for the Regularization of Landholding; the National Fund for Popular Dwellings; the National Fund for Supporting Artisanship; the Ministry of Agriculture, Livestock, Rural Development, Fisheries, and Food; the National Indigenous Institute; and the National Commission for the Development of Indigenous Peoples, among others (Kearney 2000).

29. Frente Indígena Oaxaqueño Binacional (1996).

30. Bacon (2013).

31. The project was run by the National Fund for Popular Dwellings, which provided housing for the poor.

32. INEGI (1970, 1990).

33. Maxine Molyneux (2006) likewise shows that resources from Oportunidades made people more receptive to women's inclusion.

34. Maldonado and Rodríguez (2004).

35. Barrera-Bassols (2006).

36. Ray (1998).

37. Eisenstadt (2007).

38. See Perry et al. (2009) for details.

39. Kearney (1998).

40. Wolf (1957).

CONCLUSION

1. Another eleven to fifteen million legal immigrants also faced disenfranchisement and deportation, because they did not have citizenship.

2. Dreby (2015); Massey, Durand, and Pren (2016); Menjívar and Abrego (2012).

3. Chatterjee (2004); Evans (2008); Keck and Sikkink (1998); Tarrow (2005).

4. Others make similar points about African Americans and the poor (Alexander 2012; Dowling and Inda 2013; Redclift 2013). Around the world such

excluded groups are variously known as "bare life" (Agamben 1998), "human refuse" (Bauman 2004), and "urban outcasts" (Wacquant 2013).

5. Armenta (2017); Beckett and Evans (2015); Chavez (2008); de Genova (2002); Dreby (2015); Ngai (2004); Stumpf (2006).

6. Social movement scholars have long recognized that mobilization hinges on political opportunities (McAdam 1999; Tarrow 1993). Scholars such as Peggy Levitt (2008) and Eva Østergaard-Nielsen (2003) also highlight that institutions shape migrant civic engagement.

7. Levitt (2001); R. Smith (2006); Waldinger (2015).

8. Some other scholars also note that migrants' prior political and labor experiences shape their engagement with the United States. (Hagan, Hernández-León, and Demonsant 2015; Levitt and Lamba-Nieves 2011).

9. Rogers Brubaker and Jaeeun Kim (2011) and Jaeeun Kim (2016) show that sending states make and unmake "transnational" populations.

10. FitzGerald (2008); Iskander (2010).

11. Abrego (2014); Dreby (2015); Schmalzbauer (2014); R. Smith (2006).

12. Berry (2018); Tripp (2015); Viterna (2013).

13. Andrews (2014).

14. The goal of this reflexive approach is not to tell a "representative" story (as in positivist studies) but instead to use cases to build theory (for a cogent explanation, see R. Smith 2006, 280–83).

15. Duquette-Rury (2016).

16. Gleeson and Gonzales (2012); Marrow (2009).

17. Chauvin and Garcés-Mascareñas (2012); Coleman (2012); Landolt (2008); Martiniello and Lafleur (2008).

18. Provine et al. (2016).

19. Talavera, Nuñez-Mchiri, and Heyman (2010).

20. Pande (2012).

21. Leerkes, Varsanyi, and Engbersen (2012).

22. For other perspectives, see Benjamin-Alvarado, DeSipio, and Montoya (2009); García (forthcoming); Zepeda-Millán (2017).

23. Desmond and Valdez (2013); Goffman (2014).

24. Salcido and Menjívar (2012).

25. Calavita (2005).

26. Fox (2005); Rivera-Salgado and Escala Rabadán (2004); R. Smith (2003).

27. Kearney and Besserer (2004).

28. Waldinger (2015)

29. Passel and Cohn (2016).

30. Waldinger (2015).

31. Pedersen (2013); Zilberg (2011).

32. Østergaard-Nielsen (2003); Tarrow (2005).

33. Délano (2011); FitzGerald (2008); Portes (2007).

34. Eccarius-Kelly (2002); Landolt and Goldring (2010).

35. Horst (2008).

36. Alarcón, Escala, and Odgers (2016).

37. Mathema (2017).

38. Gutierrez (2017); R. Smith (2006).

39. In a comparison between Arizona and New Mexico, Deborah Schildkraut and her coauthors (forthcoming) show that exclusionary local laws and policing practices also have "collateral effects" on legal and second-generation immigrants, making such groups feel excluded even though the laws are not specifically directed at them.

40. Wong (2017).

METHODOLOGICAL APPENDIX

1. In contrast, some ethnographers attempt to avoid bias by writing themselves out of their research (Desmond 2016) or seeking to act like "flies on the wall" (Goffman 2014).

2. Respondents reminded me of my outsider status by addressing me almost exclusively as *guerita* (white girl), even when they knew my name.

References

Abrego, Leisy J. 2011. "Legal Consciousness of Undocumented Latinos: Fear and Stigma as Barriers to Claims-Making for First-and 1.5-Generation Immigrants." *Law & Society Review* 45 (2): 337–70.

———. 2014. *Sacrificing Families: Navigating Laws, Labor, and Love across Borders*. Stanford: Stanford University Press.

Abrego, Leisy J., and Roberto G. Gonzales. 2010. "Blocked Paths, Uncertain Futures: The Postsecondary Education and Labor Market Prospects of Undocumented Latino Youth." *Journal of Education for Students Placed at Risk* 15 (1–2): 144–57.

Agamben, Giorgio. 1998. *Homo Sacer: Sovereign Power and Bare Life*. Stanford: Stanford University Press.

Aguilera, Michael, and Douglas Massey. 2003. "Social Capital and the Wages of Mexican Migrants: New Hypotheses and Tests." *Social Forces* 82 (2): 671–701.

Alarcón, Rafael, Luis Escala, and Olga Odgers. 2016. *Making Los Angeles Home: The Integration of Mexican Immigrants in the United States*. Oakland: University of California Press.

Alba, Francisco. 1982. *The Population of Mexico: Trends, Issues, and Policies*. Livingston, NJ: Transaction Books.

Alexander, Michelle. 2012. *The New Jim Crow*. New York: New Press.

Anderson, Benedict. 1998. *The Spectre of Comparisons: Nationalism, Southeast Asia and the World*. London: Verso.

Andrews, Abigail. 2014. "Women's Political Engagement in a Mexican Sending Community: Migration as Crisis and the Struggle to Sustain an Alternative." *Gender & Society* 28 (4): 583–608.

Andrews, Abigail, Brenda Nicolás, Lucia Goin, and Melissa Karakash. 2013. "Discount Transnationalism: Recession and the Transformation of Cross-Border Ties." In FitzGerald, Hernández-Díaz, and Keyes 2013, 79–98.

Andrews, Abigail, and Nazanin Shahrokni. 2014. "Patriarchal Accommodations: Women's Mobility and Policies of Gender Difference from Urban Iran to Migrant Mexico." *Journal of Contemporary Ethnography* 43 (2): 148–75.

Aquino, Salvador. 2009. "Contesting Social Memories and Identities in the Zapotec Sierra of Oaxaca, Mexico." PhD diss., University of Arizona.

Aquino Moreschi, Alejandra. 2010. "De la Indignación Moral a las Protestas Colectivas: La Participación de los Migrantes Zapotecos en las Marchas de Migrantes de 2006." *Norteamérica* 5 (1): 63–90.

Archer, Nicole, Ana Luz Gonzalez, Kimi Lee, Simmi Gandhi, and Delia Herrera. 2010. "The Garment Worker Center and the 'Forever 21' Campaign." In *Working for Justice: The L.A. Model of Organizing and Advocacy,* edited by Ruth Milkman, Joshua Bloom, and Victor Narro, 154–66. Ithaca: Cornell University Press.

Arizpe, Lourdes. 1981. "The Rural Exodus in Mexico and Mexican Migration to the United States." *International Migration Review* 14 (5): 626–49.

Armenta, Amada. 2015. "Between Public Service and Social Control: Policing Dilemmas in the Era of Immigration Enforcement." *Social Problems* 63 (1): 111–26.

———. 2017. "Racializing Crimmigration: Structural Racism, Colorblindness, and the Institutional Production of Immigrant Criminality." *Sociology of Race and Ethnicity* 3 (1): 82–95.

Armstrong, Elizabeth A., and Mary Bernstein. 2008. "Culture, Power, and Institutions: A Multi-Institutional Politics Approach to Social Movements." *Sociological Theory* 26 (1): 74–99.

Arnold, Carrie L. 2007. "Racial Profiling in Immigration Enforcement: State and Local Agreements to Enforce Federal Immigration Law." *Arizona Law Review* 49:113–42.

Babb, Sarah. 2001. *Managing Mexico: Economists from Nationalism to Neoliberalism.* Princeton: Princeton University Press.

Bacon, David. 2013. *The Right to Stay Home: How US Policy Drives Mexican Migration.* Boston: Beacon.

Bada, Xóchitl. 2014. *Mexican Hometown Associations in Chicagoacán.* New Brunswick: Rutgers University Press.

Bada, Xóchitl, Jonathan Fox, Robert Donnelly, and Andrew Selee. 2010. *Context Matters: Latino Immigrant Civic Engagement in Nine U.S. Cities.* Washington, DC: Woodrow Wilson International Center for Scholars.

Bada, Xóchitl, Jonathan Fox, and Andrew Selee. 2006. *Invisible No More: Mexican Migrant Civic Participation in the U.S.* Washington, DC: Woodrow Wilson International Center for Scholars.

Baker-Cristales, Beth. 2009. "Mediated Resistance: The Construction of Neoliberal Citizenship in the Immigrant Rights Movement." *Latino Studies* 7 (1): 60–82.

Balderrama, Rafael and Hilario Molina II. 2009. "How Good Are Networks for Migrant Job Seekers? Ethnographic Evidence from North Carolina Farm Labor Camps." *Sociological Inquiry* 79 (2): 190–218.

Barkin, David. 2002. "The Reconstruction of a Modern Mexican Peasantry." *Journal of Peasant Studies* 30 (1): 73–90.

Barrera-Bassols, Dalia. 2006. "Mujeres Indígenas en el Sistema de Representación de Cargos de Elección: El Caso de Oaxaca." *Agricultura, Sociedad y Desarrollo* 3 (1): 19–37.

Barreto, Matt A., Sylvia Manzano, Ricardo Ramírez, and Kathy Rim. 2009. "Mobilization, Participation, and Solidaridad: Latino Participation in the 2006 Immigration Protest Rallies." *Urban Affairs Review* 44 (5): 736–64.

Bartolomé, Miguel A. 1997. *Gente de Costumbre y Gente de Razón: Las Identidades Étnicas en México.* Mexico City: Siglo XXI.

Basch, Linda, Nina Glick Schiller, and Christina Szanton Blanc. 1994. *Nations Unbound: Transnational Projects, Postcolonial Predicaments, and Deterritorialized Nation-States.* New York: Taylor and Francis.

Bauman, Zygmunt. 2004. *Wasted Lives: Modernity and Its Outcasts.* Cambridge: Polity.

Baviskar, Amita. 1995. *In the Belly of the River: Tribal Conflicts over Development in the Narmada Valley.* New York: Oxford University Press.

Bayat, Asef. 1997. *Street Politics: Poor People's Movements in Iran.* New York: Columbia University Press.

———. 2013. *Life as Politics: How Ordinary People Change the Middle East.* 2nd ed. Stanford: Stanford University Press.

Beckett, Katherine, and Heather Evans. 2015. "Crimmigration at the Local Level: Criminal Justice Processes in the Shadow of Deportation." *Law & Society Review* 49 (1): 241–77.

Benjamin-Alvarado, Jonathan, Louis DeSipio, and Celeste Montoya. 2009. "Latino Mobilization in New Immigrant Destinations: The Anti–HR 4437 Protest in Nebraska's Cities." *Urban Affairs Review* 44 (5): 718–35.

Benton, Allyson Lucinda. 2012. "Bottom-Up Challenges to National Democracy: Mexico's (Legal) Subnational Authoritarian Enclaves." *Comparative Politics* 44 (3): 253–71.

Berger, Susan. 2009. "(Un)Worthy: Latina Battered Immigrants under VAWA and the Construction of Neoliberal Subjects." *Citizenship Studies* 13 (3): 201–17.

Berry, Marie E. 2017. "Barriers to Women's Progress after Atrocity: Evidence from Rwanda and Bosnia-Herzegovina." *Gender & Society* 31 (6): 830–53.

———. 2018. *War, Women, and Power: From Violence to Mobilization in Rwanda and Bosnia-Herzegovina.* New York: Cambridge University Press.

Besserer, Federico. 2002. *Topografías Transnacionales: Hacia una Geografía de la Vida Transnacional.* 1st ed. Colección CSH. Mexico City: Plaza y Valdés, Universidad Autónoma Metropolitana, Unidad Iztapalapa.

Bosniak, Linda. 2012. "Arguing for Amnesty." *Law, Culture and the Humanities* 9 (3): 432–42.

Bourdieu, Pierre. 1989. "Social Space and Symbolic Power." *Sociological Theory* 7 (1): 14–25.

Branton, Regina. 2007. "Latino Attitudes toward Various Areas of Public Policy: The Importance of Acculturation." *Political Research Quarterly* 60 (2): 293–303.

Bravo, Jorge. 2009. "Emigración y Compromiso Político en México." *Política y Gobierno* 1:273–310.

Bray, David Barton. 1991. "Struggle for the Forest: Conservation and Development in the Sierra Juárez." *Grassroots Development: Journal of the Inter-American Foundation* 15 (3): 13–25.

Brenner, Robert. 1976. "Agrarian Class Structure and Economic Development in Pre-Industrial Europe." *Past and Present* 70:30–75.

Brown, Wendy. 1992. "Finding the Man in the State." *Feminist Studies* 18 (1): 7–34.

Brubaker, Rogers. 2010. "Migration, Membership, and the Modern Nation-State: Internal and External Dimensions of the Politics of Belonging." *Journal of Interdisciplinary History* 41 (1): 61–78.

Brubaker, Rogers, and Jaeeun Kim. 2011. "Transborder Membership Politics in Germany and Korea." *European Journal of Sociology/Archives Européennes de Sociologie* 52 (1): 21–75.

Buechler, Steven M. 2000. *Social Movements in Advanced Capitalism: The Political Economy and Cultural Construction of Social Activism.* New York: Oxford University Press.

Burawoy, Michael. 1976. "The Functions and Reproduction of Migrant Labor: Comparative Material from Southern Africa and the United States." *American Journal of Sociology* 81 (5): 1050–87.

———. 1985. *The Politics of Production: Factory Regimes under Capitalism and Socialism.* London: Verso.

———. 2009. *The Extended Case Method: Four Countries, Four Decades, Four Great Transformations, and One Theoretical Tradition.* Berkeley: University of California Press.

———. 2017. "On Desmond: The Limits of Spontaneous Sociology." *Theory and Society* 46 (4): 261–84.

Burgess, Katrina. 2016. "Organized Migrants and Accountability from Afar."
    Latin American Research Review 51 (2): 150–73.

Caballero, Juan Julián, and Manuel Ríos Morales. 2004. "Impacto de la
    Migración Transnacional entre los Ñuu Savi (Mixtecos) y los Bene Xhon
    (Zapotecos de la Sierra Norte) de Oaxaca." In *La Ruta Mixteca: El Impacto
    Etnopolítico de la Migración Transnacional en los Pueblos Indígenas de
    México*, edited by Sylvia Escárcega and Stefano Varese, 137–201. Mexico
    City: Universidad Nacional Autónoma de México.

Calavita, Kitty. 1998. "Immigration, Law, and Marginalization in a Global
    Economy: Notes from Spain." *Law & Society Review* 32 (3): 529–66.

———. 2005. *Immigrants at the Margins: Law, Race, and Exclusion in South-
    ern Europe*. New York: Cambridge University Press.

Capps, Randy, Marc R. Rosenblum, Muzaffar Chishti, and Cristina Rodríguez.
    2011. *Delegation and Divergence: A Study of 287 (g) State and Local Immi-
    gration Enforcement*. Washington, DC: Migration Policy Institute.

Careja, Romana, and Patrick Emmenegger. 2012. "Making Democratic Citi-
    zens: The Effects of Migration Experience on Political Attitudes in Central
    and Eastern Europe." *Comparative Political Studies* 45 (7): 875–902.

Castles, Stephen. 2010. "Understanding Global Migration: A Social Transfor-
    mation Perspective." *Journal of Ethnic and Migration Studies* 36 (10):
    1565–86.

Castles, Stephen, and Alastair Davidson. 2000. *Citizenship and Migration:
    Globalization and the Politics of Belonging*. New York: Routledge.

Cerrutti, Marcela, and Magalí Gaudio. 2010. "Gender Differences between
    Mexican Migration to the United States and Paraguayan Migration to
    Argentina." *Annals of the American Academy of Political and Social Science*
    630 (1): 93–113.

Cerrutti, Marcela, and Douglas S. Massey. 2001. "On the Auspices of Female
    Migration from Mexico to the United States." *Demography* 38 (2):
    187–200.

Chance, John K. 1989. *Conquest of the Sierra: Spaniards and Indians in
    Colonial Oaxaca*. Norman: University of Oklahoma Press.

———. 2003. "Haciendas, Ranchos, and Indian Towns: A Case from the Late
    Colonial Valley of Puebla." *Ethnohistory* 50 (1): 15–45.

Chand, Daniel E., and William D. Schreckhise. 2015. "Secure Communities and
    Community Values: Local Context and Discretionary Immigration Law
    Enforcement." *Journal of Ethnic and Migration Studies* 41 (10): 1621–43.

Chatterjee, Partha. 2004. *The Politics of the Governed: Reflections on Popular
    Politics in Most of the World*. New York: Columbia University Press.

Chauvin, Sébastien, and Blanca Garcés-Mascareñas. 2012. "Beyond Informal
    Citizenship: The New Moral Economy of Migrant Illegality." *International
    Political Sociology* 6 (3): 241–59.

Chavez, Leo R. 1998. *Shadowed Lives: Undocumented Immigrants in American Society*. Fort Worth: Harcourt Brace College.

———. 2008. *The Latino Threat: Constructing Immigrants, Citizens, and the Nation*. Stanford: Stanford University Press.

Cohen, Jeffrey H. 2004. *The Culture of Migration in Southern Mexico*. Austin: University of Texas Press.

Coleman, Matthew. 2012. "The 'Local' Migration State: The Site-Specific Devolution of Immigration Enforcement in the U.S. South." *Law & Policy* 34 (2): 159–90.

CONAPO (Consejo Nacional de Población). 2005. "Índice de Intensidad Migratoria México–Estados Unidos." www.conapo.gob.mx.

Cook, Maria Lorena. 1996. *Organizing Dissent: Unions, the State, and the Democratic Teachers' Movement in Mexico*. University Park: Pennsylvania State University Press.

Córdova, Abby, and Jonathan Hiskey. 2015. "Shaping Politics at Home: Cross-Border Social Ties and Local-Level Political Engagement." *Comparative Political Studies* 48 (11): 1454–87.

Cornelius, Wayne A. 1982. "Interviewing Undocumented Immigrants: Methodological Reflections Based on Fieldwork in Mexico and the U.S." *International Migration Review* 16 (2): 378–411.

Cornelius, Wayne A., David FitzGerald, Jorge Hernández-Díaz, and Scott Borger, eds. 2009. *Migration from the Mexican Mixteca: A Transnational Community in Oaxaca and California*. Boulder: Rienner.

Coronil, Fernando. 1997. *The Magical State: Nature, Money, and Modernity in Venezuela*. Chicago: University of Chicago Press.

Coutin, Susan B. 2000. *Legalizing Moves: Salvadoran Immigrants' Struggle for U.S. Residency*. Ann Arbor: University of Michigan Press.

Crenshaw, Kimberle. 1991. "Mapping the Margins: Intersectionality, Identity Politics, and Violence against Women of Color." *Stanford Law Review* 43 (6): 1241–99.

Cummings, Scott. 2009. "Hemmed In: Legal Mobilization in the Los Angeles Anti-Sweatshop Movement." *Berkeley Journal of Employment and Labor Law* 30 (1): 101–84.

Curiel, Charlynne. 2011. "'En Momentos Difíciles Nosotros Somos un Pueblo': Haciendo Política en la Mixteca de Oaxaca: Un Estudio sobre el Ritual, la Pasión, y el Poder." PhD diss., Wageningen University.

Dalton, Margarita. 1990. "La Organización Política, las Mujeres y el Estado: El Caso de Oaxaca." *Estudios Sociológicos* 8 (22): 39–65.

Danielson, Michael. 2010. "All Immigration Politics Is Local: The Day Labor Ordinance in Vista, California." In *Taking Local Control: Immigration Policy Activism in U.S. Cities and States*, edited by Monica W. Varsanyi, 239–54. Stanford: Stanford University Press.

———. 2017. *Emigrants Get Political: Mexican Migrants Engage Their Home Towns*. New York: Oxford University Press.

Danielson, Michael S., and Todd A. Eisenstadt. 2009. "Walking Together, but in Which Direction? Gender Discrimination and Multicultural Practices in Oaxaca, Mexico." *Politics & Gender* 5 (2): 153–84.

De Genova, Nicholas P. 2002. "Migrant 'Illegality' and Deportability in Everyday Life." *Annual Review of Anthropology* 31 (1): 419–47.

———. 2005. *Working the Boundaries: Race, Space, and "Illegality" in Mexican Chicago*. Durham: Duke University Press.

———. 2010. "The Deportation Regime: Sovereignty, Space, and the Freedom of Movement." In *The Deportation Regime: Sovereignty, Space, and the Freedom of Movement*, edited by Nicholas De Genova and Nathalie Peutz, 33–68. Durham: Duke University Press.

De Graauw, Els. 2014. "Municipal ID Cards for Undocumented Immigrants: Local Bureaucratic Membership in a Federal System." *Politics & Society* 42 (3): 309–30.

De Graauw, Els, and Floris Vermeulen. 2016. "Cities and the Politics of Immigrant Integration: A Comparison of Berlin, Amsterdam, New York City, and San Francisco." *Journal of Ethnic and Migration Studies* 42 (6): 989–1012.

Délano, Alexandra. 2011. *Mexico and Its Diaspora in the United States: Policies of Emigration since 1848*. New York: Cambridge University Press.

Delgado-Wise, Raúl, and James M. Cypher. 2007. "The Strategic Role of Mexican Labor under NAFTA: Critical Perspectives on Current Economic Integration." *Annals of the American Academy of Political and Social Science* 610 (1): 119–42.

Desmond, Matthew. 2014. "Relational Ethnography." *Theory and Society* 43 (5): 547–79.

———. 2016. *Evicted: Poverty and Profit in the American City*. New York: Crown/Archetype.

Desmond, Matthew, and Nicol Valdez. 2013. "Unpolicing the Urban Poor: Consequences of Third-Party Policing for Inner-City Women." *American Sociological Review* 78 (1): 117–41.

Dillingham, Alan Shane. 2012. "Indigenismo and Its Discontents: Bilingual Teachers and the Democratic Opening in the Mixteca Alta of Oaxaca, Mexico, 1954–1982." PhD diss., University of Maryland.

Domínguez Santos, Rufino. 2004. "The FIOB Experience: Internal Crisis and Future Challenges." In Fox and Rivera-Salgado 2004, 69–80.

Donato, Katharine M., and Amada Armenta. 2011. "What We Know about Unauthorized Migration." *Annual Review of Sociology* 37 (1): 529–43.

Dow, James. 1977. "Religion in the Organization of a Mexican Peasant Economy." In *Peasant Livelihood: Studies in Economic Anthropology and*

Cultural Ecology, edited by Rhoda Halperin and James Dow, 215–26. New York: St. Martin's Press.

Dowling, Julie, and Jonathan Inda. 2013. *Governing Immigration through Crime: A Reader.* Stanford: Stanford University Press.

Dreby, Joanna. 2010. *Divided by Borders: Mexican Migrants and Their Children.* Berkeley: University of California Press.

———. 2015. *Everyday Illegal: When Policies Undermine Immigrant Families.* Oakland: University of California Press.

Dreby, Joanna, and Leah Schmalzbauer. 2013. "The Relational Contexts of Migration: Mexican Women in New Destination Sites." *Sociological Forum* 28 (1): 1–26.

Duquette-Rury, Lauren. 2014. "Collective Remittances and Transnational Coproduction: The 3 × 1 Program for Migrants and Household Access to Public Goods in Mexico." *Studies in Comparative International Development* 49 (1): 112–39.

———. 2016. "Migrant Transnational Participation: How Citizen Inclusion and Government Engagement Matter for Local Democratic Development in Mexico." *American Sociological Review* 81 (4): 771–99.

Durand, Jorge, and Douglas S. Massey. 1992. "Mexican Migration to the United States: A Critical Review." *Latin American Research Review* 27 (2): 3–42.

Ebert, Kim, and Dina G. Okamoto. 2013. "Social Citizenship, Integration and Collective Action: Immigrant Civic Engagement in the United States." *Social Forces* 91 (4): 1267–92.

———. 2015. "Legitimating Contexts, Immigrant Power, and Exclusionary Actions." *Social Problems* 62 (1): 40–67.

Eccarius-Kelly, Vera. 2002. "Political Movements and Leverage Points: Kurdish Activism in the European Diaspora." *Journal of Muslim Minority Affairs* 22 (1): 91–118.

Eisenstadt, Todd A. 2007. "Usos y Costumbres and Postelectoral Conflicts in Oaxaca, Mexico, 1995–2004: An Empirical and Normative Assessment." *Latin American Research Review* 42 (1): 52–77.

———. 2011. *Politics, Identity, and Mexico's Indigenous Rights Movements.* New York: Cambridge University Press.

Escobar, Arturo. 1995. *Encountering Development: The Making and Unmaking of the Third World.* Princeton: Princeton University Press.

Esteva, Gustavo. 2007. "Oaxaca: The Path of Radical Democracy." *Socialism and Democracy* 21 (2): 74–96.

Evans, Peter. 2008. "Is an Alternative Globalization Possible?" *Politics & Society* 36 (2): 271–305.

Fanon, Frantz. 1963. *The Wretched of the Earth.* Translated by Constance Farrington. New York: Grove.

FitzGerald, David. 2008. *A Nation of Emigrants: How Mexico Manages Its Migration*. Berkeley: University of California Press.

FitzGerald, David Scott, Jorge Hernández-Díaz, and David Keyes. 2013. *The Wall between Us: A Mixteco Migrant Community in Mexico and the United States*. San Diego: Center for Comparative Immigration Studies, University of California, San Diego.

Fox, Jonathan. 1992. *The Politics of Food in Mexico: State Power and Social Mobilization*. Ithaca: Cornell University Press.

———. 2005. "Unpacking 'Transnational Citizenship.'" *Annual Review of Political Science* 8 (1): 171–201.

Fox, Jonathan, and Xóchitl Bada. 2008. "Migrant Organization and Hometown Impacts in Rural Mexico." *Journal of Agrarian Change* 8 (2–3): 435–61.

Fox, Jonathan, and Gaspar Rivera-Salgado. 2004. *Indigenous Mexican Migrants in the United States*. La Jolla: Center for U.S.-Mexican Studies / Center for Comparative Immigration Studies, University of California, San Diego.

Frente Indígena Oaxaqueño Binacional. 1996. "Propuestas de las Comunidades del Municipio de San Miguel Tlacotepec, Oax., en Torno a la Consulta Nacional sobre Derechos y la Participación Indígena." June 25. http://fiob .org/1996/06/propuestas-municipio-san-miguel-tlacotepec-oaxaca/.

Frey, John Carlos. 2012. "Escondido Profits from Undocumented Immigrants." *Huffington Post,* March 12, 2012. www.huffingtonpost.com/john-carlos-frey /escondido-undocumented-immigrants_b_1326744.html.

Friedman, Debra, and Doug McAdam. 1992. "Collective Identity and Activism." In *Frontiers in Social Movement Theory,* edited by Carol McClurg Mueller and Aldon D. Morris, 156–73. New Haven: Yale University Press.

Fujiwara, Lynn H. 2005. "Immigrant Rights Are Human Rights: The Reframing of Immigrant Entitlement and Welfare." *Social Problems* 52 (1): 79–101.

García, Angela S. Forthcoming. *Legal Passing: Navigating Undocumented Life and Local Immigration Law*. Oakland: University of California Press.

García, Angela, and David Keyes. 2012. *Life as an Undocumented Immigrant: How Restrictive Local Immigration Policies Affect Daily Life*. Washington, DC: Center for American Progress.

Garduño, Everardo. 1991. Mixtecos en Baja California: El Caso de San Quintín. *Estudios Fronterizos* 24–25:87–113.

Gibson, Edward. 2005. "Boundary Control: Subnational Authoritarianism in Democratizing Countries." *World Politics* 58 (1): 101–32.

Gleeson, Shannon. 2010. "Labor Rights for All? The Role of Undocumented Immigrant Status for Worker Claims Making." *Law & Social Inquiry* 35 (3): 561–602.

———. 2015. "'They Come Here to Work': An Evaluation of the Economic Argument in Favor of Immigrant Rights." *Citizenship Studies* 19 (3–4): 400–420.

―――. 2016. *Precarious Claims: The Promise and Failure of Workplace Protections in the United States.* Oakland: University of California Press.

Gleeson, Shannon, and Roberto G. Gonzales. 2012. "When Do Papers Matter? An Institutional Analysis of Undocumented Life in the United States." *International Migration* 50 (4): 1–19.

Glick Schiller, Nina, and Georges E. Fouron. 1999. "Terrains of Blood and Nation: Haitian Transnational Social Fields." *Ethnic and Racial Studies* 22 (2): 340–66.

Goffman, Alice. 2014. *On the Run: Fugitive Life in an American City.* Chicago: University of Chicago Press.

Golash-Boza, Tanya Maria. 2015. *Deported: Immigrant Policing, Disposable Labor, and Global Capitalism.* New York: New York University Press.

Golash-Boza, Tanya, and Pierrette Hondagneu-Sotelo. 2013. "Latino Immigrant Men and the Deportation Crisis: A Gendered Racial Removal Program." *Latino Studies* 11 (3): 271–92.

Goldring, Luin. 1992. "Diversity and Community in Transnational Migration: A Comparative Study of Two Mexico-U.S. Migrant Circuits." PhD diss., Cornell University.

―――. 1998. *From Market Membership to Transnational Citizenship? The Changing Politicization of Transnational Social Spaces.* Santa Cruz: Chicano/Latino Research Center, Merrill College, University of California, Santa Cruz.

―――. 2003. "Gender, Status, and the State in Transnational Spaces: The Gendering of Political Participation and Mexican Hometown Associations." In *Gender and U.S. Immigration: Contemporary Trends,* edited by Pierette Hondagneu-Sotelo, 341–58. Berkeley: University of California Press.

―――. 2004. "Individual and Collective Remittances to Mexico: A Multi-Dimensional Typology of Remittances." *Development and Change* 35 (4): 799–840.

Gomberg-Muñoz, Ruth. 2010. "Willing to Work: Agency and Vulnerability in an Undocumented Immigrant Network." *American Anthropologist* 112 (2): 295–307.

Goodman, Gary L., and Jonathan T. Hiskey. 2008. "Exit without Leaving: Political Disengagement in High Migration Municipalities in Mexico." *Comparative Politics* 40 (2): 169–88.

Gosse, Van. 1996. "'El Salvador Is Spanish for Vietnam': A New Immigrant Left and the Politics of Solidarity." In *The Immigrant Left in the United States,* edited by Dan Georgakas and Paul Buhle, 301–29. Albany: State University of New York Press.

Grasmuck, Sherri, and Patricia R. Pessar. 1991. *Between Two Islands: Dominican International Migration.* Berkeley: University of California Press.

Greenberg, James B. 1981. *Santiago's Sword: Chatino Peasant Economies and Rebellion*. Berkeley: University of California Press.

Grindle, Merilee Serrill. 2007. *Going Local: Decentralization, Democratization, and the Promise of Good Governance*. Princeton: Princeton University Press.

Guardino, Peter. 2005. *The Time of Liberty: Popular Political Culture in Oaxaca, 1750–1850*. Durham: Duke University Press.

Guarnizo, Luis Eduardo. 1997. "The Emergence of a Transnational Social Formation and the Mirage of Return Migration among Dominican Transmigrants." *Identities* 4 (2): 281–322.

Guarnizo, Luis Eduardo, Alejandro Portes, and William Haller. 2003. "Assimilation and Transnationalism: Determinants of Transnational Political Action among Contemporary Migrants." *American Journal of Sociology* 108 (6): 1211–48.

Guidi, Ruxandra. 2011. "DUI Checkpoints in California May Soon Be Regulated." *KPBS*, September 1, 2011. https://fronterasdesk.org/content/dui-checkpoints-california-may-soon-be-regulated.

Gulasekaram, Pratheepan, and Karthick Ramakrishnan. 2013. "Immigration Federalism: A Reappraisal." *NYU Law Review* 88:2074–145.

Gutierrez, Armand. 2017. "A Family Affair: How and Why Second-Generation Filipino-Americans Engage in Transnational Social and Economic Connections." *Ethnic and Racial Studies* 41 (2): 1–19.

Gutiérrez, David G., and Pierrette Hondagneu-Sotelo. 2008. "Introduction: Nation and Migration." *American Quarterly* 60 (3): 503–21.

Hagan, Jacqueline, Karl Eschbach, and Néstor Rodríguez. 2008. "U.S. Deportation Policy, Family Separation, and Circular Migration." *International Migration Review* 42 (1): 64–88.

Hagan, Jacqueline, Rubén Hernández-León, and Jean-Luc Demonsant. 2015. *Skills of the Unskilled: Work and Mobility among Mexican Migrants*. Oakland: University of California Press.

Hall, Andrew, Hannah Gibson, Bethany Reed, Boanerges Rodríguez, and Tanya Monroy. 2013. "A Town without Water Is Dead: Migration and Responses to Ecological Change." In FitzGerald, Hernández-Díaz, and Keyes 2013, 172–98.

Hall, Matthew T. 2012. "Escondido Chief Explains City's Illegal Immigration Policy." *San Diego Union Tribune*. June 26. www.sandiegouniontribune.com/sdut-chief-aim-of-escondidos-illegal-immigration-polic-2012jun26-htmlstory.html.

Hallett, Miranda Cady. 2012. "'Better Than White Trash': Work Ethic, Latinidad and Whiteness in Rural Arkansas." *Latino Studies* 10 (1–2): 81–106.

Hallett, Miranda Cady, and Michael Jones-Correa. 2012. "Borders of the Public: Framing the Inclusion and Bureaucratic Incorporation of Undocumented

Migrants in North Carolina." Paper presented at the Law and Society Annual Meeting, Honolulu, Hawai'i, June.

Hamilton, Nora, and Norma Stoltz Chinchilla. 2001. *Seeking Community in a Global City: Guatemalans and Salvadorans in Los Angeles.* Philadelphia: Temple University Press.

Hart, Gillian. 1991. "Engendering Everyday Resistance: Gender, Patronage and Production Politics in Rural Malaysia." *Journal of Peasant Studies* 19 (1): 93–121.

———. 2002. *Disabling Globalization: Places of Power in Post-Apartheid South Africa.* Berkeley: University of California Press.

———. 2016. "Relational Comparison Revisited: Marxist Postcolonial Geographies in Practice." *Progress in Human Geography,* December 16, 1–24.

Hernández Castillo, R. Aída. 2001. "Entre el Etnocentrismo Feminista y el Esencialismo Étnico." *Debate Feminista* 24:206–29.

Hernández-Díaz, Jorge. 2007 *Ciudadanías Diferenciadas en un Estado Multicultural: Los Usos y Costumbres en Oaxaca.* Mexico City: Siglo XXI.

Hernández-Díaz, Jorge, and Jorge Hernández Hernández. 2013. "The 'Parties' between Us: Migrant Participation in the Politics of San Miguel Tlacotepec." In FitzGerald, Hernández-Díaz, and Keyes 2013, 59–78.

Hirabayashi, Lane Ryo. 1993. *Cultural Capital: Mountain Zapotec Migrant Associations in Mexico City.* PROFMEX Series. Tucson: University of Arizona Press.

Hirsch, Jennifer. 2003. *A Courtship after Marriage: Sexuality and Love in Mexican Transnational Families.* Berkeley: University of California Press.

Hirschman, Albert O. 1970. *Exit, Voice, and Loyalty.* Cambridge: Harvard University Press.

Holmes, Seth M. 2007. "'Oaxacans Like to Work Bent Over': The Naturalization of Social Suffering among Berry Farm Workers." *International Migration* 45 (3): 39–68.

———. 2013. *Fresh Fruit, Broken Bodies: Migrant Farmworkers in the United States.* Berkeley: University of California Press.

Hondagneu-Sotelo, Pierrette. 1994. *Gendered Transitions: Mexican Experiences of Immigration.* Berkeley: University of California Press.

Hondagneu-Sotelo, Pierrette, and Angelica Salas. 2008. "What Explains the Immigrant Rights Marches of 2006? Xenophobia and Organizing with Democracy Technology." In *Immigrant Rights in the Shadows of Citizenship,* edited by Rachel Ida Bluff, 209–25. New York: New York University Press.

Hopkins, Daniel J. 2010. "Politicized Places: Explaining Where and When Immigrants Provoke Local Opposition." *American Political Science Review* 104 (1): 40–60.

Horst, Cindy. 2008. "The Transnational Political Engagements of Refugees: Remittance Sending Practices amongst Somalis in Norway: Analysis." *Conflict, Security & Development* 8 (3): 317–39.

Hulshof, Marije. 1991. "Zapotec Moves: Networks and Remittances of U.S.-Bound Migrants from Oaxaca, Mexico." PhD diss., University of Amsterdam.

Hunt, Scott A., and Robert D. Benford. 2004. "Collective Identity, Solidarity, and Commitment." In *The Blackwell Companion to Social Movements*, edited by David A. Snow, Sarah A. Soule, and Hanspeter Kriesi, 433–57. Malden, MA: Blackwell.

Ibarra Templos, Yuribi Mayek. 2003. "Espacios Alternativos de Poder: Participación de las Mujeres en una Comunidad Transnacional." Undergraduate thesis, Universidad Autónoma Metropolitana, Unidad Iztapalapa.

Immigration Advocates Network. 2017. "National Immigration Legal Services Directory." www.immigrationadvocates.org/nonprofit/legaldirectory/.

INEGI (Instituto Nacional de Estadística, Geografía e Informática). 1940. *V Censo de Población: Estado de Oaxaca.* www.inegi.gob.mx.

———. 1950. *VI Censo General de Población: Estado de Oaxaca.* www.inegi.gob.mx.

———. 1970. *IX Censo General de Población: Estado de Oaxaca.* www.inegi.gob.mx.

———. 1990. *XI Censo General de Población: Estado de Oaxaca.* www.inegi.gob.mx.

———. 2010. *XIII Censo General de Población: Estado de Oaxaca.* www.inegi.gob.mx.

Iskander, Natasha N. 2010. *Creative State: Forty Years of Migration and Development Policy in Morocco and Mexico.* Ithaca: Cornell University Press.

Itzigsohn, José, Carlos Dore Cabral, Esther Hernández Medina, and Obed Vazquez. 1999. "Mapping Dominican Transnationalism: Narrow and Broad Transnational Practices." *Ethnic and Racial Studies* 22 (2): 316–39.

Itzigsohn, José, and Silvia Giorguli Saucedo. 2002. "Immigrant Incorporation and Sociocultural Transnationalism." *International Migration Review* 36 (3): 766–98.

Jiménez, Tomás Roberto. 2010. *Replenished Ethnicity: Mexican Americans, Immigration, and Identity.* Berkeley: University of California Press.

Johnson, Kevin R. 2003. "The Case for African American and Latina/o Cooperation in Challenging Racial Profiling in Law Enforcement." *Florida Law Review* 55:341–63.

Jones-Correa, Michael. 1998. "Different Paths: Gender, Immigration and Political Participation." *International Migration Review* 32 (2): 326–49.

Joseph, Gilbert M., and Daniel Nugent. 1994. *Everyday Forms of State Formation: Revolution and the Negotiation of Rule in Modern Mexico.* Durham: Duke University Press.

Kandel, William, and Douglas S. Massey. 2002. "The Culture of Mexican Migration: A Theoretical and Empirical Analysis." *Social Forces* 80 (3): 981–1004.

Kapur, Devesh. 2005. "Remittances: The New Development Mantra?" *Remittances: Development Impact and Future Prospects,* edited by Samuel Munzele Maimbo and Dilip Ratha, 331–60. Washington, DC: World Bank.

———. 2010. *Diaspora, Development, and Democracy: The Domestic Impact of International Migration from India.* Princeton: Princeton University Press.

Kay, Cristóbal. 2004. "Rural Livelihoods and Peasant Futures." In *Latin America Transformed: Globalization and Modernity,* edited by Robert N. Gwynne and Crystobal Kay, 232–50. New York: Routledge.

Kearney, Michael. 1996. *Reconceptualizing the Peasantry: Anthropology in Global Perspective.* Critical Essays in Anthropology. Boulder: Westview.

———. 1998. "Mixtec Political Consciousness: From Passive to Active Resistance." In *Rural Revolt in Mexico: U.S. Intervention and the Domain of Subaltern Politics,* edited by Daniel Nugent, 134–46. Durham: Duke University Press.

———. 2000. "Transnational Oaxacan Indigenous Identity: The Case of Mixtecs and Zapotecs." *Identities* 7 (2): 173–95.

———. 2004. "The Classifying and Value-Filtering Missions of Borders." *Anthropological Theory* 4 (2): 131–56.

Kearney, Michael, and Federico Besserer. 2004. "Oaxacan Municipal Governance in Transnational Context." In Fox and Rivera-Salgado 2004, 449–66.

Keck, Margaret E., and Kathryn Sikkink. 1998. *Activists beyond Borders: Advocacy Networks in International Politics.* Ithaca: Cornell University Press.

Keil, Roger. 1998. *Los Angeles, Globalization, Urbanization, and Social Struggles.* New York: Wiley.

Kibria, Nazli. 1990. "Power, Patriarchy and Gender Conflict in the Vietnamese Immigrant Community." *Gender & Society* 4 (1): 9–24.

Kim, Jaeeun. 2016. *Contested Embrace: Transborder Membership Politics in Twentieth-Century Korea.* Stanford: Stanford University Press.

Klandermans, Bert. 2003. "Collective Political Action." In *Oxford Handbook of Political Psychology,* edited by Leonie Huddy, David O. Sears, and Jack S. Levy, 670–709. New York: Oxford University Press.

Klaver, Jeanine. 1997. *From the Land of the Sun to the City of Angels: The Migration Process of Zapotec Indians from Oaxaca, Mexico to Los Angeles, California.* Utrecht, Netherlands: Dutch Geographical Society.

Kresge, Lisa. 2007. "Indigenous Oaxacan Communities in California: An Overview." *California Institute for Rural Studies.* www.safsf.org/wp-content/uploads/2015/08/2015_Aug26_IndigenousHealthWeb_Report .pdf.

Krissman, Fred. 1995. "Farm Labor Contractors: The Processors of New Immigrant Labor from Mexico for Californian Agribusiness." *Agriculture and Human Values* 12 (4): 18–46.

———. 2002. "Apples and Oranges? Recruiting Indigenous Mexicans to Divide Farm Labor Markets in the Western US." Paper presented at the Indigenous Mexican Migrants in the US: Building Bridges between Researchers and Community Leaders conference, Santa Cruz, CA, October.

Krogstad, Jens Manuel, Jeffrey S. Passel, and D'Vera Cohn. 2017. "5 Facts about Illegal Immigration in the U.S." *Pew Research Center* (blog). April 27, 2017. www.pewresearch.org/fact-tank/2017/04/27/5-facts-about-illegal-immigration-in-the-u-s/.

Lacayo, A. Elena. 2010. "The Impact of Section 287(g) of the Immigration and Nationality Act on the Latino Community." *National Council of la Raza.* http://publications.unidosus.org/bitstream/handle/123456789/1067/287g _issuebrief_pubstore.pdf?sequence=1.

Lamont, Michèle, and Virág Molnár. 2002. "The Study of Boundaries in the Social Sciences." *Annual Review of Sociology* 28 (1): 167–95.

Landolt, Patricia. 2008. "The Transnational Geographies of Immigrant Politics: Insights from a Comparative Study of Migrant Grassroots Organizing." *Sociological Quarterly* 49 (1): 53–77.

Landolt, Patricia, and Luin Goldring. 2010. "Political Cultures and Transnational Social Fields: Chileans, Colombians and Canadian Activists in Toronto." *Global Networks* 10 (4): 443–66.

Lee, Ching Kwan. 1995. "Engendering the Worlds of Labor: Women Workers, Labor Markets, and Production Politics in the South China Economic Miracle." *American Sociological Review* 60 (3): 378–97.

Leerkes, Arjen, Monica Varsanyi, and Godfried Engbersen. 2012. "Local Limits to Migration Control: Practices of Selective Migration Policing in a Restrictive National Policy Context." *Police Quarterly* 15 (4): 446–75.

Levien, Michael, and Marcel Paret. 2012. "A Second Double Movement? Polanyi and Shifting Global Opinions on Neoliberalism." *International Sociology* 27 (6): 724–44.

Levitt, Peggy. 2001. *The Transnational Villagers.* Berkeley: University of California Press.

———. 2008. "Religion as a Path to Civic Engagement." *Ethnic and Racial Studies* 31 (4): 766–91.

Levitt, Peggy, and Deepak Lamba-Nieves. 2011. "Social Remittances Revisited." *Journal of Ethnic and Migration Studies* 37 (1): 1–22.

Lewis, Paul G., Doris Marie Provine, Monica W. Varsanyi, and Scott H. Decker. 2012. "Why Do (Some) City Police Departments Enforce Federal Immigration Law? Political, Demographic, and Organizational Influences on Local Choices." *Journal of Public Administration Research and Theory* 23 (1): 1–25.

Lewis, Paul G., and S. Karthik Ramakrishnan. 2007. "Police Practices in Immigrant-Destination Cities: Political Control or Bureaucratic Professionalism?" *Urban Affairs Review* 42 (6): 874–900.

Light, Ivan. 2006. *Deflecting Immigration: Networks, Markets, and Regulation in Los Angeles.* New York: Sage Foundation.

López, Felipe, and David Runsten. 2004. "Mixtec and Zapotecs Working in California: Rural and Urban Experiences." In Fox and Rivera-Salgado 2004, 249–78.

Lopez, Mark Hugo, and Susan Minushkin. 2008. *Hispanics See Their Situation in U.S. Deteriorating; Oppose Key Immigration Enforcement Measures.* Washington, DC: Pew Research Center.

López Bárcenas, Francisco, and Guadalupe Espinoza Sauceda. 2003. *Derechos Territoriales y Conflictos Agrarios en la Mixteca: El Caso de San Pedro Yosutatu.* Mexico City: Centro de Orientacion y Asesoria.

Mahler, Sarah J., and Patricia R. Pessar. 2006. "Gender Matters: Ethnographers Bring Gender from the Periphery toward the Core of Migration Studies." *International Migration Review* 40 (1): 27–63.

Mahoney, James. 2000. "Path Dependence in Historical Sociology." *Theory and Society* 29 (4): 507–48.

———. 2010. *Colonialism and Postcolonial Development: Spanish America in Comparative Perspective.* New York: Cambridge University Press.

Maldonado, Centolia, and Patricia Artía Rodríguez. 2004. "'Now We Are Awake': Women's Political Participation in the Oaxacan Indigenous Binational Front." In Fox and Rivera-Salgado 2004, 495–510.

Mallon, Florencia E. 1995. *Peasant and Nation: The Making of Postcolonial Mexico and Peru.* Berkeley: University of California Press.

Marcos, Sylvia. 2005. "The Borders Within: The Indigenous Women's Movement and Feminism in Mexico." In *Dialogue and Difference: Feminisms Challenge Globalization,* edited by Marguerite Waller and Sylvia Marcos, 81–112. New York: Palgrave Macmillan.

Marcus, George E. 2009. "Multi-Sited Ethnography: Five or Six Things I Know about It Now." In *Multi-Sited Ethnography: Problems and Possibilities in the Translocation of Research Methods,* edited by Simon Coleman and Pauline von Hellermann, 16–32. New York: Routledge.

Marosi, Richard. 2011. "Escondido's City-Federal Effort to Oust Illegal Immigrants Draws Praise, Criticism." *Los Angeles Times,* February 4, 2011. http://articles.latimes.com/2011/feb/04/local/la-me-adv-immigration-crackdown-20110206.

Marrow, Helen B. 2009. "Immigrant Bureaucratic Incorporation: The Dual
Roles of Professional Missions and Government Policies." *American Sociological Review* 74 (5): 756–76.

———. 2011. *New Destination Dreaming: Immigration, Race, and Legal Status
in the Rural American South*. Stanford: Stanford University Press.

Martin, Deborah, and Byron Miller. 2003. "Space and Contentious Politics."
Mobilization: An International Quarterly 8 (2): 143–56.

Martínez, Konane M. 2005. "Health across Borders: Mixtec Transnational
Communities and Health Care Systems." PhD diss., University of California,
Riverside.

Martínez, Lisa M. 2005. "Yes We Can: Latino Participation in Unconventional
Politics." *Social Forces* 84 (1): 135–55.

———. 2008. "The Individual and Contextual Determinants of Protest among
Latinos." *Mobilization: An International Quarterly* 13 (2): 189–204.

Martiniello, Marco, and Jean-Michel Lafleur. 2008. "Towards a Transatlantic
Dialogue in the Study of Immigrant Political Transnationalism." *Ethnic and
Racial Studies* 31 (4): 645–63.

Massey, Douglas S. 2012. "The New Latino Underclass: Immigration Enforcement as a Race-Making Institution." Working paper, Stanford Center on
Poverty and Inequality.

Massey, Douglas S., Rafael Alarcón, Jorge Durand, and Humberto González. 1987.
*Return to Aztlan: The Social Process of International Migration from Western
Mexico*. Studies in Demography 1. Berkeley: University of California Press.

Massey, Douglas S., Joaquin Arango, Graeme Hugo, Ali Kouaouci, Adela
Pellegrino, and J. Edward Taylor. 1993. "Theories of International Migration: A Review and Appraisal." *Population and Development Review* 19 (3):
431–66.

Massey, Douglas S., Jorge Durand, and Karen A. Pren. 2016. "Why Border
Enforcement Backfired." *American Journal of Sociology* 121 (5): 1557–600.

Massey, Douglas, and Kristin Espinosa. 1997. "What's Driving Mexico-U.S.
Migration? A Theoretical, Empirical, and Policy Analysis." *American
Journal of Sociology* 102 (4): 939–99.

Massey, Douglas S., Mary J. Fischer, and Chiara Capoferro. 2006. "International Migration and Gender in Latin America: A Comparative Analysis."
International Migration 44 (5): 63–91.

Massey, Douglas, Luin Goldring, and Jorge Durand. 1994. "Continuities in
Migration: An Analysis of Nineteen Mexican Communities." *American
Journal of Sociology* 99 (6): 1492–522.

Massey, Douglas S., and Nolan J. Malone. 2003. "Pathways to Legalization."
Population Research and Policy Review 21:473–504.

Mathema, Silva. 2017. "Keeping Families Together: Why All Americans Should
Care about What Happens to Unauthorized Immigrants." Center for

American Progress. March 16, 2017. www.americanprogress.org/issues /immigration/reports/2017/03/16/428335/keeping-families-together/.

Maya, Theodore. 2002. "To Serve and Protect or to Betray and Neglect? The LAPD and Undocumented Immigrants." *UCLA Law Review* 49:1611–53.

McAdam, Doug. 1999. *Political Process and the Development of Black Insurgency, 1930–1970*. Chicago: University of Chicago Press.

McKenzie, David. 2005. "Beyond Remittances: The Effects of Migration on Mexican Households." In *International Migration, Remittances and the Brain Drain*, edited by Çaglar Özden and Maurice Schiff, 123–47. New York: Palgrave Macmillan.

Meissner, Doris, Donald M. Kerwin, Muzaffar Chishti, and Claire Bergeron. 2013. "Immigration Enforcement in the United States: The Rise of a Formidable Machinery." Washington, DC: Migration Policy Institute.

Menjívar, Cecilia. 2000. *Fragmented Ties: Salvadoran Immigrant Networks in America*. Berkeley: University of California Press.

Menjívar, Cecilia, and Leisy J. Abrego. 2012. "Legal Violence: Immigration Law and the Lives of Central American Immigrants." *American Journal of Sociology* 117 (5): 1380–421.

Menjívar, Cecilia, and Olivia Salcido. 2002. "Immigrant Women and Domestic Violence: Common Experiences in Different Countries." *Gender & Society* 16 (6): 898–920.

Merry, Sally Engle. 2003. "Human Rights Law and the Demonization of Culture (and Anthropology along the Way)." *Political and Legal Anthropology Review* 26 (1): 55–76.

Meseguer, Covadonga, and Katrina Burgess. 2014. "International Migration and Home Country Politics." *Studies in Comparative International Development* 49 (1): 1–12.

Meyer, David S. 2004. "Protest and Political Opportunities." *Annual Review of Sociology* 30:125–45.

Meyer, David S., and Suzanne Staggenborg. 1996. "Movements, Countermovements, and the Structure of Political Opportunity." *American Journal of Sociology* 101 (6): 1628–60.

Michelson, Melissa R. 2016. "Healthy Skepticism or Corrosive Cynicism? New Insights into the Roots and Results of Latino Political Cynicism." *Russell Sage Foundation Journal of the Social Sciences* 2 (3): 60–77.

Milkman, Ruth. 2006. *L.A. Story: Immigrant Workers and the Future of the U.S. Labor Movement*. New York: Sage Foundation.

———. 2007. "Labor Organizing among Mexican-Born Workers in the U.S.: Recent Trends and Future Prospects." *Labor Studies Journal* 32 (1): 96–112.

Milkman, Ruth, and Veronica Terriquez. 2012. "'We Are the Ones Who Are Out in Front': Women's Leadership in the Immigrant Rights Movement." *Feminist Studies* 38 (3): 723–52.

Miller, Byron A. 2000. *Geography and Social Movements: Comparing Antinuclear Activism in the Boston Area.* Minneapolis: University of Minnesota Press.

Mines, Richard, Sandra Nichols, and David Runsten. 2010. *California's Indigenous Farmworkers.* Final Report of the Indigenous Farmworker Study (IFS) to the California Endowment. www.indigenousfarmworkers .org/final_report.shtml.

Molyneux, Maxine. 2006. "Mothers at the Service of the New Poverty Agenda: Progresa/Oportunidades, Mexico's Conditional Transfer Programme." *Social Policy & Administration* 40 (4): 425–49.

Monaghan, John, Arthur Joyce, and Ronald Spores. 2003. "Transformations of the Indigenous Cacicazgo in the Nineteenth Century." *Ethnohistory* 50 (1): 131–50.

Mutersbaugh, Tad. 2002. "Migration, Common Property, and Communal Labor: Cultural Politics and Agency in a Mexican Village." *Political Geography* 21 (4): 473–94.

Nader, Laura. 1991. *Harmony Ideology: Justice and Control in a Zapotec Mountain Village.* Stanford: Stanford University Press.

Nagengast, Carole, and Michael Kearney. 1990. "Mixtec Ethnicity: Social Identity, Political Consciousness, and Political Activism." *Latin American Research Review* 25 (2): 61–91.

Narro, Victor. 2005. "Impacting Next Wave Organizing: Creative Campaign Strategies of the Los Angeles Worker Centers." *New York Law School Law Review* 50:465–513.

Nevins, Joseph. 2002. *Operation Gatekeeper: The Rise of the "Illegal Alien" and the Making of the U.S.-Mexico Boundary.* New York: Routledge.

Newdick, Vivian. 2005. "The Indigenous Woman as Victim of Her Culture in Neoliberal Mexico." *Cultural Dynamics* 17 (1): 73–92.

Ngai, Mae M. 2004. *Impossible Subjects: Illegal Aliens and the Making of Modern America.* Princeton: Princeton University Press.

Nicholls, Walter Julio. 2003. "Forging a 'New' Organizational Infrastructure for Los Angeles' Progressive Community." *International Journal of Urban and Regional Research* 27 (4): 881–96.

———. 2008. "The Urban Question Revisited: The Importance of Cities for Social Movements." *International Journal of Urban and Regional Research* 32 (4): 841–59.

———. 2013. *The DREAMers: How the Undocumented Youth Movement Transformed the Immigrant Rights Debate.* Stanford: Stanford University Press.

Novo, Carmen. 2004. "The Making of Vulnerabilities: Indigenous Day Laborers in Mexico's Neoliberal Agriculture." *Identities* 11 (2): 215–39.

Okamoto, Dina, and Kim Ebert. 2010. "Beyond the Ballot: Immigrant Collective Action in Gateways and New Destinations in the United States." *Social Problems* 57 (4): 529–58.

Orloff, Leslye E., Mary Ann Dutton, Giselle Aguilar Hass, and Nawal Ammar. 2003. "Battered Immigrant Women's Willingness to Call for Help and Police Response." *UCLA Women's Law Journal* 13:43–100.

Østergaard-Nielsen, Eva. 2003. "The Politics of Migrants' Transnational Political Practices." *International Migration Review* 37 (3): 760–86.

Pande, Amrita. 2012. "From 'Balcony Talk' and 'Practical Prayers' to Illegal Collectives: Migrant Domestic Workers and Meso-Level Resistances in Lebanon." *Gender & Society* 26 (3): 382–405.

Parrado, Emilio A., and Chenoa A. Flippen. 2005. "Migration and Gender among Mexican Women." *American Sociological Review* 70 (4): 606–32.

Parreñas, Rhacel Salazar. 2001. *Servants of Globalization: Women, Migration and Domestic Work*. Stanford: Stanford University Press.

Passel, Jeffrey S., and D'Vera Cohn. 2011. *Unauthorized Immigrant Population: National and State Trends, 2010*. Washington, DC: Pew Research Center.

———. 2016. *Unauthorized Immigrant Totals Rise in 7 States, Fall in 14*. Washington, DC: Pew Research Center.

Pastor, Manuel, Pierrette Hondagneu-Sotelo, Alejandro Sanchez-Lopez, Pamela Stephens, Vanessa Carter, and Walter Thompson-Hernández. 2016. "Roots/ Raíces: Latino Engagement, Place Identities, and Shared Futures in South Los Angeles." USC Dornsife Center for the Study of Immigrant Integration. https://dornsife.usc.edu/assets/sites/731/docs/RootsRaices_Full_Report _CSII_USC_Final2016_Web_Small.pdf.

Pastor, Rodolfo. 1986. *Campesinos y Reformas: La Mixteca, 1700–1856*. Mexico City: Colegio de México.

Patler, Caitlin. 2018. "'Citizens but for Papers': Undocumented Youth Organizations, Anti-Deportation Campaigns, and the Reframing of Citizenship." *Social Problems* 65 (1): 96–115.

Paul, Anju Mary. 2011. "Stepwise International Migration: A Multistage Migration Pattern for the Aspiring Migrant." *American Journal of Sociology* 116 (6): 1842–86.

Pedersen, David. 2013. *American Value: Migrants, Money, and Meaning in El Salvador and the United States*. Chicago: University of Chicago Press.

Pedraza, Francisco, Gary Segura, and Shaun Bowler. 2011. "The Efficacy and Alienation of Juan Q. Public: The Immigrant Marches and Orientation toward American Political Institutions." In Voss and Bloemraad 2011, 233–49.

Pedraza, Silvia. 1985. *Political and Economic Migrants in America: Cubans and Mexicans*. Austin: University of Texas Press.

———. 2007. *Political Disaffection in Cuba's Revolution and Exodus*. New York: Cambridge University Press.

Pérez-Armendáriz, Clarisa. 2014. "Cross-Border Discussions and Political Behavior in Migrant-Sending Countries." *Studies in Comparative International Development* 49 (1): 67–88.

Pérez-Armendáriz, Clarisa, and David Crow. 2010. "Do Migrants Remit Democracy? International Migration, Political Beliefs, and Behavior in Mexico." *Comparative Political Studies* 43 (1): 119–48.

Perry, Elizabeth, Nishma Doshi, Jonathan Hicken, and Julio Ricardo Méndez-García. 2009. "Between Here and There: Ethnicity, Civic Participation, and Migration in San Miguel Tlacotepec." In Cornelius et al. 2009, 207–35.

Pfutze, Tobias. 2012. "Does Migration Promote Democratization? Evidence from the Mexican Transition." *Journal of Comparative Economics* 40 (2): 159–75.

Piore, Michael J. 1979. *Birds of Passage: Migrant Labor and Industrial Societies*. New York: Cambridge University Press.

Polletta, Francesca. 1999. "'Free Spaces' in Collective Action." *Theory and Society* 28 (1): 1–38.

Polletta, Francesca, and James M. Jasper. 2001. "Collective Identity and Social Movements." *Annual Review of Sociology* 27 (1): 283–305.

Portes, Alejandro. 1999. "Conclusion: Towards a New World; The Origins and Effects of Transnational Activities." *Ethnic and Racial Studies* 22 (2): 463–77.

———. 2007. "Migration, Development, and Segmented Assimilation: A Conceptual Review of the Evidence." *Annals of the American Academy of Political and Social Science* 610 (1): 73–97.

Portes, Alejandro, and Robert L. Bach. 1985. *Latin Journey: Cuban and Mexican Immigrants in the United States*. Berkeley: University of California Press.

Portes, Alejandro, and Jozsef Borocz. 1989. "Contemporary Immigration: Theoretical Perspectives on Its Determinants and Modes of Incorporation." *International Migration Review* 23 (3): 606–30.

Portes, Alejandro, Cristina Escobar, and Alexandria Walton Radford. 2007. "Immigrant Transnational Organizations and Development: A Comparative Study." *International Migration Review* 41 (1): 242–81.

Portes, Alejandro, Luis E. Guarnizo, and Patricia Landolt. 1999. "The Study of Transnationalism: Pitfalls and Promise of an Emergent Research Field." *Ethnic and Racial Studies* 22 (2): 217–37.

Portes, Alejandro, and Rubén G. Rumbaut. 2006. *Immigrant America: A Portrait*. Berkeley: University of California Press.

Portes, Alejandro, and Min Zhou. 1993. "The New Second Generation: Segmented Assimilation and Its Variants." *Annals of the American Academy of Political and Social Science* 530 (1): 74–96.

———. 2012. "Transnationalism and Development: Mexican and Chinese Immigrant Organizations in the United States." *Population and Development Review* 38 (2): 191–220.

Provine, Doris Marie, Monica Varsanyi, Paul George Lewis, and Scott H. Decker. 2016. *Policing Immigrants: Local Law Enforcement on the Front*

Lines. Chicago Series in Law and Society. Chicago: University of Chicago Press.

Pulido, Laura. 1996. *Environmentalism and Economic Justice: Two Chicano Struggles in the Southwest.* Tucson: University of Arizona Press.

Quereshi, Ajmel. 2010. "287(g) and Women: The Family Values of Local Enforcement of Federal Immigration Law." *Wisconsin Journal of Law, Gender, and Society* 25 (2): 261–300.

Ramakrishnan, S. Karthik, and Tak Wong. 2010. "Partisanship, Not Spanish: Explaining Municipal Ordinances Affecting Undocumented Immigrants." In *Taking Local Control: Immigration Policy Activism in U.S. Cities and States,* edited by Monica Varsanyi, 73–96. Stanford: Stanford University Press.

Ray, Raka. 1998. *Fields of Protest: Women's Movements in India.* Minneapolis: University of Minnesota Press.

Redclift, Victoria. 2013. "Abjects or Agents? Camps, Contests and the Creation of 'Political Space.'" *Citizenship Studies* 17 (3–4): 308–21.

Ribas, Vanesa. 2015. *On the Line: Slaughterhouse Lives and the Making of the New South.* Oakland: University of California Press.

Riosmena, Fernando, and Douglas S. Massey. 2012. "Pathways to El Norte: Origins, Destinations, and Characteristics of Mexican Migrants to the United States." *International Migration Review* 46 (1): 3–36.

Rivera-Salgado, Gaspar. 1999. "Welcome to Oaxacalifornia: Transnational Political Strategies among Mexican Indigenous Migrants." PhD diss., University of California, Santa Cruz.

Rivera-Salgado, Gaspar, and Luis Escala Rabadán. 2004. "Collective Identity and Organizational Strategies of Indigenous and Mestizo Mexican Migrants." In Fox and Rivera-Salgado 2004, 145–78.

Rodriguez, Antonio, and Stella M. Rouse. 2012. "Look Who's Talking Now! Solidarity, Social Networks and Latino Political Participation." Working Paper, University of Maryland, College Park.

Rother, Stefan. 2009. "Changed in Migration? Philippine Return Migrants and (Un)Democratic Remittances." *European Journal of East Asian Studies* 8 (2): 245–74.

Roy, Ananya. 2010. "Millennial Woman: The Gender Order of Development." In *The International Handbook of Gender and Poverty: Concepts, Research, Policy,* edited by Silvia Chant, 548–56. Cheltenham, UK: Elgar.

Rubin, Jeffrey. 1996. "Decentering the Regime: Culture and Regional Politics in Mexico." *Latin American Research Review* 31 (3): 85–126.

Ryo, Emily. 2013. "Deciding to Cross: Norms and Economics of Unauthorized Migration." *American Sociological Review* 78 (4): 574–603.

———. 2015. "Less Enforcement, More Compliance: Rethinking Unauthorized Migration." *UCLA Law Review* 62:624–70.

Salcido, Olivia, and Cecilia Menjívar. 2012. "Gendered Paths to Legal Citizenship: The Case of Latin-American Immigrants in Phoenix, Arizona." *Law & Society Review* 46 (2): 335–68.

Salzinger, Leslie. 2003. *Genders in Production: Making Workers in Mexico's Global Factories.* Berkeley: University of California Press.

Sanchez, Gabriel R., and Natalie Masuoka. 2010. "Brown-Utility Heuristic? The Presence and Contributing Factors of Latino Linked Fate." *Hispanic Journal of Behavioral Sciences* 32 (4): 519–31.

Sassen, Saskia. 1990. *The Mobility of Labor and Capital: A Study in International Investment and Labor Flow.* New York: Cambridge University Press.

Schildkraut, Deborah J., Tomás R. Jiménez, John F. Dovidio, and Yuen J. Huo. Forthcoming. "A Tale of Two States: How State Immigration Climate Affects Belonging to State and Country among Latinos." *Social Problems.*

Schlosser, Eric. 1995. "In the Strawberry Fields." *Atlantic,* November 1995. www.theatlantic.com/magazine/archive/1995/11/in-the-strawberry-fields/305754/.

Schmalzbauer, Leah. 2009. "Gender on a New Frontier: Mexican Migration in the Rural Mountain West." *Gender & Society* 23 (6): 747–67.

———. 2014. *The Last Best Place: Gender, Family, and Migration in the New West.* Stanford: Stanford University Press.

Schussman, Alan, and Sarah Anne Soule. 2005. "Process and Protest: Accounting for Individual Protest Participation." *Social Forces* 84 (2): 1083–108.

Scott, James C. 1985. *Weapons of the Weak: Everyday Forms of Resistance.* New Haven: Yale University Press.

Scott, Joan Wallach. 1988. *Gender and the Politics of History.* New York: Columbia University Press.

Selee, Andrew D. 2011. *Decentralization, Democratization, and Informal Power in Mexico.* University Park: Pennsylvania State University Press.

Shaw, Katerina. 2009. "Barriers to Freedom: Continued Failure of U.S. Immigration Laws to Offer Equal Protection to Immigrant Battered Women." *Cardozo Journal of Law and Gender* 14 (65): 663–89.

Sifuentes, Edward. 2011. "Escondido Woman Turned over to Immigration after Domestic Violence Incident." *North County Times,* October 9, 2011. www.sandiegouniontribune.com/sdut-exclusive-escondido-woman-turned-over-to-2011oct19-story.html.

Singer, Audrey, and Douglas Massey. 1998. "The Social Process of Undocumented Border Crossing among Mexican Migrants." *International Migration Review* 32 (3): 561–92.

Smith, Benjamin T. 2005. "Anticlericalism and Resistance: The Diocese of Huajuapam de León, 1930–1940." *Journal of Latin American Studies* 37 (3): 469–505.

———. 2007. "Defending 'Our Beautiful Freedom': State Formation and Local Autonomy in Oaxaca, 1930–1940." *Mexican Studies/Estudios Mexicanos* 23 (1): 125–53.

———. 2009. *Pistoleros and Popular Movements: The Politics of State Formation in Postrevolutionary Oaxaca.* Lincoln: University of Nebraska Press.

Smith, Jackie, Charles Chatfield, and Ron Pagnucco. 1997. *Transnational Social Movements and Global Politics: Solidarity beyond the State.* Syracuse: Syracuse University Press.

Smith, Robert C. 2003. "Migrant Membership as an Instituted Process: Transnationalization, the State and the Extra-Territorial Conduct of Mexican Politics." *International Migration Review* 37 (2): 297–343.

———. 2006. *Mexican New York: Transnational Lives of New Immigrants.* Berkeley: University of California Press.

Snow, David A., and Sarah Anne Soule. 2010. *A Primer on Social Movements.* New York: Norton.

Soyer, Daniel. 1997. *Jewish Immigrant Associations and American Identity in New York, 1880–1939.* Cambridge: Harvard University Press.

Spivak, Gayatri. 1988. "Can the Subaltern Speak?" In *Marxism and the Interpretation of Culture,* edited by Cary Nelson and Lawrence Grossberg, 271–313. Urbana: University of Illinois Press.

Spores, Ronald. 1967. *Mixtec Kings and Their People.* Norman: University of Oklahoma Press.

Stephen, Lynn. 2005. *Zapotec Women: Gender, Class, and Ethnicity in Globalized Oaxaca.* Durham: Duke University Press.

———. 2007. *Transborder Lives: Indigenous Oaxacans in Mexico, California, and Oregon.* Durham: Duke University Press.

———. 2013. *We Are the Face of Oaxaca: Testimony and Social Movements.* Durham: Duke University Press.

Stepick, Alex, and Carol Dutton Stepick. 2010. "The Complexities and Confusions of Segmented Assimilation." *Ethnic and Racial Studies* 33 (7): 1149–67.

Stern, Steve J. 1983. "The Struggle for Solidarity: Class, Culture and Community in Highland Indian America." *Radical History Review* 27:21–45.

Sterngold, James. 2006. "A City That Thrives on Immigration / Huntington Park Offers a Base for New Arrivals. It's Bustling." *SFGate,* May 28, 2006. www.sfgate.com/news/article/A-city-that-thrives-on-immigration-Huntington-2534276.php.

Stuart, James and Michael Kearney. 1981. *Causes and Effects of Agricultural Migration from the Mixteca of Oaxaca to California.* La Jolla: Center for U.S.-Mexican Studies, University of California, San Diego.

Stumpf, Juliet P. 2006. "The Crimmigration Crisis: Immigrants, Crime, and Sovereign Power." *American University Law Review* 56 (2): 367–419.

Talavera, Victor, Guillermina Gina Nuñez-Mchiri, and Josiah Heyman. 2010. "Deportation in the U.S.-Mexico Borderlands: Anticipation, Experience and Memory." In *The Deportation Regime: Sovereignty, Space, and the Freedom of Movement*, edited by Nicholas de Genova and Nathalie Peutz, 166–95. Durham: Duke University Press.

Tarrow, Sidney. 1993. "Cycles of Collective Action: Between Moments of Madness and the Repertoire of Contention." *Social Science History* 17 (2): 281–307.

———. 2005. *The New Transnational Activism*. New York: Cambridge University Press.

Taylor, Edward J., Antonio Yuñez-Naude, Fernando Barceinas Paredes, and George Dyer. 2005. "Transition Policy and the Structure of Agriculture in Mexico." In *North American Agrifood Market Integration: Situation and Perspectives*, edited by Karen M. Huff, Karl D. Meilke, Ronald D. Knutson, Rene F. Ochoa, James Rude, and Antonio Yuñez-Naude, 86–118. College Station: Texas A&M University Press.

Taylor, Paul, Mark Hugo López, Jeffrey S. Passel, and Seth Motel. 2011. *Unauthorized Immigrants: Length of Residency, Patterns of Parenthood*. Washington, DC: Pew Research Center.

Terriquez, Veronica. 2015. "Intersectional Mobilization, Social Movement Spillover, and Queer Youth Leadership in the Immigrant Rights Movement." *Social Problems* 62 (3): 343–62.

Thompson, Gary D., and Philip L. Martin. 1989. *The Potential Effects of Labor-Intensive Agriculture in Mexico on United States–Mexico Migration*. U.S. Commission for the Study of International Migration and Cooperative Economic Development, Working Paper No. 11, Washington, DC.

Tilly, Charles. 1995. *Popular Contention in Great Britain, 1758–1834*. Cambridge: Harvard University Press.

Tramonte, Lynn. 2011. *Debunking the Myth of 'Sanctuary Cities': Community Policing Policies Protect American Communities*. Washington, DC: American Immigration Council.

Tripp, Aili Mari. 2015. *Women and Power in Postconflict Africa*. New York: Cambridge University Press.

Tyner, James A. 2004. *Made in the Philippines: Gendered Discourses and the Making of Migrants*. New York: Routledge.

U.S. Census Bureau. 2012. "Census Briefs: The American Indian and Alaska Native Population: 2010." www.census.gov/prod/cen2010/briefs/c2010br-10.pdf.

———. 2017. "Quick Facts: United States." www.census.gov/quickfacts/fact/table/US/PST045217.

U.S. Department of Homeland Security. 2012. *Yearbook of Immigration Statistics*. Washington, DC: Office of Immigration Statistics.

VanWey, Leah Karin, Catherine M. Tucker, and Eileen Diaz McConnell. 2005. "Community Organization, Migration, and Remittances in Oaxaca." *Latin American Research Review* 40 (1): 83–107.

Vargas, Jose Antonio. 2011. "My Life as an Undocumented Immigrant." *New York Times*, June 22, 2011. www.nytimes.com/2011/06/26/magazine/my-life-as-an-undocumented-immigrant.html.

Varsanyi, Monica W. 2005. "The Paradox of Contemporary Immigrant Political Mobilization: Organized Labor, Undocumented Migrants, and Electoral Participation in Los Angeles." *Antipode* 37 (4): 775–95.

Velasco Ortiz, Laura. 2002. *El Regreso de la Comunidad: Migración Indígena y Agentes Étnicos; Los Mixtecos en la Frontera México–Estados Unidos.* Mexico City: Colegio de México/Colegio de la Frontera Norte.

———. 2005a. *Desde Que Tengo Memoria: Narrativas de Identidad en Migrantes Indígenas Oaxaqueños.* Mexico City: Colegio de México/Colegio de la Frontera Norte.

———. 2005b. *Mixtec Transnational Identity.* Tucson: University of Arizona Press.

Velásquez, Maria Cristina. 2004. "Comunidades Migrantes, Género y Poder Político en Oaxaca." In *Indígenas Mexicanos Migrantes en los Estados Unidos,* edited by Jonathan Fox and Gaspar Rivera-Salgado, 519–23. Mexico City: Universidad Autónoma de Zacatecas.

Ventura Luna, Silvia. 2010. "The Migration Experience as It Relates to Cargo Participation in San Miguel Cuevas, Oaxaca." *Migraciones Internacionales* 5 (3): 44–70.

Verba, Sidney, Kay Lehman Schlozman, and Henry E. Brady. 1995. *Voice and Equality: Civic Voluntarism in American Politics.* Cambridge: Harvard University Press.

Vertovec, Steven. 2009. *Transnationalism.* New York: Routledge.

Villalón, Roberta. 2010. *Violence against Latina Immigrants: Citizenship, Inequality, and Community.* New York: New York University Press.

Viterna, Jocelyn. 2013. *Women in War: The Micro-Processes of Mobilization in El Salvador.* New York: Oxford University Press.

Voss, Kim, and Irene Bloemraad, eds. 2011. *Rallying for Immigrant Rights: The Fight for Inclusion in 21st Century America.* Berkeley: University of California Press.

Voss, Kim, and Michelle Williams. 2012. "The Local in the Global: Rethinking Social Movements in the New Millennium." *Democratization* 19 (2): 352–77.

Wacquant, Loïc. 2013. *Urban Outcasts: A Comparative Sociology of Advanced Marginality.* Cambridge: Polity.

Waldinger, Roger. 2007. *Between Here and There: How Attached Are Latino Immigrants to Their Native Country?* Washington, DC: Pew Research Center.

———. 2008. "Between 'Here' and 'There': Immigrant Cross-Border Activities and Loyalties." *International Migration Review* 42 (1): 3–29.

———. 2013. "Immigrant Transnationalism." *Current Sociology* 61 (5–6): 756–77.

———. 2015. *The Cross-Border Connection: Immigrants, Emigrants, and Their Homelands.* Cambridge: Harvard University Press.

Waldinger, Roger, and Lauren Duquette-Rury. 2016. "Emigrant Politics, Immigrant Engagement: Homeland Ties and Immigrant Political Identity in the United States." *Russell Sage Foundation Journal of the Social Sciences* 2 (3): 42–59.

Waldinger, Roger, and David FitzGerald. 2004. "Transnationalism in Question." *American Journal of Sociology* 109 (5): 1177–95.

Walker, Kyle E. 2014. "The Role of Geographic Context in the Local Politics of US Immigration." *Journal of Ethnic and Migration Studies* 40 (7): 1040–59.

Walker, Kyle E., and Helga Leitner. 2011. "The Variegated Landscape of Local Immigration Policies in the United States." *Urban Geography* 32 (2): 156–78.

Walter, Nicholas, Philippe Bourgois, and H. Margarita Loinaz. 2004. "Masculinity and Undocumented Labor Migration: Injured Latino Day Laborers in San Francisco." *Social Science & Medicine* 59 (6): 1159–68.

Waters, Mary C., and Marisa Gerstein Pineau. 2015. "The Integration of Immigrants into American Society." Panel on the Integration of Immigrants into American Society, Committee on Population, Division of Behavioral and Social Sciences and Education. Washington, DC: National Academy of Science.

White, Marceline, Carlos Salas, and Sarah Gammage. 2003. *Trade Impact Review: Mexico Case Study; NAFTA and the FTAA: A Gender Analysis of Employment and Poverty Impacts in Agriculture.* Women's Edge Coalition. www.iatp.org/files/NAFTA_and_the_FTAA_A_Gender_Analysis_of_Employ.pdf.

Wilkerson, Isabel. 2010. *The Warmth of Other Suns: The Epic Story of America's Great Migration.* New York: Random House.

Wolf, Eric R. 1957. "Closed Corporate Peasant Communities in Mesoamerica and Central Java." *Southwestern Journal of Anthropology* 13 (1): 1–18.

———. 1969. *Peasant Wars of the Twentieth Century.* Norman: University of Oklahoma Press.

Wolford, Wendy. 2003. "Producing Community: The MST and Land Reform Settlements in Brazil." *Journal of Agrarian Change* 3 (4): 500–520.

Wong, Tom K. 2017. *The Effects of Sanctuary Policies on Crime and the Economy.* Washington, DC: Center for American Progress.

Worthen, Holly. 2012. "The Presence of Absence: Indigenous Migration, a Ghost Town, and the Remaking of Communal Systems in Oaxaca, Mexico." PhD diss., University of North Carolina, Chapel Hill.

———. 2015. "Indigenous Women's Political Participation: Gendered Labor and Collective Rights Paradigms in Mexico." *Gender & Society* 29 (6): 914–36.

Wright, Angus Lindsay. 2005. *The Death of Ramón González: The Modern Agricultural Dilemma.* Austin: University of Texas Press.

Yinger, Nancy V. 2006. *Feminization of Migration.* Washington, DC: Population Reference Bureau.

Yoo, Grace J. 2008. "Immigrants and Welfare: Policy Constructions of Deservingness." *Journal of Immigrant & Refugee Studies* 6 (4): 490–507.

Young, Kate. 1978. "Changing Economic Roles of Women in Two Rural Mexican Communities." *Sociologia Ruralis* 18 (2–3): 197–216.

Yukich, Grace. 2013. "Constructing the Model Immigrant: Movement Strategy and Immigrant Deservingness in the New Sanctuary Movement." *Social Problems* 60 (3): 302–20.

Yuval-Davis, Nira. 2006. "Belonging and the Politics of Belonging." *Patterns of Prejudice* 40 (3): 197–214.

Zabin, Carol. 1992. *Mixtec Migrant Farm Workers in California Agriculture: A Dialogue among Mixtec Leaders, Researchers and Farm Labor Advocates.* San Diego: Center for U.S.-Mexican Studies, University of California, San Diego; Davis: California Institute for Rural Studies.

———. 1997. "U.S.-Mexico Economic Integration: Labor Relations and the Organization of Work in California and Baja California Agriculture." *Economic Geography* 73 (3): 337–55.

Zepeda-Millán, Chris. 2017. *Latino Mass Mobilization: Immigration, Racialization, and Activism.* New York: Cambridge University Press.

Zilberg, Elana. 2011. *Space of Detention: The Making of a Transnational Gang Crisis between Los Angeles and San Salvador.* Durham: Duke University Press.

Index

Page references followed by an italicized *fig.* indicate illustrations or material contained in their captions.